W9-CGN-623

Public Economics

Politicians, Property Rights, and Exchange

Public Economics

Politicians, Property Rights, and Exchange

Adam Gifford, Jr.
California State University

Gary J. Santoni
California State University

The Dryden Press
Hinsdale, Illinois

For Ann, Nina, Adam III, Matthew, Melisa, and Michael

Copyright © 1979 by The Dryden Press
A division of Holt, Rinehart and Winston
All rights reserved
Library of Congress Catalog Card Number: 78-56195
ISBN: 0-03-021646-X
Printed in the United States of America
9 039 987654321

Preface

Government activity is an important, growing and pervasive influence determining, at least in part, the composition of output, allocation of resources, and distribution of product within the economy of the United States. The purpose of this book is to introduce the reader to an economic theory of government activity. In other words, the book develops an analytical framework that explains and predicts the choices of individuals as they function as voters, elected representatives, and bureaucrats and the effect that these choices have on resource allocation.

Some of the specific topics include a rather extensive discussion of public goods and problems associated with their supply, externalities, property rights, and taxation. Furthermore, many issues that have been raised by recent literature in the area of public choice are treated. These include economic hypotheses regarding the behavior of individuals as voters, members of political parties, elected representatives, and bureaucrats as well as the economics of campaign expenditures.

Economics is a science. Consequently, economic theory is positive. Its purpose is to serve as an aid to the individual in explaining and predicting real-world outcomes. Scientific theories are either accepted or rejected depending upon how well they do this job. In other words, the theory is tentatively accepted if the hypotheses it generates survive repeated tests against the evidence. In keeping with this approach, we have included application sections in each chapter. These applications consist of short reviews of empirical studies that have been published in the professional literature. They have been included to illustrate and to provide evidence regarding the theory developed in the text. Clearly, we do not exhaust the evidence and, for a scientist, the evidence is never conclusive.

Chapters 1-4 review some fundamental economic concepts, define public goods, and discuss problems associated with the supply of public goods. Chapters 5-8 treat the collective decision-making process, what has come to be called public choice. We believe that our discussion of this topic is considerably more extensive than has been the case in previous texts. Chapters 9-12 analyze taxation. We focus on the incidence of the various taxes and the effect of these taxes on resource allocation.

We, of course, are indebted to many individuals who helped in the development of this book. In particular, we would like to thank Professors Joseph Cordes of George Washington University, Robert Main of California State University at Hayward, T. Norman Van Cott of Ball State University, and Kenneth R. Vogel of The State University of New York, Buffalo. Each has read the entire manuscript and all have provided us with helpful advice, comments, corrections and constructive criticisms. Thanks are also due to Professors Richard Friedman and Jora Minasian, both of California State University at Northridge, who have provided criticism, encouragement, and enlightening discussion in the early stages of the book's development. The students in several of our Public Finance classes have been helpful to us in improving the clarity and readability of the manuscript. Finally, we owe special thanks to our typist, Judy Shulman, who maintained her good cheer through the manuscript's many stages.

June 1978   A. Gifford, Jr.
                                             G. J. Santoni

Contents

Chapter 6

Representative Democracy   105

Chapter 7

Public Allocation—Bureaucracy   123

Chapter 8

The Distribution of Income and the Structure of Rights   143

Chapter 9

Personal Income Tax   171

1

Introduction

In the United States, total government expenditure, expressed as a percentage of gross national product, has increased from 9.9 percent in 1929 to approximately 34.0 percent in recent years. An understanding of the interrelationship between government and the private economy is of increasing importance to individuals interested in explaining resource allocation as government involvement in this arena becomes more pervasive.

This book examines the interaction that takes place between the public and private sectors of the economy. Specifically, it examines how taxation and expenditure decisions are made in a democratic system and how these decisions affect the allocation of resources. Since these decisions are, essentially, microeconomic in nature (that is, they concern individual choices regarding the allocation of scarce resources), we have adopted the fundamental assumptions and analysis of microeconomic theory.

Individualistic Methodology

Microeconomic theory takes the individual as the unit of analysis, focusing on the causes and effects of decisions made by individuals. Consequently, the analysis is individualistic in nature. It rules out the possibility of a public interest that is divorced from the interests of individuals. Our analysis of public decisions begins and ends with the individual.

Individuals are assumed to pursue self-interest when making decisions in the public sector, just as they do in the private sector. That is, individuals (as voters, bureaucrats, or politicians) will make choices (decisions) that have the effect of maximizing their utility subject to the constraints they face. We do not assume, in other words, that individuals have two modes of behavior, one for private-sector decisions and one for public-sector decisions. *All* decisions made by an individual are made to maximize his or her utility. If observed behavior in the public sector is different from that in the private sector, it is because individuals face a different set of constraints in the public sector—not because their objectives are different. We are not saying that behavior motivated by true altruism does not exist. We are asserting that this behavior is not pervasive enough to warrant complicating the theory to account for it.

Positive Economic Framework

The basic approach of any science—and economics is a science—is a positive one. Employing this science, we will attempt to explain and predict how individuals make decisions regarding the allocation of resources in the public sector. Economic science can say nothing about how or what decisions *should* be made. Our approach will be to present and, to a certain extent, develop a testable economic theory concerning the public sector. In addition, we will present some of the evidence supporting this theory in the application sections of each chapter.

The only normative judgment we make is that individual tastes and preferences should count in public decision making; that is, our theory of the public sector is based on the concept that public decisions should be made by individuals acting collectively. This judgment will color our evaluation of the predicted results that follow from certain government policies. It does not, however, affect the predictions themselves. The predictions follow from the application of a strictly positive analysis.

We limit our analysis to "what is" rather than "what ought to be" because the study of public economics, if it is to be an aid in explaining and predicting real-world observations, must be a positive science. Chemistry is a positive science. Therefore, chemists are not interested in what elements ideally *should* combine to make water; they are interested in what elements *do* combine to make water. That is, they want to explain and predict real-world events. In a similar fashion, public economics attempts to determine or predict what will happen when specific public policies are pursued. It follows, then, that positive theories are judged on the basis of their ability to predict real-world occurrences. You are encouraged to judge the theory presented here on this basis. You may, of course, be tempted to judge it on the basis of its assumptions; for instance, do they strike you as being realistic? You would be wrong, however, if you used this as a basis for judgment because all testable scientific theories are formulated by making assumptions that simplify reality. Unfortunately, the world is too complex to understand by simple observation. Theories must simplify reality to produce results; they must be based on simplifying assumptions. If the assumptions were realistic, they would not simplify; hence the purpose of making them would be defeated.

Scarcity and Competition

Economics can be defined as the study of the allocation of scarce resources among unlimited and competing wants. The key to this definition is the reality that resources are scarce. If resources were not scarce, there would be no need to economize in their use. Scarcity forces any user of resources in the public or the private sector to make choices about the use of those resources. That is, trade-offs must be made among the alternative uses to which the resources may be put.

The fact that choices must be made among alternative uses leads directly to the concept of cost as employed by economists. Because of scarcity, productive capacity is limited. This limitation affects both the public and the private sectors. The limitation of productive capacity means that if one chooses to increase the output of the public sector he or she necessarily chooses to decrease the output of the private sector. Alternatively, one might choose to increase output in one area of the public sector, defense for example, at the expense of another, say, subsidized housing. The fact that these choices must be made implies that production of goods and services involves costs. Consequently, we define the cost of any good, service, or action as the highest valued alternative good, service, or action necessarily forsaken as a result of the one selected. This concept of cost is referred to as *opportunity cost*.

The economic concept of cost is not limited to monetary outlays. For example, the cost of going to a baseball game is not simply the $5 ticket price. Not only are you giving up $5 worth of other goods and services by going to the game, but you are also giving up your time. The full cost of going to the game includes the value of your time spent going to and from the game and the time spent at the game. If, for example, the next highest valued use of your time has an approximate market value of $250, your full cost of going to the game is $255.

Social Costs and Private Costs

In economics we are primarily concerned with the social cost of any action, that is, the full cost of all alternatives forsaken. The private costs of an action are only those costs borne by the individual taking the action. In the baseball example, the private cost is $255. In most situations, the social costs and private costs of an action are the same. Put another way, the private costs are the social costs.

When a decision maker does not bear the full economic cost of his or her decision or action, we say that an *externality* exists. When externalities occur, other individuals bear some of the costs of the action taken by the decision maker. For example, if my motorcycle does not have a muffler and I ride it down the street, I impose costs on those people I ride past who are sensitive to loud noise. Therefore, I do not bear the full cost of riding my motorcycle. In this situation, the social cost of my action exceeds the private costs. As we will see, these divergences between social and private costs (externalities) sometimes create problems regarding the efficient allocation of resources.

Scarcity and the Economic System

Scarcity means that individuals are not going to be able to satisfy all of their wants. Consequently, individuals will compete among themselves for the scarce goods and services which are produced. This competition is a result, not a cause, of scarcity. Scarcity does *not* result from the economic system. Economic systems are designed to deal with scarcity.

Different economic systems—socialism, communism, capitalism—are simply alternative mechanisms for dealing with scarcity. Essentially, these systems define the basis upon which the competition will take place. Although the system defines the rules of the game, scarcity requires the game to be played.

In the United States, we, for the most part, employ a private property, free enterprise, market system (a capitalistic system) to allocate resources in the private sector. In the public sector, resource allocation is determined through the democratic process.

Property and Other Rights

Our economic system is based, in part, on the concept of private property rights. A property right grants the individual the right to use, possess, and dispose of his or her property. In this sense, property refers to any physical asset or good. Property rights are a part of a set of rights granted to individuals in democratic, free enterprise societies. Other individual rights, such as copyrights, patents, and free speech, grant individuals the rights to intangible things, such as ideas, processes, and human interaction.

Rights grant individuals certain freedoms. However, they also restrict the actions of individuals. The right to maintain possession of your property places the restriction on others that they may not take it or use it without your permission. A right is a guaranty that has the force of tradition, moral code, or formal law behind it. Rights, by granting a guaranty, increase the value of social and economic interaction among individuals by reducing certain harmful actions. Theft is an example of a harmful activity that is restricted by the assignment of private property rights.

The possession of rights by or the granting of rights to individuals is not sufficient to increase the value of social and economic interaction. Rights must also be enforced or protected. Governments protect rights from both external and internal forces by devoting resources to national defense and by maintaining and enforcing laws through the court system and the police force. Better protection of property rights will increase the value of property. Better protection means that individuals can expect with greater certainty that their decisons regarding the use of the property will be effective. Two identical automobiles will sell for different prices if one of them carries a two-year guaranty against a breakdown and the other carries no guaranty. The automobile example is analogous to improving the protection of property rights. If the incidence of auto theft is reduced because the police become more efficient in enforcing the law, the value of autos (the price that individuals are willing to pay to acquire the rights to an automobile) will rise. This is true because the reduction in the incidence of auto theft gives the individual a better guaranty that his or her decisions regarding the use of the auto will be effective. The individual is now more certain that, when he or she parks the car in the driveway after returning home from work, it will still be there the next morning. Of course, devoting resources to the protection of property rights is costly. It only pays to devote additional resources to improving protection if the increase in the value of property covers the cost.

It is necessary to protect rights if efficient rates of production are to occur. This is also true with respect to the exchange of goods because what is exchanged is the bundle of rights that accrue to the owner of the good. Individuals must have some guaranty that they will maintain control of the goods they produce or purchase. Producing or purchasing goods is costly because other goods are given up in the process, and unless the individuals have a guaranty that they will maintain control of the goods acquired through production or exchange, they will not incur the cost.

It is important to keep in mind that all rights, including property rights, are rights of individuals. It is incorrect to consider property rights as being separate or different from human rights; all rights are human rights. All rights have the same purpose, that is, to increase the well-being of individuals.

In the next chapter we will examine, briefly, the allocation of resources in a free enterprise system. We will see how prices and markets coordinate the production, allocation, and distribution of resources in an efficient manner.

The remainder of this book is devoted to explaining and analyzing government within a democratic, free enterprise economy. We will examine the means by which individuals take collective action in an attempt to satisfy their tastes and preferences for goods not provided through the interaction of individuals in private markets. We will spend a great deal of time analyzing the *effectiveness* of this collective action in performing its task.

Questions and Exercises

1. List the costs of your college education. Are the social costs of your education equal to the private costs? Explain.

2. Why don't we test theories in economics by the realism of their assumptions?

3. Explain the relationship between scarcity and competition.

4. Scarcity forces us to choose among alternatives. How are these choices related to cost?

5. What role does the individual play in the analysis in this book? Why is the assumption that individual preferences should count normative?

Additional Readings

Alchian, Armen, and Allen, William R. *Exchange and Production: Competition, Coordination, and Control.* 2d ed. Belmont, Calif.: Wadsworth Publishing Co., 1977. Chapter 1.

Buchanan, James M., and Tullock, Gordon. *The Calculus of Consent.* Ann Arbor, Mich.: Ann Arbor Paperbacks, 1971. Chapters 1–4.

Friedman, Milton. *Essays in Positive Economics.* Chicago: The University of Chicago Press, 1970.

2

Efficiency and Gains from Exchange and Specialization

In this chapter, we review some of the principles of economic analysis that will be used in subsequent chapters of this book. The discussion of these principles will not be comprehensive; consequently, you might find it useful to review the list of additional readings provided at the end of the chapter.

The science of economics is based on the proposition that resources are scarce relative to the wants of individuals. Throughout history, individuals have devised many different methods for dealing with the problem of scarcity.

One method of dealing with the problem of scarcity is the free exchange of private property rights. The following discussion deals with this method exclusively because it has always been an important way of dealing with scarcity and because, as we will argue later, it forms the underpinning for any practical method of dealing with the problem.

The Fundamental Theorem of Exchange

Why do individuals exchange goods that are scarce (goods, which in some sense, they do not have enough of) and how does this exchange mitigate (make less onerous or burdensome) the effects of scarcity? The Fundamental Theorem of Exchange suggests an answer to this question. The theorem states that the parties to any free exchange will benefit from the exchange. Since the exchange is voluntary, any party that would not benefit from the transaction would refuse to exchange. The theory of exchange is based on the following propositions: (1) that individuals are always willing to substitute some of one good for more of another good; (2) that the more of one good, say, good A, that an individual consumes per unit of time relative to some other good, say, good B, the fewer units of good B he or she is willing to give up for an additional unit of good A; and (3) that individuals are rational in the sense that, if they express a preference for alternative X over alternative Y and alternative Y over alternative Z, they will express a preference for X over Z.

A term we will employ in discussing the fundamental theorem is marginal value in use. The marginal value in use of units of good A to an individual is the *maximum* number of units of good B that the individual would *willingly* give up in exchange for an additional unit of good A. The value of good A is measured in terms of units of good B, and that value is completely subjective with respect to the individual. The second proposition implies that the marginal value in use declines as more of the good is consumed per unit of time.

To illustrate, consider the following example. Suppose that Tom is endowed with a given amount of beer and bourbon per unit of time. Given this mix, he is just willing to give up five units of beer to obtain one more unit of bourbon. We would say that the marginal value in use of units of bourbon to Tom is five units of beer. This is expressed in the following ratio:

$$\frac{5 \text{ fewer beers}}{1 \text{ more bourbon}} = 5 \text{ beers per bourbon}$$

At the margin, Tom values a unit of bourbon at five units of beer. If he were to exchange at this rate, he would consider that he made an even trade. In Tom's view, he would be no better nor worse off. Once we know Tom's marginal value in use of bourbon measured in terms of beer, we can obtain his marginal value in use of beer measured in terms of bourbon. If Tom values an additional bourbon at five beers, he must value an additional unit of beer at 1/5 of a unit of bourbon.

Suppose Bill, who is also endowed with a given amount of bourbon and beer, is willing to give up ten units of beer for an additional unit of bourbon. This is expressed in the following ratio:

$$\frac{10 \text{ fewer beers}}{1 \text{ more bourbon}} = 10 \text{ beers per bourbon}$$

Bill values an additional unit of bourbon at ten units of beer. Alternatively, he values one unit of beer at 1/10 unit of bourbon. At the margin, Bill values bourbon more than Tom does, which is another way of say that Bill places a lower value on beer than does Tom.

Bill is willing to pay as many as ten units of beer for an additional unit of bourbon. Tom, who values a unit of bourbon at five units of beer, would willingly accept as few as five beers as an inducement to give up one unit of bourbon.[1] It is possible, then, for these two individuals to engage in an exchange which is mutually beneficial. And, if they are aware of this circumstance or opportunity, they will do so. The spread between the ten beers, which is the maximum that Bill is willing to pay, and the five beers, which is the minimum that Tom will accept, is called the potential gain from exchange. Any price of bourbon falling between ten beers and five beers will make both individuals better off. As long as both individuals are free to refuse any offer made by the other, agreement will only occur at a price between ten and five beers. Consequently, any exchange that occurs will benefit both parties even though each is giving up scarce goods which both value. The important point is, however, that each gives up goods that are valued less highly than the goods received. Because this is the case, exchange mitigates the problem of scarcity.

Suppose that the price agreed to is seven units of beer per unit of bourbon. When Bill buys his first bourbon from Tom, he will gain three beers. This is true because he values the additional bourbon at ten beers but pays only seven beers. On the other hand, Tom gives up a unit of bourbon, which he values at five beers, in exchange for seven beers. Tom gains two beers in the transaction. As viewed by the participants in the exchange, each is better off.

It is clear from this discussion that free exchange will allow resources (goods) to flow to their highest valued uses. Bill values an additional bourbon at ten beers while Tom values an additional bourbon at only five beers. Bourbon has a higher valued use to Bill, so he receives bourbon in the exchange. Alternatively, Tom values an additional beer at 1/5 of a unit of bourbon, while Bill values beer at only 1/10 of a unit of bourbon. Beer has a higher valued use to Tom, so he receives beer in the exchange.

Trade need not cease with one exchange. It will continue as long as a potential gain exists (as long as the individuals value bourbon differently at the margin). As the trade proceeds, Bill acquires additional bourbon. His marginal value in use of bourbon will decline (see the second proposition). Tom, on the other hand, gives up bourbon and acquires beer. His marginal value in use of bourbon will rise. This is another way of saying that his marginal value in use of beer measured in terms of bourbon will decline.

---

[1]When discussing exchanges of discrete amounts, one should distinguish between the value associated with having one more unit and the amount necessary to induce the transactor to give up one of the units he or she already possesses. These two amounts will be slightly different. For the moment, we are ignoring this problem.

Consequently, the potential gain from each subsequent exchange will shrink until it vanishes. Trade will cease when this has occurred, that is, when marginal values in use are equal between the two individuals.

To illustrate this point, suppose that Tables 2.1(a) and 2.1(b) give the marginal values in use that Tom and Bill attach to bourbon at different rates of bourbon consumption. Remember, each individual begins with a certain mix. Let Tom begin with twenty units of beer and seven units of bourbon, and let Bill begin with thirty units of beer and eight units of bourbon. Given the initial endowments, the potential gain from exchange of the first unit of bourbon is three units of beer. Remember that the potential gain is the difference between the marginal value in use that Bill attaches to nine units of bourbon (Bill gains the ninth unit in the exchange) and the marginal value in use that Tom attaches to seven units of bourbon (Tom gives up the seventh unit in the exchange). Exchanging this unit will reduce Tom's bourbon to six units and increase Bill's quantity to nine units. At the margin, Tom now values bourbon at 5.5 units of beer while Bill values bourbon at 8 units of beer. The potential gain from further exchange is 0.5 units of beer. The marginal value in use that Bill attaches to an additional unit

Table 2.1

(a)		(b)	
Tom's Marginal Value in Use of Bourbon (Expressed in Terms of Beer)		Bill's Marginal Value in Use of Bourbon (Expressed in Terms of Beer)	
Units of Beer per Unit of Bourbon	Units of Bourbon	Units of Beer per Unit of Bourbon	Units of Bourbon
8.0	1	24	1
7.5	2	22	2
7.0	3	20	3
6.5	4	18	4
6.0	5 Equilibrium quantity	16	5
		14	6
5.5	6	12	7
5.0	7 Initial quantity	10	8 Initial quantity
4.5	8	8	9
4.0	9	6	10 Equilibrium quantity
3.5	10		
3.0	11	4	11
2.5	12	2	12

of bourbon (bringing his consumption to 10) is 6 units of beer. The marginal value in use that Tom attaches to 6 units of bourbon is 5.5 beers (Tom gives up the sixth unit in the exchange). The difference is 0.5 beers. When this exchange has occurred, Tom is left with 5 units of bourbon which, at the margin, he values at 6 units of beer. Bill has 10 units of bourbon which, at the margin, he values at 6 units of beer. In this case, the gain from exchange vanishes when two units of bourbon have been traded.

Consumer and Seller Surplus

The above points are shown graphically in Figure 2.1. The curves MV_B and MV_T relate the marginal value in use of bourbon measured in terms of beer for Bill and Tom and are obtained from Tables 2.1(a) and 2.1(b). In Figure 2.1, we assume that the exchange of bourbon is made at a uniform price of six beers per bourbon. Bill is endowed initially with eight units of bourbon. The exchange moves him from point A to point E. He increases his consumption by two units of bourbon. The additional units of bourbon cost him twelve units of beer in total. This is given by the area $ABDE$ in Figure 2.1. The value (measured in terms of beer) of these additional two units to him is the larger area $ACDE$. Bill's gain from the exchange is given by the difference between the value of the additional units to him and his cost of obtaining

Figure 2.1

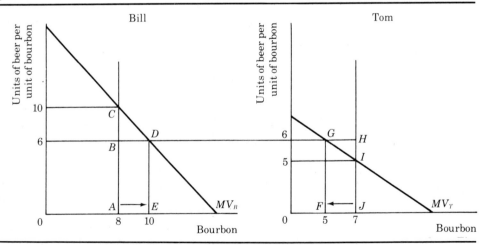

them—the area *BCD*. This area reflects Bill's consumer surplus that results from the exchange and is the same as Bill's gain from exchange.

Tom, on the other hand, receives twelve beers for the two units of bourbon he trades to Bill. This is given by the area *FGHJ* in Figure 2.1. The value of these two units to Bill is given by the area *FGIJ*. Tom's gain from the exchange is the difference between the number of beers he receives and the value that he places on the bourbon (measured in terms of beer) that he foregoes. Tom's gain is given by the area *GHI* in Figure 2.1. This area reflects the seller surplus that results from the exchange.

The information given in Figure 2.1 may be presented in more traditional form by rotating the horizontal axis, which gives Tom's bourbon consumption, to the left around the vertical axis and then sliding the two horizontal axes together until the resulting length is equal to the sum of the two endowments (15 units of bourbon). This is shown in Figure 2.2. The curve giving Tom's marginal value in use of bourbon, MV_T, becomes the supply curve confronting Bill. It follows that, in a pure exchange model, downward-sloping demand curves (curves relating marginal value in use) imply upward-sloping supply curves.

In summary, free exchange of private rights in property will result in the following: (1) each party to the exchange will share in the potential gain from exchange; (2) each party gives up goods that are considered valuable; (3) goods (resources) will be allocated

Figure 2.2

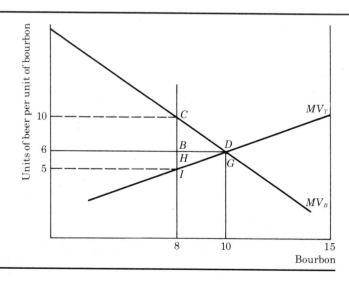

to their highest valued use; (4) when exchange ceases, the marginal value in use of bourbon to Bill is equal to Tom's, and the same is true for beer; (5) the self-interest of individuals, which motivates them in the pursuit of gain, is the force that brings about these results.

A Qualification: Information Costs and External Effects

The above analysis depicts a world in which information regarding the offers of sellers and the bids of buyers is costless. In the real world this is, of course, not true. Neither is it true that information regarding the quality of products being offered is free. The additional costs incurred in shopping for products reduce the extent of and gains from trade. With positive information, or transaction cost, trades cease when the gain from an additional exchange is just enough to cover the additional costs of forming the exchange.

The existence of middlemen (agents, brokers, wholesalers, retailers, etc.) attests to the fact that shopping costs are positive. It is an error, however, to argue that these individuals add to shopping costs. If they did, producers and consumers would choose to avoid the additional middlemen cost by "dealing direct." Middlemen services are employed in most exchanges because middlemen are able to reduce shopping costs. Middlemen serve to increase the extent of exchange—not, of course, to the point that would exist if the shopping cost were zero, but further than would be the case if their services were not employed. By reducing information and transaction costs, middlemen reduce the spread between the marginal values in use of the product between individuals when these costs are positive.

Information costs and the problem of external effects mentioned in Chapter 1 require a qualification of certain predictions of the theory of exchange discussed in the preceding example. These problems are dealt with at length in the remaining chapters of this book.

Production and Specialization

To this point, our discussion has not included production. The two individuals were endowed with given amounts of goods per unit of time which they exchanged to reach preferred combinations.

Goods, of course, have to be produced, and this is the problem we now turn to. Typically, individuals produce more of one particular good than they consume—they specialize in production. The residual (the amount produced in excess of their own consumption) is traded for other goods for which their own consumption exceeds their own production. Why is this the case? Why aren't individuals self-sufficient?

In order to answer these questions, we consider two individuals in isolation. Each one catches fish and picks berries. Initially, they do not exchange with one another. Production is costly. Catching more fish means that fewer berries can be picked. Generally speaking, the greater the rate of production, the more costly it is, in terms of goods foregone, to increase the rate further. That is, marginal cost increases as the rate of production increases. Marginal cost is the change in total cost (here, measured in terms of pounds of berries foregone) that results when the rate of production (pounds of fish per unit of time) changes by a small amount (here, one pound).

Table 2.2 summarizes the situation confronted by two individuals. The marginal value in use, *MV,* of pounds of fish expressed in terms of pounds of berries is given in column two of Table 2.2(a) and 2.2(b). Remember, this is the maximum quantity of berries the individual would willingly forego for an additional pound of fish. Table 2.2 presents the marginal values of fish in use to two individuals at different rates of fish consumption. The marginal cost, *MC,*

Table 2.2

(a)			(b)		
Ann			Diane		
Fish	*MV*	*MC*	Fish	*MV*	*MC*
1	10.0	2.5	1	11.0	2.0
2	9.0	3.0	2	10.0	4.0
3	8.0	3.5	3	9.0	6.0*
4	7.0	4.0	4	8.0	8.0
5	6.0*	4.5	5	7.0	10.0
6	5.0	5.0	6	6.0*	12.0
7	4.0	5.5	7	5.0	14.0
8	3.0	6.0*	8	4.0	16.0
9	2.0	6.5	9	3.0	18.0
10	1.0	7.0	10	2.0	20.0

*Values at equilibrium.

of catching fish measured in terms of pounds of berries foregone is given in column 3 of each table. This column indicates the quantity of berries the individual *necessarily* foregoes by catching additional fish.

If no exchange occurs between the two individuals, Ann and Diane, Ann will choose to produce and consume 6 pounds of fish per unit of time. This is true because, at consumption rates up to 6 pounds of fish, she values additional pounds of fish measured in terms of pounds of berries more highly than the cost of obtaining additional fish measured in terms of pounds of berries. She will not produce the seventh pound of fish because she values this at only 4 pounds of berries and it costs her 5.5 pounds of berries to obtain it. Diane, for similar reasons, will produce and consume 4 pounds of fish per unit of time.

The total value of 10 pounds of fish to the two individuals is 83 pounds of berries. This is obtained by summing over the marginal values in use up to the quantity of fish consumed by each individual. The total cost of 10 pounds of fish is 42.5 pounds of berries (the sum over the marginal cost of producing fish). The social dividend from production is the difference between total value in use and total cost, or 40.5 pounds of berries.

In the absence of exchange, Ann and Diane have reached an equilibrium. You should note that, in this equilibrium, the marginal values in use and marginal costs are not equal between the two individuals. While Ann's *MV* equals her *MC* and Diane's *MV* equals her *MC*, Diane's *MV* and *MC* are higher than Ann's. At the margin, Diane values fish more highly than does Ann. It is also true that obtaining additional pounds of fish is more costly to Diane than it is to Ann. We have shown that if marginal values in use are not the same between individuals, a potential gain from exchange exists and that it is in the interest of individuals to exploit this. The same is true when there is a difference in marginal costs.

Suppose that we allow exchange and, for the moment, suppose production is held at 10 pounds of fish. Ann continues to produce 6 units and Diane produces 4 units. Ann values fish at the margin at 5 pounds of berries, while Diane values an *additional* pound of fish at 7 pounds of berries. The potential gain from exchange is 2 pounds of berries; therefore, the two individuals will make this trade. After this exchange, each consumes 5 pounds of fish. Further reallocation of the existing 10 pounds of fish between the two will produce no further gains *given the allocation of production*. Note, however, that the marginal cost of producing fish to Ann is 5 pounds of berries when 6 pounds of fish are produced. When Diane produces 4 pounds of fish, her marginal cost is 8 pounds of berries. If Diane were to reduce fish production by 1 pound, she, alternatively, could produce 8 pounds of berries. If Ann were to increase fish production by 1 pound to 7 pounds, she would forego the production of only 5.5 pounds of berries. Diane would be willing to pay a maximum of 8 pounds of berries (the amount she can produce by reducing fish production by 1 pound) for 1 pound of fish. Ann, on the other hand, would willingly accept as few as 5.5 pounds of berries as an inducement to produce an additional pound of fish for Diane. Reallocating the production of 1 pound of fish away from Diane to Ann will save foregoing 2.5 pounds of berries. This saving will motivate them to engage in an exchange that will accomplish the reallocation.

Ann is now producing 7 pounds of fish at a marginal cost of 5.5 pounds of berries, and she is consuming 5 pounds of fish. Ann is specializing in the production of fish. Diane is producing 3 pounds of fish at a marginal cost of 6 pounds of berries and is consuming 5 pounds of fish. Her fish consumption exceeds her production. She is trading berries for the additional fish. Hence, Diane is specializing in berry production.

Further reallocation of fish production will not result in an increase in berry production. The increase in berry production that results from reallocating the production of 10 pounds of fish is 2.5 pounds of berries. A further exchange will occur that will increase fish production above 10 pounds.

Ann values an additional pound of fish (the sixth pound) at 5 pounds of berries. Since she is already producing 7 pounds of fish, producing another pound would cost her 6 pounds of berries. Clearly, she will not produce the additional pound of fish for her own consumption. However, Diane could induce Ann to produce the additional pound of fish since Diane would be willing to pay 6 pounds of berries (Diane's marginal value in use of an additional pound of fish).

After this exchange has occurred, Ann consumes 5 pounds of fish and produces 8 pounds. Her marginal value in use and marginal cost of fish are equal. Diane consumes 6 pounds of fish and produces 3 pounds. Her marginal value in use and marginal cost are equal and are also equal to Ann's. Total fish production is 11 pounds per unit of time. The total quantity of berries foregone is 46 pounds. No other allocation of production or distribution of fish between the two individuals would result in a larger difference between total value in use (the sum over the marginal values) and total cost (the sum over marginal cost). The total value in use of fish after these exchanges is 91 pounds of berries. The total cost of producing fish is 46 pounds of berries. The social dividend from production and exchange is 45 pounds of berries. This is 4.5 pounds of berries more than was obtained in the absence of exchange.

By exploiting the gains from exchange, individuals take actions which result in maximizing this social dividend. The above argument is summarized in Figure 2.3. The curves D and S are obtained by horizontally summing Ann's and Diane's MV and MC curves. Diane's gain (profit) from specializing in the production of fish is the area ABC. Diane's gain from exchanging berries for fish is the area DEF. Diane's gain results from the fact that she obtains more fish (6 rather than 4) at a lower price (6 rather than 8 pounds of berries per pound of fish). Note that higher profits for the seller are not inconsistent with lower prices for the buyer. To illustrate, Ann, who is the seller, had a net gain (profit) when she was self-sufficient of 22.5 pounds of berries. This is the difference between the *sum* of her marginal values in use and marginal cost of producing and consuming 6 pounds of fish. When Ann specializes in the production of fish and exchanges with Diane, her net gain (profit) is 24 pounds of berries. Note that Ann produces 5 pounds of fish for her *own* consumption, which she values in total at 40 pounds of berries. In addition, Ann produces 3 pounds of fish that she trades to Diane at a price of 6 pounds of berries per pound of fish for a total of 18 pounds of berries. Ann's total gain resulting from the production of 8 pounds of fish is 58 pounds of berries. Her total cost (the sum over her marginal cost) of producing 8 pounds of fish is 34 pounds of berries. Her net gain or profit is 24 pounds of berries $(24 = 58 - 34)$. Ann's profits are 1.5 pounds of berries greater when she specializes and exchanges with Diane than they are when she is self-sufficient.

Figure 2.3

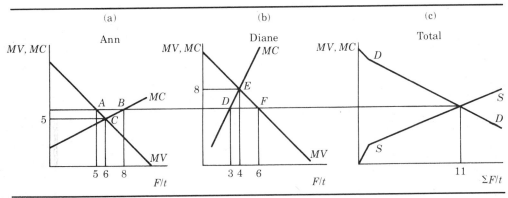

Diane, on the other hand, receives fish at a lower price (6 pounds of berries rather than 8 pounds of berries) when she exchanges with Ann. This results in a gain to Diane of 3 pounds of berries. Note that Ann's gain from specialization and exchange (1.5 pounds of berries) and Diane's gain from specialization and exchange (3.0 pounds of berries) sum to 4.5 pounds of berries, which is equal to the increase in the social dividend that we computed above.

Exchange and Efficiency

Free exchange maximizes the social dividend, that is, the difference between total value in use and total cost for each good produced.[2] In other words, after all gains from exchange have been exhausted, it is impossible to reallocate production or the distribution of products between individuals without making at least one individual worse off. Put still another way, it means that making one individual better off *necessarily* means that some other individual or individuals will be made worse off. When this is true, resources (goods) are said to be allocated efficiently. Free exchange, then, leads to an efficient allocation of resources, or, as it is sometimes called, a Pareto optimal allocation of resources.

When resources (goods) are allocated efficiently, marginal values in use are equal between consumers and equal to marginal costs, which are equal between producers. Check the example given in Table 2.2. The asterisk denotes each individual's marginal use value, or marginal cost, for her respective rates of consumption and production. This may be put more formally as follows:

$$MV_{ij} = MC_{kj}; \quad i = 1, \ldots, m; \quad k = 1, \ldots, n; \quad j = 1, \ldots, p.$$

MV and *MC* are defined as before. The subscripts *i, j,* and *k* indicate the *i*th consumer, *j*th product, and *k*th producer, respectively. In other words, the marginal value in use that each individual associates with, say, fish is equal to the marginal value in use of fish for every other individual. If this were not the case, further gains from exchange resulting in the reallocation of the consumption of fish would be possible. A similar statement holds for marginal cost. The equation indicates that the marginal cost of producing fish for

---

[2]External effects may cause this result to break down. We will begin to deal with this problem in Chapter 3. For now, we ignore it.

each individual is equal to the marginal cost of producing fish for every other individual. If this were not the case, further gains from exchange resulting in the reallocation of the production of fish would be possible. Likewise, marginal value in use is equal to marginal cost for each individual and between individuals. If this were not the case, further gains would be possible from increasing the production of fish if *MV* exceeds *MC* or from reducing the production of fish if *MC* exceeds *MV*.

The Budget Constraint and Indifference Curves: A Brief Review

We will find it convenient, at times, to present the analysis of exchange somewhat differently. As you are well aware, most real-world exchanges are not conducted by barter (exchanging goods for goods). Rather, individuals exchange money for goods and goods for money. The introduction of money into the exchange process, however, does not alter the essential aspects of exchange that were discussed previously. When money is employed as a medium of exchange, individuals select a particular quantity of goods per unit of time subject to the constraint imposed by the money income they receive per unit of time and the money prices of the commodities.[3] The individual's money income and the money prices that he or she faces are taken as given. The ratio of any two money prices indicates the rate at which the individual *can* substitute the two commodities in the budget. For example, if the money price of a one-pound box of candy is two dollars and the money price of one gallon of ice cream is one dollar, the individual must forego two gallons of ice cream when he or she purchases a box of candy.

$$\frac{\text{Money price of one-pound box of candy}}{\text{Money price of one gallon of ice cream}} = \frac{\$2.00}{\$1.00} = \frac{2 \text{ gallons of}}{\text{ice cream}}$$

Two gallons of ice cream is the *relative* price of candy in terms of ice cream. The relative price of ice cream in terms of candy is one-half box of candy or the reciprocal of the relative price of candy in terms of ice cream. The money prices and, consequently, the relative prices of these commodities are determined by market forces.

---

[3]We ignore, here, the particular source of the money income received by the individual. In general, the income will result from the sale of other commodities or services. Also, the discussion of exchange in this section does not treat explicit exchange between individuals as we have discussed previously but exchange between individuals at market determined prices.

The individual takes them as given since his or her actions alone are not sufficient to alter them appreciably.

The money prices of commodities together with the individual's money income indicate the various combinations of commodities the individual can purchase. For example, if the individual's money income is $100 per unit of time and the money prices of candy and ice cream are as above, the individual can purchase 50 boxes of candy and no ice cream or 100 gallons of ice cream and no candy or 25 boxes of candy and 50 gallons of ice cream, as well as many other combinations. These combinations and any other combination that exhausts the individual's budget may be plotted as in Figure 2.4. Units of ice cream per unit of time are plotted along the vertical axis. Units of candy per unit of time are plotted along the horizontal axis. The straight line *AA,* which connects the point 100 gallons of ice cream and no candy to the point 50 boxes of candy and no ice cream, indicates all of the combinations of ice cream and candy that, when purchased, will exhaust the money income of the individual. The slope of the budget constraint, *AA,* is equal to the relative price of candy in terms of ice cream. It indicates the rate at which ice cream *can* be substituted for candy in the individual's budget.

Combinations of ice cream and candy, which are indicated by points interior to the budget constraint (such as point *B*), are, of

Figure 2.4

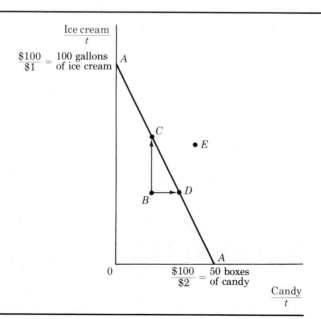

course, attainable to the individual. They are, however, not desirable since the individual could move to point C and consume more ice cream without reducing consumption of candy. Alternatively, he or she could move to point D and consume more candy without reducing consumption of ice cream. Points that are exterior to the budget constraint are not attainable to the individual. The individual will choose a combination of the two commodities that lies along the budget constraint. In order to determine which particular combination he or she will choose, it is necessary to introduce indifference curves.

An indifference curve indicates all those combinations of two goods which are equally preferred by the individual.[4] We expect indifference curves to be negatively sloped. This indicates that if the individual's consumption of one good (ice cream) were reduced, he or she would have to be compensated with some more of some other other good (candy) if he or she is to prefer the new combination equally to the original combination. Note that this is consistent with our first proposition regarding individual behavior. We also expect indifference curves to be convex with respect to the origin. This indicates that if the consumption of, say, ice cream is successively reduced by one unit, per unit of time, the individual will require successively larger amounts of candy to maintain indifference. This is consistent with our second proposition regarding individual behavior.

Figure 2.5 depicts two indifference curves. Units of ice cream per unit of time are measured along the vertical axis while units of candy per unit of time are measured along the horizontal axis. U_0 indicates those combinations of ice cream and candy which are equally preferred by the individual. The same is true for those combinations indicated by U_1. However, the combinations indicated by U_1 are preferred to those indicated by U_0. This is easily shown to be true. Since all combinations indicated by U_0 are equally preferred by the individual, they are equally preferred to the combination indicated by point a. Since all of the combinations indicated by U_1 are equally preferred by the individual, they are equally preferred to the combination indicated by point b. However, the combination indicated by point b must be preferred to the combination indicated by point a, since the combination indicated by point b contains the same amount of ice cream but more candy than does the combination at point a.

---

[4]An indifference surface could be constructed for three goods, and the concept of indifference can be applied to combinations of many goods. For the purpose of simplicity, we deal with only two goods.

Figure 2.5

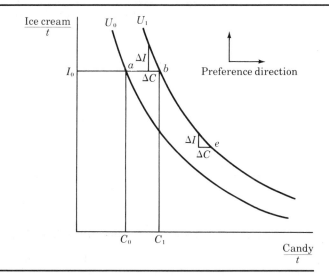

The slope of the indifference curve indicates the rate at which the individual is *willing* to substitute the two commodities. Our second proposition regarding the behavior of the individual states that this rate will change as the mix in which the two commodities are consumed changes. In the neighborhood of point e along U_1, a reduction in the individual's consumption of candy by ΔC requires an increase in consumption of ice cream by ΔI to maintain indifference. In this neighborhood, the individual consumes relatively more candy and less ice cream than in the neighborhood of point b along U_1. Note that, in the neighborhood of point b, a reduction in consumption of candy, ΔC, by the same amount that it was reduced at point e, will require a much greater increase in consumption of ice cream to maintain indifference. The individual values candy more highly in terms of ice cream in the neighborhood of point b (where he or she consumes relatively more ice cream and less candy) than at point e.

Two further comments are important regarding indifference curves. First, there is an indifference curve which passes through every combination of ice cream and candy indicated in Figure 2.5. Second, indifference curves cannot intersect one another. If they were to intersect, it would imply that the combination of goods indicated by the point of intersection is preferred to itself (can you show why?). Clearly, this makes no sense.

It is now possible to determine the combination of ice cream and candy that the individual will select. Figure 2.6 combines the

Figure 2.6

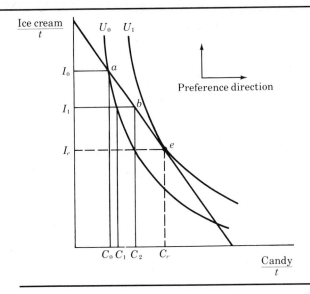

indifference map with the budget constraint. The budget constraint indicates all the combinations of candy and ice cream that are attainable. We know that the individual will select a combination somewhere along this line. The combination of ice cream and candy that he or she selects will be the one that allows him or her to reach the highest possible indifference curve that is also consistent with the budget constraint. This is the combination indicated by point e in Figure 2.6. At point e, indifference curve U_1 is tangent to the budget constraint. If the indifference curve were to cut the budget constraint, as U_0 does at point a, it would indicate that the individual could attain a more preferred combination of the two commodities.

Note that if the individual were to reduce consumption of ice cream from I_0 to I_1, the indifference curve indicates that he or she would require an increase in candy consumption from C_0 to C_1 in order to maintain indifference. The budget constraint indicates, however, that it is possible to obtain an increase in candy consumption equal to the difference between C_2 and C_0. Since this is more than is necessary to maintain indifference, the individual will substitute C_2-C_0 units of candy for I_1-I_0 units of ice cream. The gain from this substitution is C_2-C_1 units of candy. Thus, the individual will move from point a to point b on the budget constraint. The indifference curve that passes through point b (not shown) is a higher indifference curve than the one passing through point a. It is higher because the combinations that lie along it are more preferred than those indicated by U_0. The individual will continue to substitute as long as he or she experiences a gain from doing so. There is a gain from substitution as long as the indifference curve cuts the budget constraint at the selected combination. When the individual reaches point e, no further gains from substitution are possible. The combination indicated by point e is the combination the individual will continue to select as long as he or she is confronted with the same budget constraint and has the same tastes and preferences.

Should the budget constraint change because the prices of the commodities change or because income changes, the individual will select a different combination. It is by examining changes in the budget constraint that economists predict changes in the combinations of goods that individuals select.

Questions and Exercises

1. How does the free exchange of private property rights mitigate the effects of scarcity?

2. What is the Fundamental Theorem of Exchange? What is it that motivates individuals to exchange?

3. "Trade between the Mediterranean and the Baltic developed when each area produced a surplus of some good." What do you think this means? Can you propose an alternative explanation?

4. "If middlemen make a profit, it must result from charging higher prices to consumers and paying lower prices to producers." Higher (lower) than what prices? Comment on this statement.

5. What does it mean to say that an individual specializes in the production of a good?

6. Specialization results in producers obtaining higher prices for their goods while consumers pay lower prices. How is this possible?

7. What does it mean to say that resources are allocated efficiently?

8. The increased output that results from specialization is distributed as profits and as a lower price to consumers. What determines the proportion of each?

9. Making the United States self-sufficient in energy will almost certainly make U. S. citizens poorer. Why?

10. Every profit represents a gain from moving resources to a higher valued use. Do you agree? If so, why? If not, why not?

Additional Readings

Alchian, Armen, and Allen, William R. *Exchange and Production: Competition, Coordination, and Control.* 2d ed. Belmont, Calif.: Wadsworth Publishing Co., 1977.

Hirshleifer, Jack. *Price Theory and Applications.* Englewood Cliffs, N.J.: Prentice-Hall, Inc., 1976.

Stigler, George J. *The Theory of Price.* New York: The Macmillan Company, 1969.

3

Public Goods

Market Failure vs. Failure to Produce Desired Results

The theory of exchange, which was developed in the previous chapter, predicts that the forces of demand and supply will operate to allocate resources efficiently. Efficiency, here, means that it is impossible to alter the allocation of resources to make someone better off without making someone else worse off. There are many individuals, economists in particular, who consider this result desirable. As a consequence, much effort has been devoted to formulating the marginal conditions necessary to assure the desired outcome.[1] This outcome will be produced by market forces if private property rights are well defined, there are no public goods,[2] transaction costs are zero, and no individuals possess monopoly power. Given this environment, economic theory predicts that the interaction of consumers and producers in the market will result in an efficient allocation of resources.

The real world, however, is never quite as perfect as the theories constructed to explain it. If public goods are present in the economy, the market process may not result in establishing the marginal conditions predicted by the theory. As a result, some observers claim that markets fail. The market did not produce the predicted (desired) results. This is not a market failure but a failure of the theory. The theory failed to predict some outcomes because some complicating factors were intentionally excluded. The purpose of a theory is *to predict* real-world results. Theories are, generally, very poor standards by which to *judge* real-world results.

In this chapter we examine the phenomena of public goods and positive transaction costs. Our purpose is to begin to modify the theory discussed in Chapter 2 in a way that will allow it to predict real-world outcomes regarding these phenomena.

---

[1]These marginal conditions are discussed in Chapter 2.

[2]Public goods are defined later in this chapter.

Public Goods and Private Goods

A public good is one that is nonrival in consumption. These goods have the characteristic that consumption of the good by one individual does not reduce the amount available to others. *Once a pure public good is produced,* it can be consumed by many individuals.

For example, national defense is a good that is nonrival in consumption. All residents of the U.S. consume the total output of the public good, national defense. Furthermore, additional individuals can be defended without reducing the defense available to others.

The characteristic of nonrival consumption can be expressed mathematically.

$$X^s = X_1 = X_2 = X_3 = \ldots = X_N \tag{1}$$

$$MC_i(X) = 0 \tag{2}$$

In Equation (1), X^s is the total supply of the public good, X. The population for which it is technically possible to consume the public good, X, is of size N. X_1 is the first individual's consumption of X, and so on. Equation (1) states that the *total quantity* of public good X that is produced, X^s, is consumed by each individual in the population. In Equation (2), $MC_i(X)$ is the cost of providing the public good X to an additional individual (labeled i). If X is nonrival in consumption, the cost of providing an additional individual with the good is zero.

There are two important points that must be kept in mind when considering Equations (1) and (2). The first concerns Equation (1). The fact that the individuals consume the same quantity of public good X does not mean that they all get the same amount of satisfaction from their consumption of X. Individuals are different, and the degree of enjoyment or satisfaction they get from a given amount of a public good (or any good) will be different. In fact, some individuals may feel worse off by the provision of a good, even though their share in the costs of providing the good is zero.

The second point concerns Equation (2). Although Equation (2) states that the cost of providing a public good to an additional individual is zero *once the good is produced,* the opportunity cost of producing the public good is not zero. Production of public goods, like production of all goods, uses scarce resources. When these scarce resources are used in the production of a public good, they cannot be used to produce other goods. Therefore, the cost of producing an additional unit of a public good is equal to the value of the other goods that cannot be produced as a consequence of producing the public good.

Pure private goods are rival in consumption. These are the goods we discussed in Chapter 2. When a good is rival in consumption, the amount consumed by one individual is *not* available for consumption by others. The ice cream that is consumed by one person cannot be consumed by anyone else.

Equation (3) expresses mathematically the concept of rivalry in consumption.

$$Y^s = Y_1 + Y_2 + Y_3 + \ldots + Y_N \qquad (3)$$

In Equation (3), Y^s is the total supply of the private good available. Once again we have N individuals in the economy, and Y_1 is the amount of Y consumed by the first individual, etc. An individual benefits from the provision of a private good only to the extent of his or her personal consumption of the good. Equation (3) states that the first individual consumes Y_1 units of the private good. Benefit from the private good arises only from the amount *he or she* consumes (Y_1). It is not in any way related to the amount consumed by others (Y_2, Y_3, . . . , Y_n), nor is it related to the total amount produced (Y^s). Furthermore, the amount consumed by the first individual cannot be consumed by any other individual. We can see this by rewriting Equation (3).

$$Y^s - Y_1 = Y_2 + Y_3 + \ldots + Y_N \qquad (4)$$

Equation (4) is derived by subtracting the amount of the private good consumed by the first individual from both sides of Equation (3). By rearranging Equation (3), we see that the amount consumed by the first individual (or any other individual) must be subtracted from the total amount produced (Y^s) when calculating the amount available for consumption by the other individuals (2, 3, . . . , N).

A characteristic of *some* public goods (and some private goods) is that, once the good is produced, it is extremely costly to prevent individuals from consuming the good. When the consumption of a good (such as defense) involves high exclusion costs, any quantity of defense sold privately to one individual will be consumed by all other individuals, even if they choose not to pay for it.

Property Rights

Goods that have high exclusion costs are goods for which private property rights are costly to define and enforce. When a good involves high exclusion costs, its suppliers have incomplete property rights. It may be impossible for them to exclude individuals who benefit from the good but do not pay for it. As a consequence, the market price of the good will not accurately indicate the marginal value of the good to individuals.

We have argued (see Chapter 2) that free exchange of private property will cause resources to be allocated (rationed) to their highest valued use, thus maximizing the net social dividend. Goods are rationed to their highest valued use by this process because free exchange of private property *excludes* individuals on the basis of willingness to pay. Consequently, individuals are induced to reveal information regarding the value of the goods to them through the bids they make. If they do not reveal this information by bidding, they will not obtain the goods they wish to have. These bids (information regarding individual valuation of goods employed in alternative uses) transmits information to the present owner of the good concerning the alternative cost of continuing to employ the good in its present use. If the bids are high enough (if the payment will *at least* compensate for the loss incurred by selling), the present owners will sell. In markets these bids are called prices. Free exchange of private property, because it excludes on the basis of willingness to pay, causes individuals to internalize (take into account in their decisions) the costs (benefits) that their actions impose on others.

Prices reveal information not only to present owners of goods but also to producers. If the prices currently being offered for a particular good, beer for example, are high enough to compensate producers for the other goods necessarily forsaken by increasing the rate of production, brewers will increase the quantity of beer produced per unit of time. Brewers will continue to increase beer production as long as there are individuals who are willing to *at least* compensate the brewers for the other goods necessarily forsaken. That is, they will continue to increase beer production as long as individuals indicate that they value additional resources employed in the production of beer more highly than those same resources employed elsewhere. Exclusion on the basis of willingness to pay causes individuals to allocate goods to their highest valued uses in consumption and resources to their highest valued uses in production. Also, because it causes individuals to internalize the costs that their actions impose on others, it assures that adjustments in the rate of production will take place when the total cost of producing a particular good is different from the value of that good.

As we have noted, public goods, like private goods, are scarce.

This means that producing more of a particular public good necessarily means producing less of some other good, public or private. However, public goods differ from private goods in that they are nonrival in consumption. Unlike private goods, *once public goods are produced,* no rationing problem exists. As a consequence, there is no necessity on the grounds of efficiency to ration the public good to higher valued uses. Once it is produced, it is equally available for all uses.

It is sometimes argued that goods which are nonrival in consumption and for which exclusion costs are low will not be provided efficiently by the market. The argument runs as follows. Goods provided through the market will require exclusion so that suppliers can extract a payment from consumers to cover the cost of producing the good. However, if the good being produced is nonrival in consumption, supplying the good to additional individuals *once it is produced* is possible at zero cost. Consequently, excluding any individual who values the good is inefficient because supplying the good to the additional individual will make him or her better off while making no one else worse off. Rationing by price will lead to too few individuals consuming the good. This argument has some merit. However, it begins from a point after the good is produced and, thus, ignores the *opportunity cost* of producing public goods. As we stated before, producing public goods means producing fewer other goods. Furthermore, unless exclusion by price is used, there is no practical way of determining the value of the public good to consumers. Exclusion by price provides the only way we know of to determine whether it pays to produce the good. If consumers are willing to pay an amount equal to or greater than the total cost of producing the good, it follows that the value of the good to consumers exceeds the cost. Hence, while it may be inefficient to exclude individuals from consuming a public good on the basis of willingness to pay once the good is produced, it is impossible to determine whether producing the good will contribute to the welfare of the community without exclusion. This dilemma results from the fact that we live in an imperfect world.

Excluding nonpayers is important for all goods (public and private) because resources are scarce. Producing more of one good necessarily means producing less of some other. Information regarding the value of goods (where value is measured in terms of other goods *willingly* forsaken) is important in determining how much and what kinds of goods (public and private) to produce.

Excluding nonpayers by assigning and enforcing private property rights is costly. This is true for all goods, both public and private. The courts, legislature, and police force exist, in part, to define and enforce the private property rights of individuals, be it their cars, houses, furniture, or ideas. If the costs of excluding non-payers exceeds the value of the property, no net benefit will result from excluding nonpayers. In other words, the value of the information obtained by excluding nonpayers does not warrant the cost of doing so. The provision of free parking in some shopping centers is an example of a private good for which the costs of excluding nonpayers is high relative to the value of the information—regarding the value to individuals of space employed for parking—generated by excluding. National defense is an example of a public good for which exclusion costs are relatively high. When exclusion costs are high, there is no guaranty that the quantity of resources allocated to the production of the good is the quantity that maximizes the difference between the value of the good to individuals and the cost of obtaining it. "Too" much or "too" little of the good may be produced. This is one of the reasons why people argue about the quantity of resources devoted to the production of defense but do not argue about the quantity of resources devoted to the production of movies. Both movies and defense are public goods, but low cost exclusion is possible only with the movies.

When the costs of assigning and enforcing private property rights in a particular good are relatively high, so that exclusion on the basis of willingness to pay is too costly, common property rights in that good are said to exist. If the good is a private good, a rationing problem exists. Exclusion will occur on some basis other than willingness to pay. The good will not be allocated to its highest valued uses in consumption and, in general, too much or too little of the good will be produced. If the good is a public good, a rationing problem does not exist *once the good is produced*. However, because no information is revealed regarding the value of the good to individuals through a bidding process, too much or too little of the good will be produced. Figure 3.1 summarizes the arguments we have made to this point.

You should not become confused by our use of the terms public goods and private goods. Public goods are goods that are nonrival in consumption. As our examples have indicated, this does not imply that they will or should be produced through collective or government action. Many public goods are privately produced. It is also true that many private goods are provided by the government. Nor does the ability to exclude at low cost determine whether the good will be provided privately or by government. Goods that are both public and private and for which exclusion costs are either high or low are provided through both private and government action. The same is true regarding private provision of goods. A

Figure 3.1

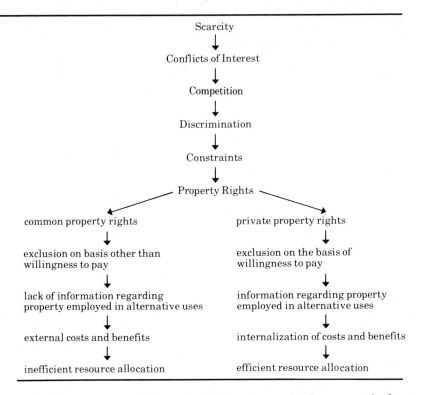

partial answer concerning what determines whether a particular good will be provided by government action or by private action will be developed in Chapters 5, 6, and 7. For now, Table 3.1 gives some examples that fall into the various categories.

Table 3.1

	High Cost Exclusion		Low Cost Exclusion	
	Public Provision	**Private Provision**	**Public Provision**	**Private Provision**
Public good	Defense	A mathematical theorem	Bridges Public TV	Movies Plays Songs Sports events
Private good	Residential curbside parking	Free parking at shopping centers	Food stamps Public housing	Bread Beer Shoes Cars

Externalities

Public goods create what are called externalities. An external effect, or externality, is said to exist when the activity of one party benefits (damages) another party that does not pay (receive compensation) for the benefit (damage). The externality can be generated by either the consumption or production processes and can affect either consumers or producers. Air pollution, water pollution, and traffic accidents are examples of harmful externalities.

Public goods have external effects that involve large numbers of people. If John Doe purchases national defense, he will externally benefit all U.S. citizens. The purchase of defense, D, generates an external effect that can be expressed by the following equation.

$$U_i (D, Y_1, Y_2, Y_3 \ldots Y_N). \quad i = 1, N$$

The *total quantity* of national defense supplied enters into the utility of *all N* citizens.

Realistically speaking, few, if any, goods fit our definition of pure public goods. If an activity generates an external effect that benefits large numbers of individuals (that is, is nonrival in consumption), and if excluding nonpayers from the benefits is costly, the activity (good) *may* not be provided by the market. In this case, government provision *may* be called for.

However, for nearly all public goods, exclusion is possible at a cost. State parks are an example of a good provided by the government where exclusion is not only possible but actually takes place. The good is rationed through the use of entrance fees.

Voluntary Solutions and Private Property Rights

In many cases, voluntary agreements among parties, when external effects are present, can lead to efficient outcomes. This proposition is known as the Coase Theorem.[3]

The Coase Theorem is relevant in situations for which the costs of reaching agreement (transaction costs) between the parties are low and where income effects are absent. When these conditions hold, the theorem implies that resource allocation will be

---

[3]See R. H. Coase, "The Problem of Social Cost," *Journal of Law and Economics,* Vol. 3 (1960), pp. 1–44.

efficient and will not be affected by the initial assignment of property rights. The initial assignment of property rights needs some explanation. Assume there are two parties involved in an external damage situation, a factory generating smoke and a nearby nursery that has plants and flowers damaged by the smoke. The factory could be assigned the property right to generate smoke, thus damaging the nursery without restraint. Alternatively, the nursery could be assigned the right to remain completely free of smoke damage. The Coase Theorem says that whichever of these initial right assignments exist, the final allocation of resources will be identical and the outcome optimal.

The requirement of the Coase Theorem that transaction costs be low is satisfied when the parties involved are few in number. Income effects are absent when the parties involved are profit-maximizing firms. When one or more of the participants are consumers, income effects are not absent because the initial assignment of property rights influences the wealth positions of the individuals involved. Changes in wealth change the response of the consumer to the externality and the bargaining process. This will change the allocation of resources. If consumers are involved in the externality, the final resource allocation will be different with different assignments of property rights. Even though the allocation of resources is different under alternate initial right assignments, the final outcome will still be efficient. That is, the first and most important result of the Coase Theorem holds even if income effects are present.

A Numerical Example

The Coase Theorem can be illustrated by using a simple numerical example.[4] Suppose that a grain farmer suffers damages (in the sense that his profits are reduced) when his neighbor's cattle wander onto his farm. Assume the cattle rancher bears no liability for the loss suffered by the farmer. If the rancher does not take the farmer's loss into account when deciding how many cattle to raise, he will be inclined to raise too many cattle (see Table 3.2). If the rancher bears no liability for the damages experienced by the farmer, he will choose to raise 14 cattle per year. The rancher's profit will be $112. Note, however, that the net benefit that results from raising cattle is only $97. The net benefit of raising cattle is

---

[4]This example is discussed by R. H. Coase, "The Problem of Social Cost," *Journal of Law and Economics,* Vol. 3 (1960), pp. 1-44; and by G. J. Stigler, *The Theory of Price* (New York: The Macmillan Company, 1969), pp. 110-14.

Table 3.2

Cattle	Profit of Rancher	Loss to Farmer	Net Benefit
9	$ 94	$ 0	$ 94
10	100	2	98
11	105	3	102
12	109	6	103
13	111	10	101
14	112	15	97
15	111	21	90

less than the rancher's profit because he is imposing a cost on the farmer which results from his wandering cattle.[5]

In this case, the *rancher has the right* to allow his cattle to wander. If the costs of negotiating contracts is low, the farmer and the rancher will find that there are mutual gains to be had from voluntary agreements regarding the number of cattle raised. When the rancher produces 14 cattle, the farmer will be willing to pay him to reduce the size of his herd. The farmer would be willing to pay as much as $5 for the rancher's agreement to reduce the herd to 13. This is true because the farmer's loss is $5 less (or his profits $5 higher) with a herd of 13 rather than 14. Reducing the size of the herd to 13 will cause the rancher's profit to fall by $1. Consequently, he must be compensated by at least this amount for his agreement to reduce production by one head. Any payment between $1 and $5 will make both individuals better off. The negotiation will continue. The farmer would benefit from a further reduction in the size of the herd. If the size of the herd is reduced to 12, the farmer's cost falls by $4. He would be willing to pay this much for the rancher's agreement to reduce the herd size. Further, the rancher will accept any offer greater than $2 since this is the amount by which his profits fall as a result of reducing the herd size to 12. Once the herd size reaches 12, no further trades will take place because continued reduction in herd size will harm the rancher by more than it benefits the farmer.

Suppose, on the other hand, that the rights had been assigned the other way around. That is, the *farmer has the right* to be free of wandering cattle. In the absence of any agreement between the two, the farmer will wish to restrict the rancher's herd to no more than 9 head. Again, it will pay the two to form an agreement. Note that the increment in profit to the rancher of increasing the size of

---

[5]In this example, we assume the cost of fencing is prohibitively high.

his herd up to and including 12 head exceeds the increment in damages to the farmer. For example, if the rancher were to increase the size of his herd from 9 head to 10, his profits would rise by $6. The farmer's damages would increase by only $2. The rancher could buy the farmer's agreement to allow the herd size to increase and still be better off. This is true until the number of cattle has been increased to 12.

As predicted by the Coase Theorem, the initial assignment of rights makes no difference in the final size of the herd when transaction costs are low. Furthermore, when transaction costs are low, the number of cattle that are raised will maximize the net benefit of cattle production. When 12 cattle are raised, the net benefit is $103. No other size herd will yield so high a net benefit. The implication of this analysis is that the existence of what seems to be an external effect does not imply that an outside authority (the government) should impose a solution. When transaction costs are low, a solution can be reached through private agreement once the initial right has been defined.

Some Geometry

The analysis of externalities and the Coase Theorem may be presented in the form of a simple geometrical model.[6] Figure 3.2 shows

Figure 3.2

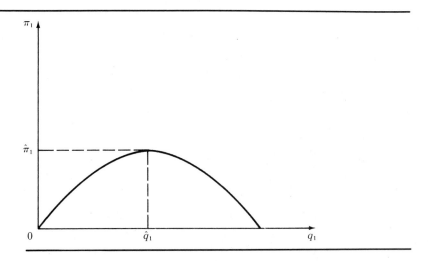

[6]This model first appeared in Adam Gifford, Jr., "Externalities in the Coase Theorem: A Graphical Analysis," *The Quarterly Review of Economics and Business* Vol. 14 (1974), pp. 7-21.

the rancher's profit, which we will call π_1, measured along the vertical axis. Measured along the horizontal axis is the size of the rancher's herd depicted by q_1. As in Table 3.2, the rancher's profit increases with increases in herd size up to a maximum, $\hat{\pi}_1$, then decreases as herd size increases. The herd size that results in the rancher's maximum profit is $\hat{q}_1$.

When the rancher increases his herd size, the crop damage suffered by the farmer increases. The economic damage that results from the increase in herd size is the decrease in the farmer's profit. This is depicted graphically in the top half of Figure 3.3. As the herd size is increased, the maximum profit the farmer can make, π_2, decreases.

As a result of the externality, the farmer's profit is inversely related to the rancher's herd size. As the damage to the farmer increases, he will reduce his crop size, q_2, to minimize the impact of the damage. The relationship between herd size and the farmer's profit-maximizing crop size is shown in the bottom half of Figure 3.3. We can see why there is an inverse relationship between q_1 and q_2 by examining Figure 3.4. In Figure 3.4, P_2 is the market price of grain. When the farmer faces the marginal cost given by the curve MC_2', his profit-maximizing output is q_2'. This is the output that equates price and marginal cost. Because of the externality, when the rancher increases his herd size, the cost of growing grain increases at each rate of output. This will increase the marginal cost faced by the farmer. As q_1 increases, MC will shift from MC_2' to MC_2''. This causes the farmer's profit-maximizing output to de-

Figure 3.3

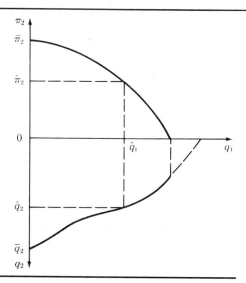

Figure 3.4

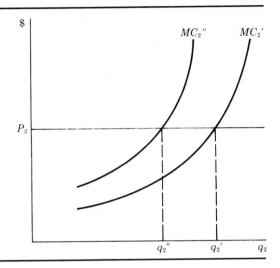

crease to q_2''. The external damage caused by the wandering herd of cattle causes the farmer's marginal cost curve to shift upward. The farmer will respond by reducing his output. This reduces the extent of crop damage at the same time it maximizes the farmer's profit *given that the herd size is now larger* than before.

When the rancher has the property right he, in essence, has the right to ignore the damage he imposes on the farmer. The rancher has the right to the profit $\hat{\pi}_1$ (see Figure 3.2) and to a herd size of $\hat{q}_1$. When the rancher maintains a herd size of $\hat{q}_1$, the farmer, by maintaining a crop size of $\hat{q}_2$, can earn a maximum profit of $\hat{\pi}_2$ (see Figure 3.3).

The damage that the wandering cattle impose on the farmer will induce him to work out some agreement with the rancher to reduce the damage.

The analysis will now focus on the sum of the profits of the two firms (the ranch and the farm). Maximizing the sum of the profits of the two firms will maximize the social dividends. Inverting Figure 3.2 and superimposing it on Figure 3.3 so that the profit functions of the two firms are just tangent gives us Figure 3.5. The vertical height of the top half of Figure 3.5 measures the maximum sum of the profits of the two firms. We can now demonstrate that any decrease in $\hat{q}_1$ (herd size) that increases the profit of the farmer by more than it lowers the profit of the rancher can be secured by exchange of agreements between the farmer and rancher. Any change that increases the summed profits of the two firms can be made mutually advantageous to the two parties through a bargaining process.

When the rancher possesses the right to the profit $\hat{\pi}_1$, it is possible for the farmer to make a payment to him that will induce him to cut back $\hat{q}_1$ (herd size), thus resulting in a reduction of the external damage to the farmer. The minimum payment the rancher would accept to reduce his herd size would have to be at least as large as his reduction in profits resulting from the decrease in $\hat{q}_1$. The maximum payment the farmer would be willing to pay to secure a reduction in the herd size and, hence, in the crop damage is the increase in profit he attains by such a reduction. The

Figure 3.5

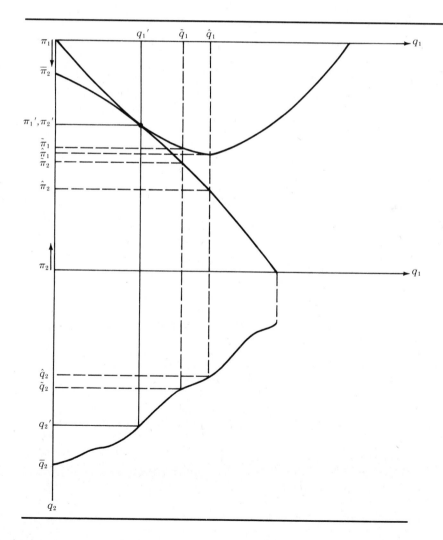

rancher would demand a payment of at least $\hat{\pi}_1 - \tilde{\pi}_1$, his loss of profit, to reduce his herd size to $\tilde{q}_1$. The farmer would be willing to pay at most $\tilde{\pi}_2 - \hat{\pi}_2$, his gain in profit, to induce the rancher to cut back his herd size from $\hat{q}_1$ to $\tilde{q}_1$. The farmer's profit-maximizing crop size, when the rancher has a herd size of $\tilde{q}_1$, is $\tilde{q}_2$.

Examination of Figure 3.5 reveals that the move to the point $(\tilde{q}_1, \tilde{q}_2)$ is mutually advantageous to the farmer and the rancher. The gain to the farmer exceeds the loss to the rancher, and the farmer can make a payment to the rancher out of that gain, leaving them both better off.

However, the bargaining between the parties will not stop with the reduction of the herd size to $\tilde{q}_1$. Only when the parties have moved to the output levels (q_1', q_2'), will they have exhausted all gains from trade. Examination of Figure 3.5 reveals that any decrease in herd size from $\hat{q}_1$ up to q_1' increases the summed profits of the firms (the gap between π_1 and π_2 decreases). If herd size is reduced beyond q_1', summed profits begin to decline. A decrease in herd size below q_1' could not be secured by the farmer because a reduction of herd size below q_1' reduces the rancher's profit by more than it increases the farmer's.

Both the rancher and farmer gain from the move to the herd size q_1'. If they stop short of this herd size, the continued existence of gains from trade will induce them to continue bargaining. The point (q_1', q_2') yields the maximum sum of the farmer's and rancher's profits and results in an efficient allocation of resources.

The actual payment made by the farmer to the rancher cannot be determined from the diagram. The payment will, however, be somewhere between the gain to the farmer, which resulted from the reduction in the herd size from $\hat{q}_1$ to q_1', $(\pi_2' - \hat{\pi}_2)$, and the loss to the rancher, resulting from the reduction $(\hat{\pi}_1 - \pi_1')$. The exact amount will be determined by the bargaining abilities of the two parties.

If the farmer possesses the property right, he has the right to be free of any external damage imposed on him by the rancher. The farmer has the right to a profit of $\bar{\pi}_2$, which corresponds to a crop size of $\bar{q}_2$. In this example, unlike the numerical example in the previous section, the rancher must reduce his herd size to zero to prevent all damage to the farmer. This, of course, will leave the rancher with a zero profit as well. However, both the farmer and the rancher can gain through an agreement that allows the rancher to raise some cattle. When the farmer has the property right to be free of damage, the rancher will have to compensate him for any damage the herd does.

The minimum payment the farmer would accept as compensation for crop damage is the reduction in profit caused by that damage. The maximum payment the rancher would be willing to make is equal to his increase in profit resulting from increasing his herd size. Once again there will be unexploited gains from trade that will compel further negotiation until the herd size q_1' is reached. The maximum payment the rancher will make to increase his herd size from zero to q_1' is π_1', his increase in profit resulting from the increase in herd size. The minimum payment the farmer would accept is $\bar{\pi}_2 - \pi_2'$, the decrease in his profit which results from the increase in herd size. Note that the maximum payment the rancher will make is greater than the minimum payment the farmer will accept; this assures successful negotiation.

As before, the exact level of the payment is indeterminant. However, the rancher and farmer are moved by the gains from trade to the point (q_1', q_2'). The initial assignment of the property right has no effect on the final allocation of resources. Further, the allocation that results is efficient.

Two additional points must be made to complete the discussion of the Coase Theorem. The first point is that actions by the farmer can damage the rancher, just as actions by the rancher can damage the farmer. We actually have a reciprocal damage situation. When the farmer has the property right, he can force the rancher to reduce his herd size to zero. This damages the rancher since it reduces his profits. Reducing the amount of external damage, in fact, damages those individuals who produce that damage.

The second point is that property rights are valuable. The farmer is much better off when he has the property right than he is when the rancher has it. When the farmer has the property right to be free of crop damage, he is guaranteed a profit of $\bar{\pi}_1$. An agreement with the rancher to allow some damage can leave him better off. When the rancher has the property right, the farmer is guaranteed a profit of only $\hat{\pi}_2$. Reaching an agreement with the rancher to reduce his herd size will allow the farmer to achieve a gross profit of π_2'. Out of this profit, however, must come the payment to the rancher. The minimum payment the rancher would accept is $\hat{\pi}_1 - \pi_1'$. Examination of Figure 3.5 reveals that if the farmer makes only the minimum payment, he will be left with a net profit equal to the vertical distance from the lower origin of Figure 3.5 (shown by the symbol π_2) to the point indicated by $\hat{\pi}_1$. This is the maximum net profit the farmer can attain when he does not have the property right, which is less than the minimum profit plus payment attainable when he does have the property right. Using similar analysis, it is easy to show that the rancher is better off when he has the property right than he is when he does not.

Application

Nonzoning in Houston[7]

Most cities have adopted detailed and complex zoning laws to deal with externalities in land usage. These zoning laws supposedly protect the property owner from decreases in land values due to changes in the use of adjoining land, for example, a slaughter house opening up in the middle of a residential neighborhood. Houston, Texas, instead of employing zoning laws, relies on the type of voluntary agreements predicted by the Coase Theorem to deal with these externality problems. In Houston, voluntary agreements between buyers and developers protect the buyer from harmful external effects. These agreements are known as restrictive covenants. All potential buyers of land in a development sign these covenants, binding themselves and future buyers to maintain the land in its current use. The covenants can only be changed by agreement of 51 percent of the landowners in a development. The restrictive covenant is economically efficient because it induces developers of a tract of land to pick the highest valued use for that tract. Buyers of the land are better off and are willing to pay more since they know that the current use will continue as long as it is the highest valued use to them.

The forces of supply and demand control land use in Houston and assure that land is used in its highest valued use. Zoning, on the other hand, arbitrarily tends to reduce the supply of land available for one use and increase the amount available for other uses. This leads to arbitrary high prices for some parcels and low prices for others, which results in a distortion of the allocation of resources.

The major findings of the study of nonzoning in Houston can be summarized as follows:

1. Economic forces and the use of restrictive covenants separate incompatible land uses so that businesses are located in one area, industry in another, and residences in still another. Zoning does not appear to separate uses as efficiently, especially in large cities.

---

[7] Taken from Bernard Siegan, "Non-zoning in Houston," *Journal of Law and Economics,* Vol. 13 (1970), pp. 71–147.

2. Zoning is a legislative function and, as such, is susceptible to the forces of special interests, which can induce inefficient outcomes. This tends to expose the landowner to arbitrary decreases in land values, a situation that does not occur in Houston where land prices are determined by supply and demand.

The Optimal Solution When Transaction Costs Are Zero

In this section, we examine the conditions necessary for an efficient allocation of resources when public goods are present. In this case, exclusion costs, which may be considered as part of transaction costs, are assumed to be zero. Understanding this simple case will aid in understanding the more complex case of high exclusion costs.

To examine the necessary conditions for efficient resource allocation when exclusion costs are zero, we will use a model first developed by Paul Samuelson.[8] Assume that the economy is composed of two individuals, Robinson (R) and Friday (F), and two goods, breadfruit (B) and defense (D). Figure 3.6(a) details the production possibility curve, BD, which indicates the optimal trade-off between B and D, assuming that all resources are employed efficiently. Figure 3.6(b) shows R's indifference curves between goods B and D. Figure 3.6(c) shows the indifference curves for F. Defense—the public good—will benefit both Friday and Robinson. They will both consume all of the defense that is produced. On the other hand, the two will have to divide the breadfruit output between them.

There will be a whole series of efficient points in an economy with public goods. The point that is finally reached in the trading process depends on the initial endowments of the parties involved and their relative bargaining strengths. The purpose of the following exercise is to determine what the conditions of an optimum are. To do this, we pick an arbitrary optimum point and examine its characteristics.

Suppose R is initially placed on indifference curve IR_2 [in Figure 3.6(b)] at point (D', B_R'). R will be consuming D' defense and B_R' breadfruit. Defense is a public good, so if D' is available to R, D' can be consumed by F. To determine how much breadfruit is pro-

[8]Paul Samuelson, "A Diagrammatic Exposition of a Theory of Public Expenditure," *The Review of Economics and Statistics,* Vol. 37 (Nov. 1955), pp. 350–56.

48   *Public Goods*

duced when D' defense is produced, follow the vertical line up from the point D' in 3.6(b) to D' in 3.6(a) and then up to the production possibility curve. This shows that when the economy produces D' defense, it can produce B' breadfruit [follow the horizontal line

Figure 3.6

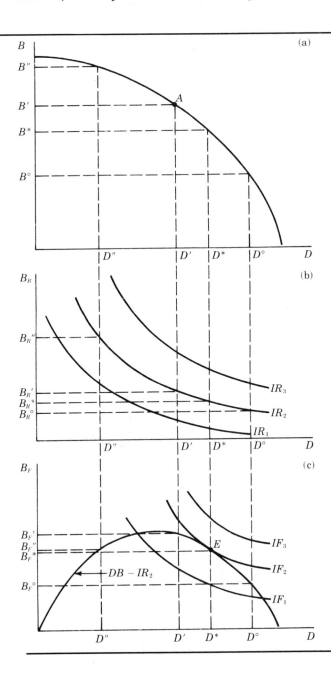

from point A over to the vertical axis in Figure 3.6(a)]. Since we know that R is consuming B_R' breadfruit because of our initial placement of R at point (B_R', D') in Figure 3.6(b), F will be able to consume $B' - B_R'$, since the sum of F's consumption of the private good, breadfruit, plus R's consumption must equal the total produced. Moving to other points along IR_2 where this relationship holds, place R at (D°, B_R°). This placement allows F to consume D° defense and B_F° breadfruit, (D°, B_F°), where $B_R^\circ + B_F^\circ = B^\circ$. Finally, put R at (D'', B_R'') and F at (D'', B_F''), where $B_R'' + B_F'' = B''$. These three points satisfy the conditions that the amount of D consumed is equal for both R and F, and that the sum of the amounts of B consumed by each equals the amount produced. All points that satisfy these conditions as R moves along IR_2 are found when F follows the curve labeled $DB - IR_2$. An efficient point will be attained when F reaches the highest indifference curve tangent to $DB - IR_2$. Since R's utility is held constant at the level signified by indifference curve IR_2, we find an efficient outcome by maximizing F's utility subject to the constraint that it must be a point on $DB - IR_2$. This efficient outcome occurs at point E. At point E, F consumes D^* defense and B_F^* breadfruit and R consumes D^* defense and B_R^* breadfruit. Both consume the same level of defense and, since $B_R^* + B_F^* = B^*$, the sum of their consumptions of breadfruit equals the total output of breadfruit.

To find other efficient points, pick a new indifference curve for R and trace out a new $DB - IR$ curve in the same way. Next, find the indifference curve for F that is tangent to this new $DB - IR$ curve. All optimums found in this manner will satisfy the following conditions.

$$MV_{DF} + MV_{DR} = MC_D \tag{5}$$

$$B = B_F + B_R \tag{6}$$

$$D = D_F = D_R \tag{7}$$

Equation (5) gives the optimal marginal conditions for a public good. It says that, at an optimum, the marginal value to Friday of D in terms of B plus the marginal value to Robinson of D in terms of B must equal the marginal cost of D in terms of B.

The condition described will hold at an optimum in the model since the $DB - IR$ curve is derived by subtracting the indifference curve on which we initially place R from the production possibility curve BD. Since at the optimum, F's indifference curve is tangent to the $DB - IR$ curve, the slopes of these two curves are equal.

Slope IF = Slope $(DB - IR)$

or

$$\text{Slope } IF + \text{Slope } IR = \text{Slope } DB,$$

which is nothing more than Equation (5). Furthermore, Equation (6) holds because of the way $DB - IR$ was derived, and Equation (7) holds because of the way the graphs were set up.

Equation (5) states that an optimum is reached when the marginal benefit of an additional unit of defense equals the marginal cost. The only difference between the public goods case and the private goods case is that, with the former, an additional unit of the good benefits all individuals rather than only one, as in the latter. In this situation, we derive the marginal benefit of the public good by summing the benefits of the good that accrue to all individuals in the economy. If there are N individuals in the economy, Equation (5) would become:

$$MV_{D1} + MV_{D2} + \ldots + MV_{DN} = MC_{D}. \tag{8}$$

The Coase Theorem implies that when transaction costs (including exclusion) are zero, R and F will arrive at one of these optimum points by voluntary agreement. Which optimum point they reach will depend on the initial endowments and the relative bargaining strengths of the two individuals.

When exclusion costs are high, Equations (5) through (8) and the Samuelson model are useful only as a starting point for finding the optimums. The model must be modified when transaction costs are high for two reasons. First, if transaction costs affect the per unit cost of producing the public good, the DB curve will shift as the level of D changes. This is because bargaining and information costs involve the use of real resources, which must be taken into account when determining the final outcome. Second, and more important, if transaction costs are high, voluntary agreement will not be effective in reaching an optimum. A problem arises because high exclusion costs imply that any solution will not be cost free. Consequently, should the government intervene in order to move the market-determined outcome toward the Samuelson solution, it will only pay to invest resources up to the point at which a dollar's worth of real resources invested yields a dollar's worth of return. This implies that the actual result will fall short of the Samuelson ideal since it will not "pay" to achieve this ideal. The second part of this book will deal with this problem.

To further aid in understanding the nature of the problem, let us cast the Samuelson model in terms of demand and supply analysis. To do this we must start with a specific initial endowment that will yield a single equilibrium. In Figure 3.7, D_R is R's demand curve for the public good and D_F is F's. The height of these curves measures the marginal benefit of each level of D to F and R. We know from Equation (7) that, to find the Samuelson solution, we sum the marginal valuations (MV's) of the two individuals for the public good and equate this sum to marginal cost. In terms of demand and supply analysis, we add the individual curves vertically (as opposed to horizontally in the case of private goods) to derive the market demand curve. To find the optimum, we equate this market curve ($D_R + D_F$ in Figure 3.7) to the marginal cost of D (*MC* in Figure 3.7). The optimal output of defense will be D^*. The marginal value of D^* to R is T_R^* and the marginal value to F is T_F^*, and $T_R^* + T_F^* = MC$. When transaction costs are zero, voluntary agreement between R and F will lead to this outcome. Furthermore, each individual is willing to pay a price per unit for the public good equal to the marginal benefit, as in the private good case. R is willing to pay T_R^* and F is willing to pay T_F^*.

The difference between the public good solution and that of private goods is that, in the case of public goods, each individual consumes the same quantity of the public good. Hence, if marginal values differ between individuals when each consumes the same quantity, the individuals will pay different prices. This is illustrated in Figure 3.7. Each individual consumes the same quantity of defense, D^*. Because marginal values differ, however, Friday pays a unit price of T_F^* while Robinson pays a unit price of T_R^*. The

Figure 3.7

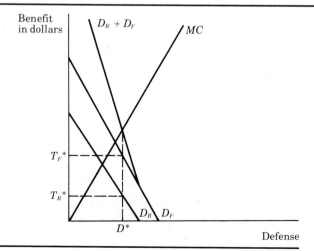

voluntary solution will be viable if the amount paid $T_F^* D^* + T_R^* D^*$ covers the total cost of providing D^*. Only if there is some total payment that consumers of the public good are willing to pay which covers the total cost of the good at output D^* will we know that D^* is both viable and optimal. We included optimal here since the maximum total payment consumers would pay measures their total benefit, and only if this exceeds total cost will we be at an optimum.

Application

Defense Expenditures of NATO Nations

The above analysis suggests two points. First, in an environment in which contracting is possible, the equilibrium quantity of public goods may be provided through voluntary arrangements. This is true particularly if the number of transactors is small. Second, if public goods are provided in this fashion, the prices paid by the parties will be related to the benefits derived.

NATO is a voluntary defense arrangement entered into by certain countries. Defense has certain public good attributes. One might expect the benefits of this defense agreement to be related to the quantity of wealth protected. The defense expenditures by the parties to the agreement are listed below along with the country's GNP (a proxy for wealth).[9] If defense is, indeed, a public good such that each party consumes the entire quantity, each country's total expenditure on defense is a proxy of the price paid. Our hypothesis is that defense expenditures will rise with the GNP (see Table 3.3). The relationship is obvious and in the predicted direction. However, it is not proportional. This may be due to small countries attempting to "free-ride" on large countries or it may be that defense is a superior good.

Application

The Lighthouse in Economics

The lighthouse example has occupied a relatively prominent position in discussions of public goods because of the public-good attributes of lighthouses. Once the light is produced, it is available to

---

[9]M. Olson, Jr., and R. Zeakhauser, "An Economic Theory of Alliances," *The Review of Economics and Statistics*, Vol. 48 (August 1966), p. 267.

Table 3.3

	GNP 1964		Defense Expenditures		As a Percentage of GNP	
	In Billions	Rank	In Billions	Rank	Percent	Rank
United States	569.03	1	51.2	1	9.0	1
Germany	88.87	2	4.8	3	5.5	6
United Kingdom	79.46	3	5.5	2	7.0	3
France	73.40	4	4.8	4	6.7	4
Italy	43.63	5	1.7	5	4.1	10
Canada	38.14	6	1.6	6	4.4	8
Netherlands	15.00	7	0.73	7	4.9	7
Belgium	13.43	8	0.48	8	3.7	12
Denmark	7.73	9	0.25	10	3.3	13
Turkey	6.69	10	0.38	9	5.8	5
Norway	5.64	11	0.21	13	3.9	11
Greece	4.31	12	0.22	11	4.2	9
Portugal	2.88	13	0.22	12	7.7	2
Luxembourg	0.53	14	0.009	14	1.7	14

any ship in the area, and consumption by one does not reduce the amount of light available to others. It has been argued that this characteristic would make it difficult, if not impossible, to collect fees for the use of lighthouses. As a consequence, the services of lighthouses would not be provided under a system of voluntary agreements among private individuals. R. H. Coase, however, found that this was not the case in at least one instance.[10] In studying the British lighthouse system, Coase reported that during the period 1610–1675 no lighthouses were constructed by the British Lighthouse Authority, Trinity House. At least ten, however, were constructed by private individuals during this period. (The year 1610 is chosen as a starting date because it was not until this time that lighthouses, in the modern sense of the term, were employed.) Each shipowner paid a fee to the owner of the lighthouse, which varied with the size of the cargo and the number of times the ship passed the lighthouse. By 1820, there were 46 lighthouses in operation. Of the 46, 24 were operated by Trinity House and 22 were run privately. Further, of the 24 operated by Trinity House, 12 had been built and operated initially by private individuals. By 1820,

---

[10]R. H. Coase, "The Lighthouse in Economics," *Journal of Law and Economics,* Vol. 27 (October 1974), pp. 357–76.

Trinity House had been responsible for initiating the construction of only one-fourth of the lighthouses in existence.

Exclusion Costs and the Free-Rider Problem

It has been shown that if transaction costs are zero or low, externalities do not cause inefficient resource allocation. The existence of public goods externalities, on the other hand, may lead to inefficiencies. This is because public goods externalities are likely to involve high exclusion costs. When an external impact involves large numbers of individuals, the cost of getting together to reach a voluntary solution is high. When the number of individuals is large, it will be very costly to search out all those who would benefit from the provision of the good. In many public good problems, the sheer number of people involved and the cost of finding them and getting them together will make a voluntary solution difficult. Even if all the potential beneficiaries of a voluntary agreement can be assembled, it may be difficult for such a large number of people to reach an agreement.

Another component of these high transaction costs results in the free-rider problem. This occurs when many individuals are affected by the provision of a public good and when exclusion is costly. Because of the free-rider problem, voluntary provision and financing of a public good often fails. Suppose an attempt is made to reach a voluntary agreement regarding the provision of national defense. Even if each individual feels he or she would benefit from the provision of defense, no individual will volunteer to pay for it. This is the case because each individual will reason that he or she could be even better off if the defense can be secured without paying at all. If the number of individuals is large, one share will surely not be missed, and the level of national defense will be almost unchanged. The problem is that every rational individual would tend to think this way, and, thus, defense would end up underfinanced. It does not even help if each individual realizes that others will behave as free riders, since they each know that their own individual behavior will have an insignificant effect on the final outcome. No matter what one person does, the others will act as free riders.

As N, the number of individuals involved, becomes smaller, the impact each individual has on the provision of the good becomes larger, and a "free ride" actually begins to cost something. Each individual will realize that withholding his or her share must significantly reduce the amount of defense provided. Consequently, as N becomes smaller, voluntary agreements become easier to reach.

Inversely, increasing the size of the group in the allocation of public goods makes voluntary agreement more difficult to reach. Suppose it is decided that each person's share of the financing of a public good should be based on the value of the good to that person. Each person would then understate the value he or she places on the good, thus lowering his or her share of the cost. This would lead to less than optimal provision of the public good (shown in Figure 3.7). If each individual understates the value of the good, the perceived $D_R + D_F$ curve will be lower than the actual curve. This will lead to a level of defense less than D^*.

The Role of the Government

Transaction costs and exclusion costs pose a major stumbling block to the private or voluntary provision of public goods; they *may* require that public goods be provided by the government. The presumption is that the government can provide public goods at lower cost than can the private sector. How can the government accomplish this? The government has one tool that no private firm possesses—the power to coerce. The government can *force* individuals to become parties to the provision of public goods through its power of taxation. The power to coerce reduces transaction costs by eliminating the necessity of gathering information and forming individual agreements. However, if a Samuelson "equilibrium" is to be achieved by the government, information regarding individual preferences is necessary. This information, which is revealed automatically through the process of voluntary bargaining in competitive markets, is costly to obtain. Consequently, solutions imposed by government are not likely to be optimal solutions. In the absence of information regarding individual preferences, the tax "prices" charged individuals will differ from the individuals' marginal evaluations of the public good. Those individuals who are charged a price that is too high will want to reduce the output of the public good while individuals who are charged a price which is too low will want to expand output. Each will incur costs in attempts to alter the solution imposed by the government. There is no reason to presume that these costs, along with the other costs of government provision, will be lower than the information and transaction costs which result from private provision of the public good. This can only be determined on a case-by-case basis after very careful study. Private provision, even if zero, may well be optimal.

The role of the government in the provision of public goods is summarized by Paul Samuelson as follows.

> So, pragmatically all such cases have to be studied and re-solved on their complicated and controversial merits and de-merits. One cannot avoid the difficult problem of deciding whether a particular man is a murderer by posing the problem, "Does he carry the (unique) name of the man who did commit the murder?" No more can one decide what market or social mechanisms should be used for an activity by first deciding whether it is a private or public good.[11]

Questions and Exercises

1. A theater performance with several simultaneous viewers is a public good. Why?

2. It is often implied that more public goods can be produced without the production of other goods being curtailed. Evaluate.

3. "Even if it were costless to exclude nonpayers from enjoying a public good, it does not follow that nonpayers should be excluded." Explain why.

4. Under what circumstances does the "free-rider" problem emerge? How valid is the statement that all government is fundamentally a response to the free-rider problem?

5. What limits the possibility of private supply of public goods? Will public provision mean that a more nearly optimal amount of the public good will be supplied?

6. What is the Coase Theorem? What sorts of real-world considerations make some property rights ambiguous? What considerations make the costs of negotiating and enforcing contracts high?

7. What are the marginal conditions for an optimum in Samuelson's model? How will these conditions be affected by high transaction costs?

8. In the farmer-rancher example, the optimal level of the external damage was *not* zero. Why? Do you think this is a general result in external damage situations?

---

[11]Paul A. Samuelson, "Public Goods and Subscription TV: Correction of the Record," *Journal of Law and Economics,* Vol. 7 (October 1964), p. 83.

9. Since transactions costs involve real resource costs, in at least one situation, provision of a public good by the government would *not* be recommended by an economist. What is this situation?

10. If a public good provided benefits over a period of several years, how would we modify the Samuelson marginal conditions to account for this?

Additional Readings

Buchanan, J. M. *The Demand and Supply of Public Goods.* Chicago: Rand McNally and Co., 1969.

Coase, R. H. "The Problem of Social Cost." *Journal of Law and Economics,* Vol. 3 (October 1960), pp. 1–44.

Samuelson, Paul. "A Diagrammatic Exposition of a Theory of Public Expenditure." *The Review of Economics and Statistics,* Vol. 37 (November 1955), pp. 350–56.

4

Public Expenditure and Benefit-Cost Analysis

In the preceding chapter, we began to modify the theory of markets to account for public-goods externalities. We argued that, when transaction and information costs are low and private property rights are well defined, individuals will find it in their interest to internalize what would otherwise be considered the external costs or benefits of their actions.[1] By modifying the theory of markets in this way, we infuse it with a certain amount of empirical content regarding the allocation of resources to the provision of public goods. When information and transaction costs are high, the incentive to exchange is weakened and, as a result, the external effects will not be completely internalized. Since there is no a priori reason to believe that these costs will be any lower for the government, the centralization of this process will not necessarily improve the outcome. Further, it requires the faith of Abraham to believe that government officials are as diligent in monitoring the benefits and costs of their actions as are the private entrepreneurs who directly bear the gains or losses resulting from the decisions they make.

In short, we are arguing that the actual quantities of public goods supplied through government action will reflect the demands for these goods only in a very gross sense.[2] With this in mind, we will now examine some data on actual government expenditures in the United States.

Total Government Expenditures

Table 4.1 and Figure 4.1 give rough approximations of total government involvement in the provision of goods and services. In 1975

---

[1]Internalization of costs and benefits means that individuals will take these costs and benefits into consideration when making decisions regarding the allocation of resources.

[2]This statement is explained in detail in Chapters 5, 6, and 7.

Total Government Expenditures 1902-1975 (in Billions) Table 4.1

	Level of Government						
Year	Federal	State & Local	Total	GNP	Federal GNP	State & Local GNP	Total GNP
1902	.572	1.095	1.7	21.6	2%	5%	7%
1922	3.763	5.652	9.4	74.1	5%	7%	12%
1932	4.266	8.403	12.7	58.0	7%	15%	22%
1942	35.549	10.914	46.4	157.9	22%	7%	29%
1950	43.147	22.787	65.9	248.8	17%	9%	26%
1955	68.509	33.724	102.2	398.0	17%	8%	25%
1960	92.223	51.876	144.1	503.7	18%	10%	28%
1965	118.430	74.546	192.9	684.9	17%	10%	27%
1970	196.588	131.332	327.9	976.4	20%	13%	33%
1975	326.105	229.474	555.5	1,516.3	22%	15%	37%

Source: Historical Statistics of the U.S., U.S. Dept. of Commerce, Bureau of the Census and Treasury Department and Office of Management and Budget.

Federal, State, and Local Expenditure as a Percentage of GNP Figure 4.1

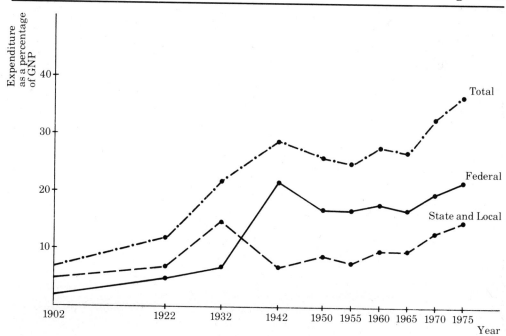

all governments—federal, state, and local—were responsible for allocating 37 percent of gross national product (GNP). This percentage has been growing over the years. In 1902 governments at all levels combined to allocate only 7 percent of GNP. Federal government expenditures have grown relative to the expenditures of state and local governments during this period. In 1902 federal expenditures amounted to less than one half of state and local expenditures. By 1975 federal expenditures were almost one-and-a-half times as large as state and local expenditures. Enactment of federal income tax legislation in 1913 has undoubtedly influenced the growth of federal expenditures relative to state and local expenditures. World War II also played an important role in increasing the relative share of federal expenditures. From the end of World War II through 1965, the relative shares of federal, state, and local expenditures in GNP remained roughly constant. Since 1970, however, both have begun to grow again, with state and local expenditures growing somewhat more rapidly than federal expenditures. Apparently, this is a result of the shift in priorities away from defense-related programs, which have been largely the responsibility of the federal government, to nondefense or domestic social programs. The responsibility for these programs has been shared by all levels of government.

Federal Government Expenditures

Table 4.2 presents federal expenditures by type of expenditure for selected years between 1960 and 1976. This table provides data on the programs in which the federal government has been involved. Although national defense absorbs a large share of federal expenditures, the share of national defense in total federal expenditures declined substantially from 1960 through 1976. This was true in spite of the fact that the United States fought a long and costly war during this period. Table 4.3 compares expenditures on national defense as a percentage of total federal expenditures to certain selected nondefense expenditures as a percentage of total federal expenditures. In 1960 national defense accounted for almost one half of all federal expenditures while community development, education and manpower, health, income security, and commerce and transportation accounted for a little more than a quarter of all federal expenditures. By 1976 the share of national defense in the total had fallen to less than a quarter while the selected nondefense expenditures had risen to more than one half. This represents a significant shift in federal government priorities. Increased federal

Federal Budget Expenditures by Type, 1960–1976 (in Millions)   Table 4.2

Type of Expenditure	Years				
	1960	1965	1970	1975	1976
Total	92,223	118,430	196,588	326,105	366,466
National Defense	45,908	49,578	80,295	86,585	89,996
International Affairs	3,054	4,340	3,570	5,862	5,067
Space Research	401	5,091	3,749	3,989	4,370
Agriculture	3,322	4,805	6,201	1,660	2,502
Natural Resources	1,019	2,056	2,568	9,537	11,282
Commerce and Transportation	4,774	7,399	9,310	16,010	17,248
Community Development	971	288	2,965	4,431	5,300
Education and Manpower	1,286	2,284	7,289	15,248	18,167
Health	756	1,704	12,907	27,647	33,448
Income Security	17,977	25,705	43,790	108,605	127,406
Veteran Benefits	5,426	5,722	8,677	16,597	18,432
Interest	8,299	10,357	18,312	30,974	34,589
Law Enforcement and Justice	—	—	—	2,942	3,320
General Government	1,327	2,210	3,336	3,089	2,927
Revenue Sharing	—	—	—	7,005	7,119
Undistributed Intragovernment Transactions	−2,297	−3,109	−6,380	−14,075	−14,704

Source: Executive Office of the President, Bureau of the Budget, The Budget of the U.S., various years.

**Federal Expenditure Priorities 1960–1976: Defense and
Selected Nondefense as a Percentage of Total Expenditure**   Figure 4.2

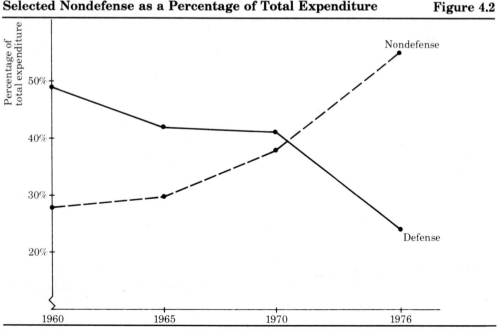

Table 4.3   **Priorities in Federal Expenditures 1960-1976 (in Millions)**

	Years					
	1960	**1965**	**1970**	**1975**	**1976**	**% 1960-76**
Total Expenditures	92,223	118,430	196,588	326,105	366,466	397%
Defense	45,908	49,578	80,295	86,585	89,996	196%
Selected Nondefense	25,764	37,377	76,261	171,941	202,753	787%
Community development	971	288	2,965	4,431	5,300	545%
Education and manpower	1,286	2,284	7,289	15,248	18,167	1,412%
Health	756	1,704	12,907	27,647	33,440	4,424%
Income security	17,977	25,702	43,790	108,605	127,406	708%
Commerce and transportation	4,774	7,399	9,310	16,010	17,248	361%
Defense as a Percentage of Total Expenditures	49%	42%	41%	26%	24%	
Selected Nondefense as a Percentage of Total Expenditures	28%	31%	38%	52%	55%	

expenditures on health, education and manpower, and income security contributed significantly to this shift.

State and Local Expenditures

Table 4.4 presents state and local expenditures by type. It is apparent from this table and Table 4.5 that the bulk of state and local expenditures is for education. Expenditure on education varied between 36 and 40 percent of state and local budgets. Unlike federal expenditures, the shares of each type of expenditure in state and local budgets have remained relatively constant between the years 1960 and 1975. The share of welfare in state and local expenditures has increased from 8.4 to 11.8 percent, while the share of highway expenditures in the total has fallen from 18.1 to 9.8 percent. Aside from these two changes, the priorities of state and local governments did not change appreciably during the period.

**State and Local Expenditures
by Type, 1960-1975 (in Millions)**   Table 4.4

Type of Expenditure	Years			
	1960	**1965**	**1970**	**1975**
Total	51,876	74,546	131,332	229,474
Education	18,719	28,563	52,718	87,858
Highways	9,428	12,221	16,427	22,528
Welfare	4,404	6,315	14,679	27,191
Health	559	836	1,806	4,428
Hospitals	3,235	4,525	7,863	14,419
Police Protection	1,857	2,549	4,494	8,387
Fire Protection	995	1,306	2,024	3,455
Natural Resources	1,189	1,730	2,752	4,223
Sanitation	1,727	2,360	3,413	7,387
Housing	858	1,250	2,138	3,457
Parks	770	1,104	1,888	3,462
Other	8,135	11,787	21,130	42,679

Source: Department of Commerce, Bureau of the Census, Census of Government
Finances, various years.

Traditionally, state and local governments have had the responsibility of providing the bulk of civilian services, such as education,
roads and transportation, welfare, health and hospitals, police, and
sanitation. In the past, the bulk of federal government expenditures was for defense. The priorities seem to be changing somewhat, with the result that in recent years the federal government
has substantially increased expenditures on civilian services. Table
4.6, which is derived from Tables 4.2 and 4.4, presents an analysis
of this change.

In 1960 state and local expenditures accounted for 58.9 percent
of total government expenditures for civilian services; federal government expenditures amounted to 41.1 percent of the total. By
1975 state and local expenditures for civilian services had shrunk to
less than one half of the total. The rise in the federal government's
share was due to its increased activity in the areas of education (6.4
percent in 1960 compared to 14.7 percent in 1975), highways and
transportation (33.6 percent in 1960 compared to 41.5 percent in
1975), police protection (0.0 percent in 1960 compared to 25.9 percent in 1975), and natural resources (46.1 percent in 1960 compared
to 69.3 percent in 1975).

The increase in total government expenditures on civilian services between the years 1960 and 1975, in large part, is accounted

Table 4.5

Government Employment for Selected Years 1929-1975 (in Thousands Except Where Noted Otherwise)

Years	Total Employment in U.S.	Employment		Percentage of Total Employment	
		Federal	State & Local	Federal	State & Local
1929	31,339	533	2,532	1.7%	8.0%
1933	23,711	565	2,601	2.3%	10.9%
1940	32,376	996	3,206	3.0%	9.9%
1945	40,394	2,808	3,137	6.9%	7.7%
1950	45,222	1,928	4,098	4.2%	9.0%
1955	50,675	2,187	4,727	4.3%	9.3%
1960	54,234	2,270	6,083	4.2%	11.2%
1965	60,815	2,378	7,696	3.9%	12.6%
1970	70,593	2,705	9,830	3.8%	13.9%
1975	84,783	2,904	12,097	3.4%	14.2%

Source: Department of Labor, Bureau of Labor Statistics.

for by increased expenditures on education and welfare. The change in total government expenditures for civilian services amounted to roughly $296 billion. The change in total government expenditures on education and welfare was $196.5 billion, accounting for 66.3 percent of the change in total government expenditures on civilian services.

Planning-Programming-Budgeting System

Planning-Programming-Budgeting System (PPBS) is an approach to federal budgeting that attempts to simulate the efficiency of private markets. PPBS was introduced by President Lyndon Johnson in an attempt to make the federal budgeting process more efficient and rational. This system requires that decision makers (1) define the budget in terms of the final product or goals of governmental activity (for example, tactical forces, flood control, and elimination of poverty); (2) make explicit comparisons and trade-offs among final goals and make explicit comparisons among alternative ways of attaining any one goal; (3) look at the full costs, as well as the benefits, of their proposals; and (4) undertake long-range planning by making explicit costs of various projects over five-year periods as opposed to computing costs for one year only.

Table 4.6

A Comparison of Federal vs. State and Local Civilian Expenditures, 1960–1975 (in Millions)

Type of Expenditure	1960					1975				
	Total	Federal	State & Local	% Federal	% State & Local	Total	Federal	State & Local	% Federal	% State & Local
Education	20,005	1,286	18,719	6.4	93.6	103,106	15,248	87,858	14.7	85.3
Highways/ Transportation	14,202	4,774	9,428	33.6	66.4	38,538	16,010	22,528	41.5	58.9
Welfare	22,381	17,977	4,404	80.3	19.7	135,796	108,605	27,191	79.9	20.1
Health	1,315	756	559	58.1	41.9	32,075	27,647	4,428	86.1	13.9
Hospitals	3,235	—	3,235	—	100.0	14,419	—	14,419	—	100.0
Police Protection	1,857	—	1,857	—	100.0	11,329	2,942	8,387	25.9	74.1
Fire Protection	995	—	995	—	100.0	3,455	—	3,455	—	100.0
Natural Resources	2,208	1,019	1,189	46.1	53.2	13,760	9,537	4,223	69.3	30.7
Sanitation	1,727	—	1,727	—	100.0	7,387	—	7,387	—	100.0
Housing	1,829	971	858	53.0	47.0	7,888	4,431	3,457	56.1	43.9
Agriculture	3,322	3,322	—	100.0	—	1,660	1,660	—	100.0	—
Total	73,076	30,105	42,971	41.1	58.9	369,413	186,080	183,333	50.3	49.7

Of course, PPBS cannot duplicate the efficiency with which resources are allocated by individuals through the process of exchange in free markets. Nevertheless, it does introduce a degree of rationality into the budgeting process that did not exist previously. To the extent that PPBS confronts decision makers with a budget constraint, it may—if coupled with a system of incentives—encourage them to try to meet their goals of producing public goods at the lowest possible cost. It may also encourage them to make trade-offs among goals in such a way that they pick the combination of outputs that provides the highest value per dollar spent. By making explicit the costs of proposals over five-year periods, PPBS allows for long-range planning of activities and for a more accurate assessment of future expenditures.

The budget itself is formulated by the executive branch of government and then it is submitted to Congress, which authorizes the various budget programs and appropriates the necessary resources. The executive branch, then, administers the various authorized programs. PPBS makes the job of Congress easier since it provides a useful basis for the evaluation of the various requests by the executive branch. Therefore, rather than authorizing expenditure by an agency for some ill-defined set of tasks, Congress authorizes expenditure only for well-defined goals or outputs. In actual practice, however, many problems are encountered in applying PPBS. Recall that the purpose of PPBS is to simulate the efficiency of private markets. One of the main reasons why private markets are efficient is that the individual transactors in these markets take into account all of the costs and benefits that result from their actions. When you buy a pair of shoes, a loaf of bread, or a hamburger, the price you pay covers the cost of supplying the good to you. In other words, the price you and others pay for, say, shoes is at least enough to cover the value of other goods foregone in supplying shoes. You implicitly take these costs (the value of other goods foregone in supplying the shoes to you) into consideration when deciding whether to buy the shoes since you will not get the shoes unless you pay the price. If you decide to purchase the shoes, *you* bear the cost of supplying the shoes. And when you purchase the shoes, you are saying that the value of the shoes to you is, at least, no lower than the value you and others place on the goods (hamburgers, bread, autos, etc.) that could have been produced with the resources devoted to producing the shoes. Additional resources, then, will not be devoted to the production of shoes unless the value (benefits experienced by individuals) of doing so exceeds the cost. If a shoe producer should make a mistake and produce too many shoes, he or she will not be able to sell them at a price that covers all of the costs and thus will incur a loss. In other words, the producer will bear the cost of the poor decision to expand production, which will result in reducing future production.

The important point here is that resources will only be devoted to the production of goods in private markets when the anticipated benefits of doing so exceed the cost and, if any mistakes are made, adjustments will take place relatively rapidly. The reason for this is that the individual empowered to make the decision (take the action) bears the cost of that decision. When decision makers bear the full costs and benefits of their decisions, resources tend to be allocated efficiently.

Compare this situation to one in which a public official is deciding whether to devote resources to the production of some good. In this case, the public official does not bear the full cost of the decisions he or she is empowered to make. When the official decides to spend public funds, the ability to purchase other goods for his or her *private* consumption is not impaired by this decision. When you buy the pair of shoes, your ability to acquire other goods declines by the price of the shoes. You buy the shoes only if the value you place on the shoes exceeds the value you place on the other goods that are necessarily foregone when you purchase the shoes. The public official, on the other hand, does not necessarily forego the *private* consumption of other goods when he or she decides to spend public funds. For example, a public official may drive a government car at a speed of 60 miles per hour and drive a personal car at 50 miles per hour under the same road conditions. An owner driving his car bears the cost of increased gas consumption, tire wear, and more rapid deterioration of the car that results from driving it at higher speeds but does not bear these costs when driving the government-owned car. The *private* costs borne by the public official of driving the government car at increased speeds are lower than the private costs of driving his or her own car. Suppose the benefit derived from driving at 60 miles per hour rather than 50 miles per hour is $20. Driving a personal car at this increased speed results in an increase in private cost of $30. Clearly, it does not pay one to drive at 60 miles per hour. If, on the other hand, private cost only increases by $10 when driving the government car at 60 miles per hour rather than 50 miles per hour, it will pay to drive the car at 60 rather than 50. If the private benefits of driving at increased speeds are the same, the official will drive the government car faster than the personal car.[3] The same argument applies to situ-

---

[3]Have you ever watched a parking attendant park cars? The principle is the same.

ations in which the public official is making decisions about more important things than the speed at which to drive.

One might contend that the above argument applies with equal force to executives and salespeople who drive company cars. To some extent this is true. They will be less careful with these cars than they are with their own. However, we must remember that the owner(s) of the company will bear the cost of the decisions (actions) of the executives and salespeople. Consequently, it will pay the owner(s) to monitor the behavior of their employees and, to the extent that it pays, the owner(s) will develop arrangements that require the employee to bear at least a portion of the cost.

A second problem with PPBS arises because, in many cases, it is very difficult to measure the output (benefits) generated by government agencies. This problem occurs because many government outputs involve significant public-goods problems. It is also the case that many publicly produced goods are supplied by a combination of agencies and this, of course, causes measurement problems. Defense, for instance, is produced by the Army, Navy, Air Force, and other agencies.

Another problem arises in the supply of publicly produced goods when making trade-offs between goals. Since the purpose of government in the first place it to provide individuals with desired goods and services that are not provided adequately by the market, these trade-offs cannot be made independently of the wishes of the constituency. As we will see in later chapters, the very reasons that yield unsatisfactory market outcomes for public goods are the same reasons that make the evaluation of the wishes of individual constituents and their aggregation extremely difficult. One tool that may be of some use in alleviating—but not solving—this problem is benefit-cost analysis.

Benefit-Cost Analysis

Benefit-cost analysis is a technique that can aid decision makers in choosing among the various projects the federal government is considering. Benefit-cost (B-C) analysis may aid the decision maker by (1) making clear what the net benefits of each project are so that those with the largest net benefits are chosen and (2) assuring that resources are *not* taken from higher valued uses in the private sector. In other words, benefit-cost analysis can be used as a test to indicate whether the resources being transferred from the private to the public sector are being transferred to a higher valued use.

B-C analysis is applied by measuring all of the benefits (present and future) of a given project in dollar terms. The benefits are then discounted at whatever is deemed the appropriate rate of interest to obtain the present value of the anticipated benefits. The same procedure is followed for the anticipated cost associated with the project. Finally, the present value of the costs is subtracted from the present value of the benefits to determine the present value of the project's net benefits. Projects are then selected in descending order of the present value of their net benefits until the proposed budget is exhausted. However, no project should be undertaken for which the present value of costs exceeds the present value of benefits. The present value of the cost of a project represents the present value of foregone alternatives. When costs exceed benefits, resources are being directed *away from* higher valued alternative uses. If costs should exceed benefits for some public projects prior to the budget being exhausted, it implies that a poor selection of projects has been made or that the budget is too large.

Many government projects involve public goods and services. Because of this, measuring the benefits that result from provision of the good will be extremely difficult in most cases, and since there will be no well-established markets for these goods, prices cannot be used to determine social value. However, when markets do exist, it is possible to measure the value to society from the provision of a good by measuring the difference between marginal value in use and marginal cost (see Chapter 2). To put this another way, the net value of a good can be measured by what people are willing to pay for it less the marginal cost of producing it when externalities and the free-rider problem are not present. When externalities are present (and they are in the case of public goods), what people are willing to pay will be different from the value of the good to them.

For some projects, external effects do not present significant problems. As an example, the benefits of irrigation projects can be measured in terms of increases in the net social dividend resulting from increased agricultural output. To do this, however, the investigator must know the elasticities of demand and supply of the agricultural commodities affected by the irrigation project. The value of the farm land, which receives water from the project, will increase as a result of the project. This increase in the value of the land should not be included in measuring the benefits of the project; land values increase because of the increased output of the land and, if included, would result in double-counting the benefits.

For most public projects, however, benefits are difficult to measure. How do we measure the dollar value of a warship or an antipoverty program? This problem is the major reason why, for the most part, benefit-cost analysis has been applied in one of two equally unsatisfactory ways in evaluating government projects. One application of the analysis includes all measurable benefits and costs. The benefits and costs that cannot be measured are simply listed and do not enter the calculation of the project's net present value. This method is of little help in evaluating government projects. If you cannot observe and measure the benefits, how can you be sure they exist? On the other hand, if the good under consideration has true public-good aspects associated with its provision and if exclusion costs are very high (for example, a new bomber or submarine), so that measuring the benefits is extremely difficult, failure to include these benefits in the calculation will bias the results against provision of the good.

Another alternative that has been employed is to have the agency which is performing the B-C analysis assign subjective values to the benefits and costs that cannot be measured and include these in the analysis. If this is done, B-C analysis is no longer an objective procedure for ranking public projects because the net present value of the project is subjective and depends upon the values of the individual who is doing the analysis.

After the values of all present and future costs and benefits are somehow determined, these values must be discounted to determine present value.

The term *discount* refers to the process of expressing the value of all costs and benefits at the same point in time (usually the present) even though the costs and benefits resulting from the provision of a particular good may be experienced at different points in time. If engineers construct a dam, the costs of construction are experienced in the present, while the benefits of having the dam will be experienced in the future and will continue for the life of the dam. A dollar's worth of future benefit is not valued as highly as a dollar's worth of present benefit, and a dollar's worth of future benefit will not offset a dollar's worth of present cost. Discounting expresses the value of future benefits in terms of their present dollar-value equivalents so that they can be compared to the costs that are incurred in the present.

If you invest $100 today at a rate of interest of 10 percent per year for one year, you will receive $110 one year from now. The future value ($110) of this investment is given by the following equation.

$$\text{Future Value} = \$100 + .10(\$100) = (1 + .10)\$100 = \$110$$

Looked at another way, $110 to be received one year from now is worth only $100 today because $100 today will grow in value to $110 in one year at an interest rate of 10 percent. The $100 that you have today is the present value of $110 to be received in one year. Note that the present value ($100) of this investment is equal to the future value ($110) divided by one plus the rate of interest, r.

$$\text{Present Value} = \frac{\text{Future Value}}{(1 + r)} = \frac{\$110}{(1 + .10)} = \$100$$

Obtaining the present value of a one-year investment requires that the future value of the investment be discounted by one plus the rate of interest.

Suppose the life of the investment had been two years instead of one year. That is, suppose you invest $100 today at a rate of interest of 10 percent per year for two years. The future value of that investment is given below.

$$\text{Future Value} = \$100 + .10(\$100) + .10[\$100 + .10(\$100)] = \$121$$

The first term on the right, $100, is the initial investment which, over the first year, grows in value at 10 percent. The growth in value over the first year is given by the second term in the equation, .10($100). At the *end* of the first year, the total amount invested is $100 plus .10($100), which will earn interest at a rate of 10 percent over the second year. This is given by the third term in the equation, .10[$100 + .10($100)]. By factoring properly, the above equation can be expressed as follows:

$$\text{Future Value} = (1 + .10)(1 + .10)\$100 = (1 + .10)^2\$100 = \$121$$

In order to obtain the future value of this investment, $100 is multiplied by $(1 + .10)^2$. Put a little differently, to obtain the present value of this investment, the future value ($121) must be divided by the term $(1 + .10)^2$.

$$\begin{aligned}\text{Present Value of a} \\ \text{Two-year Investment}\end{aligned} = \frac{\text{Future Value in Two Years}}{(1 + r)^2}$$

$$= \frac{\$121}{1.21} = \$100$$

By extension, the present value of any benefit, B, to be received at the end of n years is

$$PV = \frac{B}{(1 + r)^n}.$$

The above calculation is for a single benefit to be received at some specified future date. Suppose you were confronted with an investment opportunity that promised to pay you $50 at the end of one year and $80 at the end of the second year. In all subsequent years, benefits fall to zero. What is the maximum amount that you would be willing to pay to make this investment if the rate of interest is 10 percent? In other words, what is the present value of this stream of benefits? The present value of $50 to be received one year from now is $50/(1 +.10) and the present value of $80 to be received two years hence is $80/(1 + .10)². The present value of this stream of benefits, then, is

$$PV = \frac{\$50}{(1 + .10)} + \frac{\$80}{(1 + .10)^2} = 45.45 + 66.11 = \$111.56.$$

The maximum you would be willing to pay today for this opportunity is $111.56. If someone were to offer to sell you this opportunity for $100, you should buy it because the present value of the investment is greater than its present cost. Your present wealth would rise by the difference between present value and present cost, or by $11.56. The present value of any investment project can be calculated by employing the following equation:

$$PV = \sum_{i=1}^{n} \frac{(A_i - C_i)}{(1 + r)^i}$$

where n is the life of the project, A_i is the dollar value of gross benefits in year i, C_i is any costs that are incurred in year i $(A_i - C_i = B_i)$, and r is the rate of interest (rate of discount).

Choosing the proper rate is difficult, because there are many possible interest rates from which to choose. The correct interest rate should equal both the opportunity cost of capital in the private sector and the rate at which individuals are willing to exchange consumption today for consumption in the future.

One problem in measuring the opportunity cost of capital is in the treatment of risk. Private investment opportunities are risky. This means that the rate of return yielded by private investments that are successful will be higher than the rate of return on, for example, risk-free government bonds. In the past, the lower government bond rate has been used as the discount rate for B-C analysis. This rate is too low, however, and has resulted in an overvaluation of projects. When the benefit stream is longer than the cost stream, lower discount rates lead to a higher present value of net benefits. Using the lower government bond rate is incorrect because the cost of capital used by the government is the value of capital displaced in the private sector. The rate of return to this capital reflects its riskiness. Also, government projects (government use of capital) involve the same risk as private use of capital. Even though the government does not go out of business if it makes incorrect decisions regarding the use of capital, as may a private concern, the risky rate should still be used. This is true because the social risk involved in using the capital arises from the possibility of an incorrect valuation of future benefits. If a private firm overestimates the value of the future benefits of a potential venture, it will incur a loss on the venture and may even fail. The loss to society, however, is not the firm's loss of money. The loss to society is the loss of the benefits of a successful project that could have been undertaken with the same resources. The same is true of government projects. The fact that the government can borrow at a low, risk-free (free from the possibility of default, not from the possiblilty of the project's failure), rate of interest is a result of the government's ability to secure its bonds with its power to tax. This does not mean that a government project is free of risks in the sense that the actual benefits of the project exceed the costs.

Because of the difficulties of measuring benefits and the problems in choosing a discount rate, benefit-cost analysis and PPBS have been of limited usefulness in government decision making.

Application

The Benefits and Costs of New York City's Middle-Income Housing Program[4]

Professor J. S. DeSalvo applied benefit-cost analysis in evaluating New York City's Mitchell-Lama housing program. In essence, this program provided interest-subsidized, long-term mortgage loans to eligible developers who constructed or rehabilitated middle-income rental housing. In return for this subsidy, developers had to agree to city supervision of construction and management, including rent schedules and tenant selection. DeSalvo found that there were about 57,000 households occupying the subsidized housing. These households received net benefits from the program equal to $25.6 million, which was about $450 per household in 1968. The cost of providing these benefits was $46.9 million, or about $824 per household. Costs exceeded benefits by $21.3 million, or $374 per house-

[4]Joseph S. DeSalvo, "Benefits and Costs of New York City's Middle Income Housing Program," *Journal of Political Economy,* Vol. 83 (August 1975), pp. 792–805.

hold. It is possible, of course, that other individuals gained by knowing that these middle-income individuals benefited from the program. DeSalvo concluded that these nontenant benefits would have had to amount to $21.3 million in 1968 for the program to be considered an efficient use of resources.

Questions and Exercises

1. Is the appropriate rate of discount on government projects lower than that on private projects? Why?

2. What risk is associated with investment in a private project that is not present in public projects?

3. As long as the federal government has the power to print money, it will never default on a loan. This means that the risk associated with federal government projects is lower than for private projects. Hence, the appropriate rate of discount is less. Evaluate this statement.

4. What are some of the problems associated with measuring the benefits of public projects? Critique some of the methods that have been employed to get around these problems.

5. Is there any assurance that the application of benefit-cost analysis will prevent resources from being allocated to the public sector when they have higher valued uses in the private sector? Why?

6. What are some of the advantages of applying benefit-cost analysis to public projects?

7. Providing public goods through government action will not necessarily result in more efficient resource allocation. Why?

5

Public Allocation — Voting

This chapter and the next will concentrate on the means of communicating consumer desires to those branches of government responsible for providing public goods and services. Our analysis will be concerned with how this is done in free democratic societies (specifically in the United States) where it is assumed that the individual is important and should make the decisions.

Individual Preferences and Voting

A primary means of communicating individual preferences in democratic societies is the voting process. As in the other chapters of this book, we assume that individuals make their decisions about public goods in the same way they make decisions about private goods; that is, they consider only their own interests when making decisions in the public sector. Individuals are utility maximizers, whether their decision involves buying a new car or voting on a school bond issue.

Voting Rules

Different voting rules may generate different outcomes with respect to public good production. Majority rule, unanimity rule, plurality voting, and point voting are just some of the different systems that a community might employ in reaching collective decisions. Simple majority rule seems to be the most popular. Under this rule, each individual has one vote that he or she uses to indicate acceptance or rejection of the proposal (or candidate) under consideration. The votes are counted and the proposal is accepted if more than one half of the votes cast favor the proposal.

Unanimity rule requires that a proposal be accepted by the entire electorate. In some cases, rules that lie between simple majority and unanimity are employed. For example, the U.S. Congress requires a two-thirds majority to override a presidential veto.

A plurality voting rule is sometimes employed when there are three or more proposals (or candidates) in an election. Using this rule, the winning candidate is the one that secures the most votes, regardless of whether those votes amount to a 50% plus one majority.

Another voting system is point voting. Under this rule, each voter is assigned a given number of points. For example, if there are six proposals under consideration and only two can be accepted, each voter may receive six points. The voter is allowed to allocate those points among the proposals in whatever manner he or she chooses. He or she can decide to allocate all six points to the top choice or four points to the top choice and two points to the second choice. In this case, the two proposals receiving the most points are accepted. Point voting allows the voter to express the intensity of his or her preference for given proposals. Because of this, point voting comes closer to the system of "dollar voting" that takes place in the market for private goods than does simple majority voting. However, there are some important differences between the market outcome and the outcome of point voting. For instance, in the private market, the total number of votes (incomes) that individuals have is different.

A Simple Voting Model

In this section, we examine the outcome of the vote on a given proposal when different voting rules are employed. In order to keep the analysis simple, we assume there are only three individuals in the electorate. The question to be decided is what quantity of a public good (fire protection) is to be provided per unit of time. Suppose that each individual derives some benefit from the production of the public good and that the individual's indifference curves are normally shaped. Let fire protection be produced at constant marginal cost in terms of the private good. We assume that incomes are distributed equally and that each individual shares equally in the cost of providing the public good.

Given the last assumption, the budget constraint faced by each individual (A, B, and C) will be the same. If we define a unit of the public good so that its price in terms of a composite private good is one, the unit price of the public good to each individual is one-third private good.

We define a unit of fire protection so that giving up one unit of the composite good allows the production of one more unit of fire protection. In this case, the slope of the production possibility frontier would be -1. Since we assume that each individual pays one third of the cost of providing a unit of the public good and that each individual can consume all units produced, the cost to the individual of an additional unit of fire protection is one third of a unit of the private good. To see this more clearly, suppose each individual decides to devote his or her entire income to the purchase of the private good, G. Since the incomes of all individuals are the same, each would acquire the same quantity of the private good ($\overline{G}_A = \overline{G}_B = \overline{G}_C$). Remember that there are no spillover benefits from consumption of the private good—individuals A and C do not benefit from B's consumption of the private good. The same could be said for the effect of A's consumption of the private good on B and C, and so on. Total consumption of the private good is $\overline{G}_A + \overline{G}_B + \overline{G}_C$ in this situation. Suppose, on the other hand, that the individuals decide collectively to devote some of their income to the purchase of public good F. Since the price of a unit of the public good is one private good, one public good can be acquired for each private good foregone. However, because of the spillover benefits of the public good, purchases of a unit of the public good will benefit individuals A, B, and C. A collective decision to purchase a unit of the public good will cost the individual only $\frac{1}{3}$ of a private good. It follows that, when the individuals act jointly, each faces a price of the public good in terms of the private good of $\frac{1}{3}$ private good. If each individual devotes his or her entire income to the purchase of the public good, each will consume $\overline{F}$ units of the public good ($\overline{F} = 3\overline{G}_A = 3\overline{G}_B = 3\overline{G}_C$). The entire amount of the public good purchase is consumed by each individual. The budget constraint and indifference curves of each individual are shown in Figure 5.1.

Majority Rule

If each individual is free to propose his or her preferred quantity of fire protection services, no quantity of fire protection services will obtain a majority on the first vote. Suppose individual A proposes F_A services and individuals B and C both prefer less. They will vote down A's proposal. If individual B proposed a quantity of F_B fire protection service, individual A would vote against it because he prefers more and individual C would vote against it because she prefers less. A similar argument can be made for the proposal offered by C. The result is that no proposal wins and a zero quantity

Figure 5.1

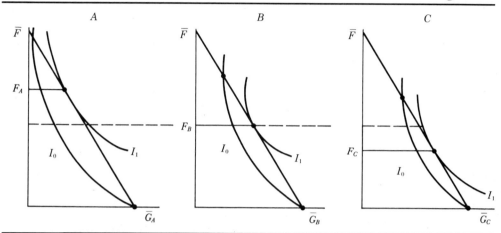

of fire protection services is produced. Clearly, this is not efficient. With a zero quantity of fire protection produced, each individual is on indifference curve I_0 at points $\overline{G}_A$, $\overline{G}_B$, and $\overline{G}_C$. A small increase in the quantity of fire protection services would allow each individual to reach a higher indifference curve. If information and transaction costs were zero, these individuals would negotiate an agreement both on the quantity of fire protection services and on the per unit price paid by each individual. A solution similar to the Samuelson equilibrium discussed in Chapter 3 would be reached. We have ruled out that possibility, however, by our assumption of high information and transaction costs.

Does this mean that the community will end up with a zero quantity of fire protection services? Note that the process of offering proposals and voting generates information about individual preferences. Individual A will recognize that F_A was too high while individual C will recognize that F_C was too low. Rather than being satisfied with a zero level of fire protection services, each will attempt to reach an indifference curve that is higher than I_0 by modifying his or her proposal. Individual A will lower his proposed amount of F and individual C will raise hers. In this manner, the proposals will converge until a majority is achieved at F_B. F_B is at equilibrium because for any other quantity of F, at least two individuals (a majority in this case) could reach a higher indifference curve by altering the quantity of the public good.

The equilibrium at F_B has some important characteristics. First, both individuals A and C are on indifference curves higher than I_0 but lower than I_1. Second, the tax prices paid by each are inefficient since the indifference curves of A and C intersect the budget constraints at F_B. Third, the process of generating information about preferences by offering alternative proposals is costly because elections are costly. These costs must be compared to the costs of reaching a negotiated solution if fire protection were left to the private market. Fourth, the solution will converge toward the quantity of fire protection services preferred by the individual with the median preference for fire protection. Fifth, if the distribution of income is changed to alter the income of the voter whose preference regarding fire protection is median, the quantity of fire protection that will obtain a majority of votes will change. If the voter's income is raised and if fire protection is a normal good, the quantity of fire protection that will obtain a majority of votes will be greater. The reverse holds if the voter's income is lowered. Of course, changing the distribution of income could cause the individual with median preference to change. And sixth, the equilibrium at F_B is stable. Any proposal to move F away from F_B will fail.

In the real world, proposals are not offered to the electorate in the manner discussed above. The cost of placing proposals before the electorate is high and most individuals never offer a proposal for consideration at the local level, not to mention the state or national level. We are sure that the reason for this is *not* that most individuals are perfectly satisfied with the operation of the government sector. The costs of becoming informed about proposals and their consequences are high. As we have argued above, these and other factors combine to give some individuals a monopoly in the right to offer proposals.

If individual A has a monopoly in the production of proposals, what effect will this have on the quantity of fire protection chosen? Any individual who has a monopoly in the right to offer proposals can confront the electorate with effective all-or-nothing alternatives.

Figure 5.2 reproduces the indifference curves and budget constraints of Figure 5.1. Individual A, when he has the monopoly power to do so, will propose quantity F_A or nothing. When individual B is confronted with this all-or-nothing proposal, he will vote in favor of it. Quantity F_A is preferred by B to no fire protection at all. Individual C will vote against the proposal, since she prefers no fire protection to quantity F_A. The proposal, however, will win a majority since A and B favor it.[1] When A has a monopoly, the quantity

---

[1] We are assuming no strategic behavior on B's part.

Figure 5.2

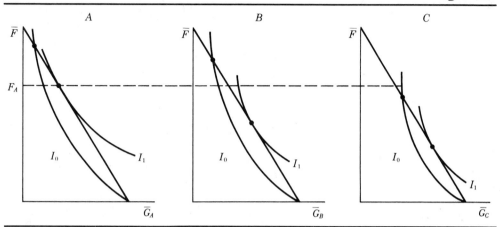

of fire protection chosen exceeds the amount chosen by the voter with median preference for the public good. Given the way we have drawn individual B's indifference map, A is able to reach his most preferred combination of fire protection and private goods. However, had indifference curve I_0 of individual B intersected his budget constraint at a quantity of F which was less than F_A, say, at F_A', individual A would have had to offer a proposal of F_A' or less to obtain a majority vote favoring the proposal. We leave it to the reader to determine the outcome when individuals B and C have the monopoly.

An important implication that should be drawn from the above discussion concerning majority rule is that it would be a pure accident if any proposal were to obtain a majority of votes in the absence of any information about the preferences of the electorate. In the first case, when no individual had a monopoly in the production of proposals, a majority was not obtained until the preferred quantity of fire protection of the median voter was discovered. In the second case, when one individual had a monopoly in the production of proposals, a majority was only obtained when he discovered the quantity of fire protection that would yield a level of utility to at least fifty percent of the electorate greater than the level yielded by no fire protection. It may be argued that the information costs associated with discovering the preferences of the electorate are lower in the second case than in the first, and lower in the first case than when a solution is reached through negotiation in a private market. Information costs, however, are lowered at the cost of leaving some individuals dissatisfied.

Unanimity Rule

Figure 5.3 reproduces the budget constraints and indifference curves of Figures 5.2 and 5.1. If no individual has a monopoly in the production of proposals, a unanimity rule will yield a quantity of fire protection between F_C and $\overline{F}_C$. Since a unanimity rule grants any individual the right to veto any proposal, no proposal can succeed that would place an individual on an indifference curve lower than I_0. Note that under unanimity rule, the quantity of fire protection chosen will make some individuals better off without damaging any other individual. This is the requirement for a Pareto optimal move. No other voting rule has this characteristic.

When no individual has a monopoly in the right to produce proposals, no quantity of fire protection proposed under unanimity rule will receive approval on the first vote. A process of repeat voting similar to that discussed under majority rule will be necessary in order to discover information concerning the preferences of all the individuals in the community. Unlike the case of majority rule, however, the process of voting does not lead to a unique solu-

Figure 5.3

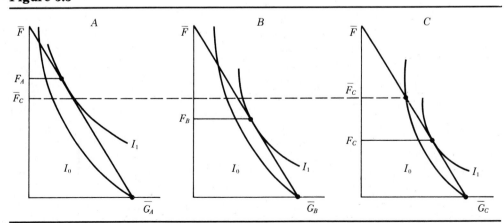

tion for fire protection. The best our model will do is to predict that the solution for F will lie between $\overline{F}_C$ and F_C. This is true because individual C will veto any quantity of F above $\overline{F}_C$, and all individuals prefer a quantity of F equal to or greater than F_C. To simplify the analysis, we are assuming fixed tax shares. If the tax share of each individual is also determined by negotiation, the final solution will be somewhat different.

If individual A has a monopoly in the right to offer proposals, he would prefer a quantity of F equal to F_A. This proposal would fail, however, since it places individual C on an indifference curve that is lower than the indifference curve associated with a zero quantity of F. The maximum quantity of F that would succeed on an all-or-nothing vote is $\overline{F}_C$. We leave it to the reader to determine the outcome when individuals B and C have a monopoly in the right to offer proposals.

Plurality and Point Voting

When proposals are voted up or down on a one-by-one basis as discussed above, plurality and point voting rules will yield an outcome identical to majority rule. These rules only become important when more than two alternatives have to be ranked. When this is the case, these rules may yield results that differ from the result obtained under majority rule. This is discussed in a subsequent section of this chapter.

The Decision to Vote

Before each major election, we hear many cries to get out and vote, and we read editorials that criticize irresponsible citizens who don't. In this section, we will try to determine why people vote.

As with all cases of individual decision making throughout the book, we assume that voters make voting decisions that are consistent with their self-interest. We assume that the voter makes decisions that will maximize his or her utility. Voting is the way individuals reveal their preferences concerning public proposals. Also, voting is the only control most individuals exercise over the political process.

If an individual votes on the basis of self-interest, then a positive model of voting behavior can be derived by looking at those factors that influence individual well-being. The factors that affect the individual voter are of two basic types: those that influence the costs of voting and those that influence the benefits to the individual from voting.

The costs of voting include the cost of acquiring information and the cost of getting to the polls. These costs also include the opportunity cost of the time spent in the voting process.

The cost of getting to the polls is probably relatively low in urban areas where polling places are easily accessible. The cost of acquiring information about elections may be more critical. If individuals are going to make rational choices at the polls, they must be able to make accurate assessments of how the outcome of the election will affect them. Typically, people pick up information about candidates and issues from campaign advertising, media reporting, and special publications put out by government agencies and by organizations like the League of Women Voters. Rational voter behavior would suggest that the higher the cost of acquiring this information, the smaller the likelihood an individual will vote.

One way the costs of voting can be lowered is by consolidating elections on issues and candidates. This reduces the number of times the individual has to physically go to the polls and vote. The evidence supports this proposition, since turnouts are usually higher in general elections where many issues and political offices are involved than in special elections where only a few are involved.

The benefits to the individual from voting are less straightforward. Aside from the feeling of doing one's duty as a citizen, an individual benefits from voting if he or she feels it might determine the outcome of the election. What this means is that a part of the potential benefits from voting depends on the probability of an individual's vote being the deciding vote. This probability diminishes as the size of the voting population increases. It also diminishes relative to how one-sided the outcome is expected to be, since any one vote would have no effect on such an outcome.

An individual may also vote to express preference for an issue or candidate even when his or her vote may not be the deciding one. If a candidate receives a mandate (that is, a large winning majority), he or she may feel more secure in office and, thus, can afford to pay less attention to opposition and devote more time to taking positions and passing legislation preferred by his or her supporters. On the other hand, if the election is close, the winner may feel compelled to adopt some of the policies and positions of the opposition to induce some of those voters to support him or her in the next election.

To the extent that this mandate phenomenon exists, supporters may still vote for their candidate even if they feel his or her election is assured. By doing so, they will increase the mandate and, therefore, reduce the extent to which their candidate adopts and supports the opposition's positions. That is, their votes will increase the probability that their candidate will push only their preferred positions after he or she is elected.

Supporters of the candidate who is expected to lose may cast their votes in order to reduce the size of the winning majority and force the winning candidate to give some weight to their positions on issues.

An individual will choose to vote if his or her expected benefit exceeds the cost of voting. The expected benefit is obtained by multiplying the potential benefit that will accrue to the individual by the probability that his or her vote will, if cast, influence the outcome. The potential benefit may take the form of a desirable change (as viewed by the voter) in the institutional structure of the community, in economic or foreign policy, or in the priorities that determine the distribution of government expenditures. It is also possible that the potential benefit may take the form of a direct gift to the voter, such as the promise of a job or contract. On the other hand, the voter may vote against a candidate who is going to raise taxes or confiscate his or her wealth. In this case, the benefit takes the form of reduced costs.

Any increase in the potential benefits of voting and/or in the probability of the vote being influential will increase the expected gains from voting and, thus, increase the likelihood that an individual will vote. Anything that increases the cost of voting will reduce the likelihood that an individual will vote.

If an individual chooses not to vote, it is because the cost of voting exceeds the benefits. Not voting is a rational act on the part of the individual. Increased voter turnout will result from either lowering the cost of voting or increasing the benefits. This suggests that increased voter turnout is more likely if easy-to-understand information about candidates and issues is made available, if polling places are made more accessible, if the vote is expected to be close, if the electorate is small, and if there are a number of issues rather than a single issue to be decided.

Application

Tests of Rational Voter Behavior

Several recent studies have tested empirically the economic theory of rational voter behavior. These studies have attempted to esti-

mate the effects on voter turnout of variables that influence the
costs and expected benefits of voting. Two such studies have been
made, one by Yoram Barzel and Eugene Silverberg in 1973[2] and
the other by Russell Settle and Burton Abrams in 1976.[3]

The Barzel-Silverberg study found a negative relationship between voter turnout in U.S. gubernatorial elections and the size of
the voting population and also the one-sidedness of the outcome.
(The negative relationship exists between voter turnout and size of
the voting population and between voter turnout and size of the
winning majority, i.e., one-sidedness.) Both of these results coin-
cide with the theory of rational voter turnout since they both indicate that the smaller the probability of a single vote being influential, the smaller the turnout. They also found an increase in the
turnout when the gubernatorial election coincided with presidential and senatorial elections. This consolidation of elections lowers
the costs of voting and the result supports the theory.

The study by Settle and Abrams looked at voter participation
in presidential elections from 1868 to 1972 (excluding the 1944 war
year election as unrepresentative). Their study included several
proxy variables to capture the effects of information on voter turnout. They assumed that campaign expenditures are correlated with
the amount of information available to voters. Further, they
assumed that the higher the campaign expenditures, the more
information transmitted. This would lower the individual's cost of
voting. Settle and Abrams found a significant and positive relationship between campaign expenditures and voter turnout.

To capture the effects of increasing expected benefits, Settle
and Abrams included a variable to measure what they called legislative profits. These are the benefits the winning candidate can
disperse to the voters. Their proxy variable for legislative profits is
federal government expenditure in constant dollars. This variable
measures the control and involvement of the government over the
economy and should reflect the ability of the government to disperse benefits to the voter. As we would expect, this variable was
found to have a positive relationship to voter turnout.

To measure the probable effectiveness of a vote, the size of the
winning majority was examined. It was found that the larger the
winning majority, the smaller the voter turnout. Income (measured by per capita GNP) was found to have a negative relationship with voter turnout. This might measure the higher opportuni-

[2]Yoram Barzel and Eugene Silverberg, "Is the Act of Voting Rational?" *Public
Choice,* Vol. 16, Fall 1973, pp. 51–58.

[3]Burton Abrams and Russell Settle, "The Determinants of Voter Participation: A
More General Model," *Public Choice,* Vol. 27, Fall 1976, pp. 81–89.

ty cost of voting. Finally, Settle and Abrams looked at the effect of women's suffrage and a third political party on voter turnout. These were found to have a positive and a negative effect, respectively, though the latter effect is very slight.

Both of these studies seem to support the theory that voters are rational utility maximizers. Voter turnouts are higher when expected benefits are higher and lower when expected costs are higher.

A Problem with Majority Voting

The evidence supports the hypothesis that individuals are rational and consistent when expressing their preferences regarding public activity. Is the political process that aggregates individual preferences also consistent? Unfortunately, this is not always the case. A problem may arise whenever three or more voters are voting on three or more issues. This is the problem of the cyclical majority, which is sometimes called the paradox of voting. This problem may arise even though *individual* decisions (voters) are rational and consistent. It is not the result of a problem with individual decision making; rather, it is the result of a problem with the mechanism used to combine individual choices into a collective choice.

To illustrate the paradox of voting, consider the following example. Suppose there are three individuals (A, B, and C) living on a private road that is in need of repair. They face the following alternatives: (1) resurfacing the road, which would cost $1000 each; (2) patching the road at $500 each; (3) doing nothing, that is, putting off repair. Assume the individuals rank these three alternatives as shown in Table 5.1.

Option (1), resurfacing the road, is the preferred choice of individual A, option (2), patching the road, is A's second choice, and option (3), doing nothing, is A's least preferred alternative. Individual B's first choice is option (2), second choice is option (3), and least preferred alternative is option (1). Individual C ranks (3) first, (1) second, and (2) third.

Table 5.1

Rank	A	B	C
High	1	2	3
Middle	2	3	1
Low	3	1	2

Assume that a simple majority voting rule is used to decide the outcome of this question. Let the voting process take the following form. Two of the three options will be matched against one another on the first vote. The winning option in this election will be placed against the remaining option, and the winner in that election will be the one selected.

Using a simple majority rule, suppose they vote on (1) and (2) first. Individuals A and C will vote for (1) over (2) and B will vote for (2) over (1). Option (1) wins since it receives two votes to option (2)'s one vote. Now suppose they vote on (1) and (3). Since B and C prefer (3) to (1), option (3) wins. Option (3) is the overall winner. If the voting process had started with options (2) and (3) instead of (1) and (2), option (2) would win the first vote. And in the vote between (2) and (1), (1) would win. In this situation, option (1) would be the final choice. If the initial vote was between (1) and

Figure 5.4

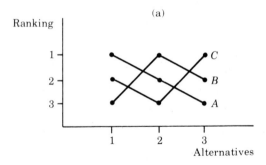

(a)

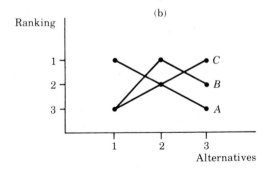

(b)

(3), option (2) would be the final choice. This is an example of a cyclical outcome; that is, the final outcome depends on the order in which the alternatives are voted upon. A cyclical outcome is distressing, because it implies that the democratic process may be arbitrary.

The cyclical majority problem will not occur when the individual rankings are single-peaked. The rankings of our example are depicted in Figure 5.4(a). Individual *C*'s ranking is double-peaked.

Double-peaked means that *C*'s ranking has two peaks; it has a peak at option (1), then it goes down to option (2), and finally, back up to option (3). The rankings of individuals *B* and *A*, on the other hand, are single-peaked.

C's ranking is somewhat unusual in that the extremes are ranked higher than the middle. If this were not the case—if *C*'s ranking was single-peaked as it is in Figure 5.4(b)—the cyclical majority problem would disappear. If individual *C* ranks option (3) first, option (2) second, and option (1) third as shown in Figure 5.4(b), then the ranking will be single-peaked. When all rankings are single-peaked, the outcome will be independent of the ordering of the vote. If the rankings of the individuals are as depicted in Figure 5.4(b), option (2) will win regardless of the voting order. As long as rankings are single-peaked, simple majority voting always results in a unique outcome. Rankings will be single-peaked as long as voters do not have extreme preferences. In fact, in the situation depicted in Figure 5.4(b), the ranking of the median voter will prevail (option 2). Furthermore, if all rankings are of equal preference intensity, the gains in utility will outweigh the losses.

When preferences are single-peaked, simple majority voting will result in the selection of that outcome preferred by the median voter. To demonstrate this, we will assume we have five voters and five increasingly expensive levels of road repair. Figure 5.5 shows the preferences of these five voters. Individual *A* prefers option (1) to all others. Individual *B*'s most preferred option is (2), and so forth. Each individual prefers options closer to his or her most preferred option to those farther away.

If the voting starts with (1) and (2), option (2) will win. Individuals *B, C, D,* and *E* will vote for option (2) over option (1). Option (1) will get only one vote, from individual *A*. If options (2) and (3) are now voted upon, option (3) will get *C, D,* and *E*'s vote and option (2) will get *A* and *B*'s vote. Option (3) wins by three votes to two. If options (3) and (4) are voted upon, option (3) will win three votes to two. Option (3) will also win against options (4) and (5). (You should verify these last two results.) Option (3), the one most prefered by the median voter, wins over all other options.

Figure 5.5

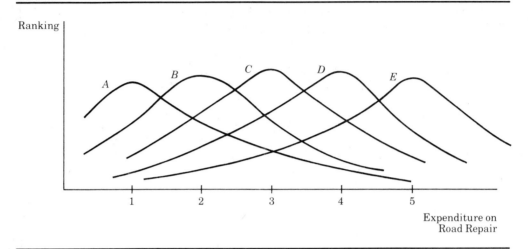

More on the Cyclical Majority

The possibility of a cyclical majority exists because majority voting does not allow voters to express the intensity of their preferences. A voter may vote for option (1) over option (2), but there is no way he can express how much he prefers option (1) to option (2). If voters could express preference intensity regarding the options, an arbitrary outcome would not occur. One way for individuals to express the intensity of their preferences is through "purchasing" quantities of public goods much as they do private goods. Suppose we allow the individuals to express their preference intensities by indicating how much they are willing to pay for one option over the other. The option with the most dollar votes wins.

Table 5.2 is identical to Table 5.1 except that the dollar figures between the ranks give the amount the individual would be willing to pay to have the higher option instead of the lower. Individual A would be willing to pay $10 for option (1) over option (2) and $20 for option (2) over option (3). Individual A would pay $30 for option (1) over option (3).

Following Table 5.2, if option (1) is run against option (2), individual A will pay $10 for (1), individual B will pay $20 for (2), and individual C will pay $15 for (1). Option (1) wins because it receives 25 dollar votes to option (2)'s 20. Pairing option (3) with option (1), option (3) receives 40 dollar votes and (1) receives 30 dollar votes. Option (3) wins. In fact, it will win regardless of the order in which the pairs are voted.

What this example demonstrates is that when the preference intensities of the rankings can be expressed, the problem of cyclical majority disappears. There are several other ways in which preference intensities can be expressed to some extent. These include point voting, vote selling, and logrolling. Logrolling will be discussed in more detail in Chapter 6.

If the community chooses to ignore preference intensity, as it does with simple majority voting, it is implicitly choosing a rule that weighs all preferences equally. If a cyclical majority should occur, one might argue that it is an expression of social indifference (that is, each option is given equal weight) given the community's rule for aggregating individual preferences. To see this, consider Table 5.3. Given the preference intensities in Table 5.3, all options receive 20 dollar votes. All options have equal value and have the same weight. In this situation, the social decision rule—simple majority voting—cannot discriminate between the options.

The implications of this analysis are several. First, if intensities are equal, as they are in Table 5.3, the cyclical majority problem can be ignored since, in a sense, society is indifferent to the outcome. This does not mean that any arbitrary option can be picked and that the election need not take place because there is no way of

Table 5.2

A		B		C	
$10	1	$10	2	$30	3
$20	2	$10	3	$15	1
	3		1		2

Table 5.3

A		B		C	
$10	1	$10	2	$10	3
$10	2	$10	3	$10	1
	3		1		2

Table 5.4

A		B		C	
$30	1	$10	2	$10	2
	2		1		1

determining whether a cyclical majority will occur beforehand. The problem may not exist, and a unique outcome may be forthcoming.

If the intensities of individual rankings are different, simple majority voting may cause problems even if the rankings are single-peaked. Suppose the rankings of the losing minority are much more intense than those of the winning majority. In this situation, the loss resulting from majority voting may exceed the gains. We do not need three options to see this. If rankings over two options are as given in Table 5.4, (2) will win over (1) under simple majority rule. In terms of dollars, A would be willing to pay $30 for (1) over (2), and B and C would be willing to pay a combined total of $20 for (2) over (1). The net loss in this situation is $10. The loss to the minority exceeds the gains of the majority.

The way to overcome the problem of the cyclical majority as well as that of intense minority preferences is to devise a voting process that allows some expression of intensities.

Application

The Probability of Intransitive Majority Rule

Several studies have attempted to look at the empirical relevance of the cyclical majority rule problem. These studies have attempted to find out how important this problem is in actual elections. The results indicate that the probability of experiencing a cyclical majority declines as the number of voters grows.

Dean Jamison asked college graduates and undergraduates to rank potential Democratic candidates for the 1972 election.[4] With three alternatives, he found that, among undergraduates, the probability of a cyclical majority ranged from .029 to .013 as the number of voters went from 3 to 15. Among graduates, the probability of a cyclical majority ranged from .028 to .018 as the number of voters went from 3 to 15.

Choice of Voting Rule

In democratic governments, voting is the means by which individual preferences are communicated to the state. The actual voting

---

[4] Dean Jamison, "The Probability of Intransitive Majority Rule: An Empirical Study," *Public Choice,* Vol. 23, Fall 1975, pp. 87-94.

process can be structured in several ways. Simple majority voting is the most common voting rule used (50 percent plus one vote is necessary for a victory), but it is only one of many possible rules. In this section, we discuss the selection of the voting rule. The approach we use was developed by James Buchanan and Gordon Tullock.[5] Buchanan and Tullock consider the choice of voting rule to be part of the process of setting up a constitution. During this stage the institutional framework within which democratic decisions are made is determined.

The formal analysis is based on the decision of the individual. We will look at the process that an individual uses to determine the voting rule he or she prefers. The choice of voting rule must be decided before votes on any issue or candidate can take place. This is because each issue will affect the individual differently. Consequently, his or her choice of rule would be different depending on the effect that the particular rule will have on the outcome. If the issue would affect the individual negatively, he or she would choose a rule that minimized its chance of passing. If the issue would benefit the individual, he or she would choose a rule that would maximize its chance of passing. Only if the choice of rule is decided before any issues are actually voted upon will it be possible to secure agreement on which rule is actually used. This is what is meant by the constitutional stage. Agreement as to choice of rule can be reached at the constitutional stage as long as each individual feels that, for the given rule, the gains will outweigh the losses. Since, at the constitutional stage, each individual will anticipate being involved in a large number of individual decisions, he or she will pick the rule that maximizes expected utility over all of them, knowing that he or she may lose on any single decision.

The Individual Choice of Rule

When deciding which voting rule to favor, individuals must look at two types of cost. Following the analysis of Buchanan and Tullock, one of these costs is the cost of having an issue pass that reduces the individual's utility. These costs are called external costs. Since state action involves coercion (if the decision rule does not require unanimous consent), an individual may be forced to abide by a decision that is contrary to his or her interests. One way in which this can happen is by a winning coalition placing the cost of the provision of a public good on the losing faction.

---

[5]James Buchanan and Gordon Tullock, *The Calculus of Consent* (Ann Arbor, Mich: The University of Michigan Press, 1971).

The cost of the tax share to the loser may exceed the benefits of the good acquired. Alternatively, the winners could vote themselves provision of a private good at the expense of the losers. If the issue involves reallocation of property, the winners could harm the losers through the expropriation of the losers' property.

External costs will decrease as the number of votes necessary for victory out of the total increases, and as the number of votes necessary for approval increases, victory will be more difficult to secure without the vote of each individual decision maker. Clearly, if the rule required unanimous consent, this component of the cost of collective action would be zero. No one would vote for any measure that made him or her worse off. Consequently, with unanimity a requirement for victory, the individual is assured that no action would pass that made him or her worse off. The external cost is depicted as *EC* in Figure 5.6. As the number of votes necessary for approval approaches *N*, the total voting population, these costs go down. When *N* is reached, the costs are zero.

The other component of the cost of collective action is what Buchanan and Tullock call decision-making costs. These costs include two elements. As the size of the group necessary for approval of a measure increases, the cost of securing an agreement goes up because of strategic bargaining. (These costs were discussed in

Figure 5.6

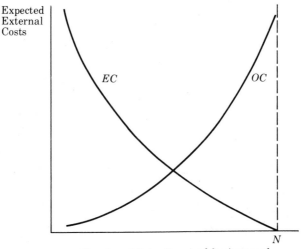

Number of Votes Required for Approval

Chapter 3.) As the number of votes necessary for approval increases, the cost of convincing the required number of individuals to vote in favor of the proposal will rise. The second element of these costs is the opportunity cost of having an issue fail. This cost represents the net benefit the individual loses as a result of having an issue he or she prefers fail to gain acceptance. This component of the cost is difficult to measure for the same reason that it is difficult to measure the benefits that arise from the provision of public goods. It is reasonable to expect, however, that these costs rise with the number of votes necessary for approval. The individual will perceive that a proposal he or she prefers will have a lesser chance of passing the larger the number of votes needed for approval. This means that the opportunity cost of having a preferred proposal fail will increase with increases in the number of votes necessary for approval. This cost is depicted as *OC* in Figure 5.6. The individual can now calculate the optimal voting rule by picking the rule that minimizes the sum of these costs. In Figure 5.7 the costs are added together, yielding the *EC* + *OC* curve.

Given the conditions depicted in Figure 5.7, the individual would, at the constitutional stage, be in favor of a rule that requires that K individuals approve any proposal before it is accepted. A voting rule of K/N minimizes the expected cost of collective action for this individual. At the constitutional stage, each individual will make this calculation, and a final decision regarding the rule must be reached. Agreement on a voting rule can be reached as long as

Figure 5.7

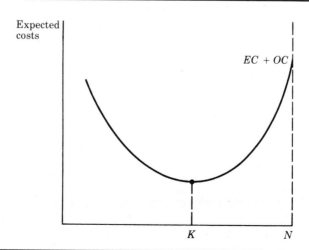

each individual gains more than he or she loses from the rule finally chosen. Several interesting implications can be drawn from the analysis of optimal individual voting rules.

First, from an individual point of view, there is no reason to expect that a simple majority rule $[N/(2 + 1)/N]$ is optimal. This rule is only one among a large number of possible rules. Though a simple majority rule may not be optimal for each individual, it may be picked for another reason. Suppose the optimal rule for each individual is a minority rule, one which requires less than a simple majority for victory. Such a rule will not work in a democracy. Suppose a 40 percent minority rule is chosen for simple "yes" or "no" elections. If "yes" gets 40 percent or more of the vote, "yes" wins; if "yes" gets less than 40 percent, "no" wins. Suppose further that a proposal to provide a public good is being voted on. The election, thus, is "yes," provide the good, or "no," don't provide it. Let's say 45 percent of the electorate vote "yes" and 55 percent vote "no." "Yes" wins. However, the "no" supporters will now propose a new election in which the issue to be decided is not to provide the public good. A vote of "yes" (which means not to provide the good) will win this election, getting 55 percent of the vote. It will not end here. The "yes" voters in the original election will offer their original proposal and win again. A never-ending cycle results. In fact, this cycle will occur unless an issue is supported by 60 percent plus one of the voters. In this case, the losers could not win in an election where a "yes" vote meant the voter was against the issue. This implies that the acceptance of a simple majority rule may be optimal when the individual calculus would lead to a minority rule.

Second, individuals will generally prefer more stringent voting rules (a larger K/N) if they expect collective decisions that tend to provide benefits for subgroups of the total population as opposed to benefits for the entire group. Further, the smaller these groups are likely to be, the more stringent the optimal voting rule is likely to be. If the individual feels that a large number of decisions will benefit others at his or her expense, he or she will perceive a higher EC curve. The result will be to increase his or her preferred K.

Some Closing Remarks

Actual political democracies, like everything else, often work less than perfectly. Votes are cast only periodically and only on some issues. At no level of government in the U.S. do individuals vote on the total size of the government budget or on how the total budget will be distributed in the provision of public goods. The cost of placing proposals before the electorate is high and the cost to the electorate of becoming informed about proposals and their consequences is significant.

Some election laws have raised these costs appreciably. Since the effect of a single individual's vote on an election is miniscule, the individual's expected benefit from voting for a preferred proposal will be very small. If the cost of voting is positive, the net benefit that would accrue to the individual from voting may be negative. If this is the case, he or she will choose not to vote. Consequently, laws that artificially raise the cost of voting will, in effect, disenfranchise part of the electorate.

Application

The Federal Election Campaign Act[6]

Public Law 92-225 restricted the expenditures of federal candidates for radio, television, newspaper, and telephone advertising to no more than ten cents per voting-aged person in the election area. Legislation of this type limits competition in two ways. First, it makes it much more difficult for little-known candidates to place their proposals before the electorate. This restricts entry into the political arena and strengthens the position of incumbents. An incumbent can obtain "free" advertising by calling a news conference or by appearing on *Face the Nation* or *Meet the Press* or any of the dozens of talk shows carried by the television networks. It is generally easier for an incumbent to take advantage of these opportunities than it is for individuals who are potential challengers. Challengers must pay to have their proposals placed before the electorate. To the extent that legislation limits expenditures on this type of advertising, the challenge becomes less effective.

Second, Abrams and Settle have shown that radio and TV advertising are relatively inexpensive means of providing the electorate with information. They estimate that the use of radio and television advertising has had the effect of reducing presidential campaign expenditures by 25 million dollars per candidate in recent elections. Consequently, limiting expenditures on this means

[6]Burton Abrams and Russell Settle, "The Effect of Broadcasting on Political Campaign Spending: An Empirical Investigation," *Journal of Political Economy,* Vol. 84 (October 1976), pp. 1095-1107.

Table 5.5		Presidential General Election Campaign Expenditures 1868-1972	
Year	Republican (in Dollars)	Democratic (in Dollars)	Expenditures per Adult
1868	150,000	80,000	.01
1872	250,000	50,000	.01
1876	950,000	900,000	.08
1880	1,100,000	360,000	.06
1884	1,300,000	1,400,000	.09
1888	1,350,000	860,000	.07
1892	1,700,000	2,350,000	.11
1896	3,350,000	680,000	.10
1900	3,000,000	430,000	.08
1904	2,100,000	700,000	.06
1908	1,660,000	630,000	.04
1912	1,070,000	1,130,000	.04
1916	2,440,000	2,280,000	.08
1920	5,420,000	1,470,000	.11
1924	4,020,000	1,110,000	.10
1928	6,260,000	5,340,000	.16
1932	2,900,000	2,250,000	.07
1936	8,890,000	5,190,000	.17
1940	3,450,000	2,780,000	.07
1944	2,830,000	2,170,000	.06
1948	2,130,000	2,740,000	.05
1952	6,610,000	5,030,000	.12
1956	7,780,000	5,110,000	.12
1960	10,130,000	9,800,000	.18
1964	16,030,000	8,760,000	.22
1968	25,400,000	11,600,000	.31
1972	35,180,000	18,480,000	.38

Source: Burton Abrams and Russell Settle, "The Effects of Broadcasting on Political Campaign Spending: An Empirical Investigation," *Journal of Political Economy,* Vol. 84 (October 1976), p. 1096. Copyright © 1976 by The University of Chicago Press. Reprinted by permission of The University of Chicago Press.

of advertising will artificially raise the cost of acquiring information about proposals and candidates. The result is to strengthen the monopoly power of those individuals already in office.

In free markets, individuals who are interested in entering a particular market are not restricted as to the source of their initial capital investment. The entrepreneur will raise this capital in the least costly manner. No one cares whether one individual contributes the whole amount or whether different amounts are raised from many different individuals. The fact that a particular entrepreneur may raise the funds from one or a few individuals does not give this firm a competitive advantage over other firms in the industry. Political entrepreneurs are not allowed to raise funds from one or a few individuals. Public Law 99-443 restricts individual contributions to not more than $1,000 to any one candidate or $2,000 if both a primary and a general election are involved. This restriction will raise the cost of entry to potential challengers and, consequently, restrict competition. The sponsors of Public Law 99-443 argue that it was necessary in order to prevent the "abuse" of power (that is, the use of the position to benefit large contributors) once the individual gains office. However, large contributions do not cause the abuse of power. Individuals in government can "abuse" their position because they have a monopoly. To the extent that limiting campaign contributions makes it more costly to raise campaign funds, it will restrict entry. Public Law 99-443 will strengthen the monopoly of government officials.

Application

Monopoly in Government[7]

If real-world political democracies are not perfect, we expect to observe individuals responsible for administering them to exhibit some of the behavior characteristics of a private monopolist. One of these characteristics is tie-in selling. Tie-in selling is the practice of requiring a buyer to purchase a full line of products in order to get any of the individual components of the line. Shops that specialize in repairing phonographs will frequently refuse to sell parts to customers without selling the service of installation also. This practice increases the revenue and profits of the firm and can only survive if the firm has some monopoly power. Tie-in selling is frequently practiced by the government. Citizens typically purchase police and fire protection, refuse collection, education, streets, and playgrounds from a single unit of government. The argument for centralizing the provision of services has been that it will reduce administrative costs. R. E. Wagner and W. E. Weber, however, have shown that, for large counties, tie-in selling has resulted in increasing the cost of the governmental units. In other words, the beneficial effect of reduced administrative cost that results from centralization is more than offset by the increase in cost of governmental

[7]R. E. Wagner and W. E. Weber, "Competition, Monopoly and the Organization of Government in Metropolitan Areas," *Journal of Law and Economics,* Vol. 18 (December 1975), pp. 661-684.

**Predicted Changes in Total Expenditure
due to Centralized Provision of Public Goods and Services**   Table 5.6

Change	Counties	Under 100,000 Population	100,000–200,000 Population	Over 200,000 Population
−	107	69	22	16
+	57	12	12	33
Total	164	81	34	49
Percentage +	34	15	35	67

provision that results from tie-in selling. However, for small counties (populations of less than 150,000) the effect of reduced administrative costs more than offsets the effect of tie-in selling. Of the 164 counties that were observed, the largest net increase in cost due to centralization was estimated to be $96 million, while the largest net decrease was $41 million.

These two applications provide some evidence that real-world political democracies exhibit some of the characteristics that are attributed to entrepreneurs who possess some monopoly power in the market for private goods. The Abrams and Settle study indicates that some election laws have served to limit competition for legislative seats by arbitrarily raising the cost of entry to potential challengers. The Wagner and Weber study provides evidence which suggests that monopoly power is exercised by government bodies through the practice of tie-in selling.

These two studies are only suggestive of the results that have been obtained by economic scholars who have studied the democratic process. However, had we taken the space to exhaust the evidence that is available, any conclusions that we would have drawn from the evidence would have been tentative. This is the nature of scientific inquiry. It is never conclusive.

Questions and Exercises

1. Increasing the individual's level of education may have an ambiguous effect on his or her voting behavior. First, a higher level of education may make it easier for the individual to acquire information about elections, thus lowering the cost of voting. But higher education often leads to a higher income and value of time for the individual. What effect will this have on the individual's voting behavior?

2. Why might a rational individual prefer a voting rule that requires a larger percentage of favorable to total votes cast for income redistribution schemes than for national defense?

3. Why might the paradox of voting actually reflect social indifference on the part of voters?

4. It was stated in the chapter that, with a unanimity rule, only those proposals that are consistent with Pareto optimal moves will be approved. If this is true, why would a rational voter approve a less stringent rule?

5. When we state in the chapter that the individual will behave just as rationally when making decisions about public goods as when making choices about private goods, what do we mean?

6. Consider Figure 5.1 and assume that the decision regarding the quantity of public goods purchased is made by majority vote. Suppose income were redistributed away from individuals B and C to A. What will happen to the quantity of the public good that receives a majority vote? What are you assuming?

7. Consider Figure 5.1. Can you think of a way to increase the equilibrium quantity of the public good that will obtain a majority vote by redistributing income? Assume a positive income elasticity of demand for public goods. How could you decrease the equilibrium quantity of the public good chosen by redistributing income?

8. Look at Figure 5.1 and suppose you were interested in maximizing the equilibrium quantity of the public good that receives a majority vote. How would you redistribute income?

9. Consider Figure 5.6. The number of individuals eligible to vote is N. It is presumed that N is also the number of individuals who actually vote. The voting rule that minimizes $OC + EC$ is K/N. Suppose that a certain number of individuals who are eligible to vote choose not to vote. Let this number be X. The number of individuals who actually vote is equal to $N_a = N - X$. What happens to the voting rule that minimizes $OC + EC$? What population are you using in your calculation, N or N_a?

10. "An efficient budget, then, is the largest tax-expenditure proposal that receives unanimous support." Evaluate this statement.

Additional Readings

Buchanan, James, and Tullock, Gordon. *The Calculus of Consent.* Ann Arbor, Mich.: The University of Michigan Press, 1971.

Downs, Anthony. *An Economic Theory of Democracy.* New York: Harper & Row, Publishers, 1957.

6

Representative Democracy

In Chapter 5, we examined the voting process as one method of communicating the tastes and preferences of individuals to those who are responsible for making decisions on public taxation and expenditure. A direct democracy was considered in which voters directly expressed their preferences for the final product of government. We assumed that voters directly expressed their desires concerning expenditure levels for such things as defense, highway construction, and welfare, as well as for the types of tax structures used to pay for them. In most modern democracies, direct voting on all governmental matters is too costly because the number and complexity of issues considered make it impossible for the individual to vote on every issue. The cost to the individual voter of acquiring information concerning all of the issues, as well as the cost of getting to the polls and voting, would be very high relative to the benefits. Because of these costs, the percentage of the voting population actually voting on most issues would be very small. To lower the cost of political decision making to the individual and to avoid the problem of low voter turnout, advanced democratic societies use a representative form of democracy.

In representative democracies, individual voters delegate most of their voting decisions to elected representatives who, with their votes, represent the tastes and preferences of the constituency on specific issues. Elected representatives are specialists who spend all their time learning about the issues in order to fulfill their responsibilities to their constituents. This arrangement lowers the cost to the individual of participating in governmental decision making, since the voter only has to select the representative who he or she feels will most faithfully represent preferred interests. This significantly reduces the number of votes in which individuals have to participate.

In *some* respects, elected representatives may be viewed as middlemen. In private markets, middlemen economize on the costs of exchange, which are the costs of discovering, negotiating, and enforcing exchange agreements. As a result of economizing on these costs, middlemen benefit both buyers and sellers. As a consequence of employing the services of middlemen, the net social dividends that result will be higher than they would be otherwise.

To illustrate, suppose you would like to purchase a three-bedroom house that is air-conditioned, has a family room, a fenced yard, and so forth. Given these specifications and others that you have in mind, you would be willing to pay as much as $40,000 for this home. Suppose, also, that there is another individual who owns such a home and who would be willing to sell it for as little as $39,000. Clearly, if the costs of discovering this offer and of negotiating the exchange are less than the potential gain from the exchange ($40,000 – $39,000 = $1,000), an advantageous exchange for both you and the seller is possible. However, searching out and negotiating this exchange will be costly for you; it will take your valuable time. The same, of course, is true for the individual who wishes to sell the house. These costs may be so high as to prevent the exchange from taking place. If they are higher than $1,000, they will absorb the potential gain from the exchange and no exchange will take place. Middlemen (real estate agents) exist because they can economize on costs by specializing in these types of transactions. If the cost of employing a real estate agent to find the house (or the buyer) and to negotiate the exchange is less than $1,000, you and the seller will benefit from having employed his or her services.

Elected representatives perform a function similar to that of real estate agents, used-car salespersons, stockbrokers, and other sales representatives. All exist because they economize on the costs of reaching advantageous exchanges. There are, however, some important differences between the set of constraints faced by the elected representatives and those faced by middlemen who function in private markets. These different constraints will cause the elected representative to behave differently than, say, a real estate agent. We will discuss these differences at length in subsequent sections of this chapter. For now, we will simply mention three important differences: (1) the elected representative is not a residual claimant; (2) the elected representative does not have salable rights in his or her office; and (3) the elected representative is not subject to as strong a force of competition as are the middlemen who function in private markets.

In order to take full advantage of gains from specialization, it is necessary to keep the number of individuals, or representatives, who actually vote on governmental issues relatively small. This means that a large number of voters will be delegating their governmental decision-making rights to each representative. Because of this, the control of any one voter over the decision-making process will be small. Each voter, by agreeing to adopt a representative form of government, accepts less control over governmental decision making in order to keep his or her cost of participating in the process low.

Many representative democracies have adopted what is known as a bicameral legislature. In this system, the representatives are divided into two houses and each voter generally has a representative in each house. Representatives in both houses may represent geographical areas based on population, as in the United States House of Representatives; or representation in one house may be based on geographical area alone, as in the United States Senate. Most bicameral legislatures have one of each type, like the United States Congress, or both of the first type, as is found in the state legislatures. In general, only the House, in which each legislator represents fewer individual voters, has the power to propose taxation bills. Other than that, any issue initiated in either house must be passed by a majority of both houses. In the United States, the president, who is an elected representative of all the voters, has veto power over any issue passed by the legislative assemblies. It has been argued that, since the president represents all of the voters, this veto power protects individuals from legislation that benefits special-interest groups at the expense of the general population. Experience, however, suggests that he is not entirely immune to the pressure of special interests. The president, who is in charge of the supply of public goods and services, is responsible for actually running the government.

Utility Maximization and the Representative

The behavior of elected representatives is motivated by self-interest. When we speak of self-interest, we do not necessarily mean some narrowly defined set of interests. Typically, self-interest will include many things. To some extent, we are all interested in the welfare of others, the stability of the political system, the quality of the environment, our stature among associates, our potential to change jobs, and the security of our property, to name just a few. Unfortunately, in the real world having more of one of these goods means having less of some other. Faced with this fact, the individual will be forced to choose among various baskets of goods. The basket that he or she selects will be the one that maximizes his or her utility or satisfaction. It is in this sense that we mean that the behavior of individuals is motivated by self-interest.

Constraints and the Representative

An important point that should be emphasized is that economic analysis predicts the choices of individuals mainly on the basis of the structure of rewards or costs that confront the individual. If a homemaker, other things being the same, prefers steak to canned beans, he or she will, nonetheless, purchase fewer steaks and more beans as the price of steak rises relative to the price of beans. The same idea applies to elected representatives. If the cost of supporting a particular public project should rise relative to the benefits, we would expect to see elected representatives shifting their support from this project to others.

The costs that confront elected representatives may take many forms. The project may make some of a representative's constituents worse off and, as a consequence, cost him or her votes in future elections. The representative will weigh the costs against the benefits that are expected in the form of votes from constituents who are helped by the project. Some of the individuals who stand to benefit or lose from the adoption of the project may be willing to offer support in addition to their votes. They may contribute to the representative's campaign fund, or they may promise to channel a certain amount of business through the representative's private law office. Of course, there is always the possibility that representatives will be offered explicit bribes of money to support or campaign against particular public projects. Representatives also may be influenced by their colleagues in the legislature. Support or nonsupport of a particular project may damage the representative's stature among associates and reduce his or her chances of influencing their behavior in the future or of being elected or appointed to certain desirable positions within the legislature.

The representative will weigh the costs and benefits associated with each alternative he or she is confronted with and will pick the alternative that yields the highest utility to him or her. If a law is passed limiting the amount of money any constituent may contribute to a representative's campaign fund but not limiting the amount of time any constituent may contribute as a voluntary worker, the law will effectively lower the relative price to the representative of ignoring the preferences of those who would have contributed money. Thus, the representative will pay less attention to the preferences of individuals who would contribute money. At the same time, the law has the effect of raising the relative price of ignoring the preferences of those who would contribute their time. The representative will pay more attention to the preferences of these individuals in the future.

If a city councilwoman runs and is elected to the office of mayor, the cost to her of supporting projects to construct city parks in her old district will rise relative to the cost of supporting projects to construct city parks in other districts. As mayor, she will devote relatively more support to park construction in other districts and less support to park construction in her old district.

If the representative, like the entrepreneur of a private firm, is successful in estimating the costs and benefits associated with the various alternatives she is confronted with, she will survive and prosper. If, on the other hand, she consistently underestimates costs and overestimates benefits, she will fail. An elected representative, as we have stated, is a political entrepreneur whose function, like that of the entrepreneur of a private firm, is to seek advantageous trades. A trade in the political arena that is advantageous to all the parties involved is called a compromise. Political compromises, like private trades, lead to outcomes that are preferred by all parties to the compromise.

Imperfections in the Political Market

The analogy between private entrepreneurs and political entrepreneurs can be pushed too far, however. When property rights are well defined and information and transaction costs are low, private entrepreneurs are forced to bear all of the costs associated with the trades they make. Suppose you buy a loaf of bread at the grocery store that sells for sixty cents. The sixty cents reflects the value of other commodities foregone in producing the loaf of bread. If you decide to hire a gardener to mow your lawn at ten dollars per week, the ten dollars reflects the value of other goods foregone that the gardener could have produced in the time it takes him to mow your lawn.

Political entrepreneurs, however, do not bear all of the costs associated with the trades they make. A trade between certain lobbyists and members of Congress for the representatives' support of legislation raising the parity price of wheat (or lowering the quota on imported shoes or steel or funding a program to build a new bomber) will be costly to large numbers of individuals. However, these costs may not be borne by the representatives. Why is this the case in the political arena and not *generally* the case in the market for private goods?

As we argued previously (see Chapter 5), the political market is not perfect. The cost imposed on any given individual by a decision to build a new bomber may be small relative to the expenses that the individual would have to incur in discovering what the costs are and in taking effective action to block the decision. Competition among elected representatives is limited. Members of Congress do not compete in the same sense as do private entrepreneurs who sell similar products. Private entrepreneurs compete for one another's customers by offering to sell at lower prices, offering higher quality products, better service, or by employing other means to attract their competitors' customers. Since private entrepreneurs can benefit from the decision to lower prices, etc., only if consumers are aware of the decision, they will find that it is in their interest to provide potential customers with this information in the least costly manner. Low-cost information to consumers about available alternatives is a result of vigorous competition among sellers. Elected representatives, however, cannot compete with one another for constituents; they serve individuals who live within particular geographic areas. The situation is analogous to one in which two firms selling similar products divide the market area between themselves and agree not to sell in the other's geographic area. Vigorous competition, of course, takes place at the time the representative must stand for reelection. As we would expect, those individuals competing (campaigning) for votes find it in their interest to provide information to the voters concerning the quality and price of the products they are peddling. This type of competition takes place only periodically, and, as pointed out in the previous chapter, the costs of entry into the political arena are kept artificially high by certain election laws.

There are other important differences between the environments in which political and private entrepreneurs operate. Private entrepreneurs must rely on voluntary transactions in furthering their own interests. Consequently, all parties to the transaction must anticipate that they will benefit, or they will refuse to exchange. This is not the case with elected representatives who can use coercion in dealing with constituents. Of course, these representatives cannot coerce all of their constituents, or even most of them, and expect to survive in office. However, it is possible for elected representatives to make decisions that benefit a majority of their constituents and themselves at the expense of the minority.

Another important difference between the environments of these two types of entrepreneurs is that private entrepreneurs have salable property rights in their firms. Because they have salable rights, they will take into account the impact of present decisions on the future profitability of the business, even though they may not anticipate owning the business when the decisions have their major impact on profits. This is true because the present price of the firm (hence, the entrepreneur's present wealth) will reflect the expected future profits of the firm. Political entrepreneurs, on the other hand, do not have salable property rights in their offices. As a consequence, the effect of their present decisions on future costs and benefits will have a relatively small impact on their present wealth. They will be less influenced by these costs and benefits than would a private entrepreneur. When compared to private entrepreneurs, political entrepreneurs will weigh present costs and benefits relatively more heavily in their decision-making calculus than they will future costs and benefits.

These points are made to caution the reader not to take the analogy between the private entrepreneur and political entrepreneur too far. Both will attempt to maximize their utility subject to the constraints they face. However, because the market in the political sector is somewhat crude, political entrepreneurs will not be forced to take into account all of the costs associated with the decisions they make.

Political Parties

Why do politicians find it in their interest to associate themselves with a particular political party? A politician could, after sampling the preferences of the electorate, establish a platform that he or she thinks will be successful without ever personally associating with a political party. Then, why is it that we seldom observe politicians running for office without a party affiliation?

In answering this question, we should remember that providing information to the electorate is costly. Politicians will find that it is in their interest to attempt to economize on these costs. Membership in a political party is one way open to politicians of providing the electorate with general information about their views on important issues at low cost. If you know that a candidate is a Republican or Democrat, this knowledge conveys some information to you about how he or she will behave when confronted with certain issues because a political party is like a brand name. The names *Republican, Democrat, Libertarian, Socialist Workers' Party* all convey information about the individual members of the parties just as the brand names *General Electric, Ford,* and *Zenith* convey information about the products that carry these names.

Of course, a politician's membership in a party will not be without cost. For example, the owners of McDonald's Corporation will attempt to protect their brand name by taking steps to assure that all individual franchise owners turn out a product of standard quality. The same will be true for the leaders of a political party. They will make it costly for any individual member of the party who, by his or her actions and decisions, would depreciate the value of the brand name. Interest in protecting the brand name implies that we will often observe representatives voting along party lines on important issues when the members of the press stand ready to inform constituents of how the representatives voted.

Application

Campaign Expenditures and Political Competition

If the individual members of political parties do attempt to maximize utility subject to certain constraints, we would expect to observe systematic behavior consistent with that objective. George Stigler has suggested that, since a party's ability to influence governmental decisions depends upon its plurality in the legislature, the value of additional seats to the party should be positive. However, as the number of seats controlled by a particular party increases, the value of controlling an additional seat should, beyond some point, decline.[1]

If the campaign expenditures of a candidate for a seat approximate the present value of the seat in the legislature, then we should expect to see candidates who are members of the minority party spending more to obtain additional seats than would candidates who are members of the majority party. W. M. Crain and R. D. Tollison tested this hypothesis by collecting data on campaign expenditures in congressional elections over a 24-year period.[2] During this time, there were 404 open seats in which paired comparisons were possible. Some of their results appear in Table 6.1. In only four of the thirteen election years observed did the mean expenditures of the majority exceed the mean expenditures of the minority. In two of these years, 1960 and 1966, the majority party

[1]Based on George Stigler, "Economic Competition and Political Competition," *Public Choice*, Vol. 13 (Fall 1972), pp. 91–106.

[2]See W.M. Crain and R.D. Tollison, "Campaign Expenditures and Political Competition," *Journal of Law and Economics*, Vol. 19 (April 1976), pp. 177–188.

Table 6.1

Election Year	Open Seat Districts	Percentage of House	Mean Expenditure (in Dollars)
1948	48	43% D	4,026
		57% R	2,374
1950	38	39% R	5,692
		61% D	3,345
1952	53	46% R	4,695
		54% D	3,429
1954	25	49% D	6,421
		51% R	6,798
1956	31	47% R	3,209
		53% D	3,502
1958	45	46% R	5,237
		54% D	3,854
1960	36	35% R	5,589
		65% D	5,750
1962	51	40% R	10,693
		60% D	8,146
1964	47	41% R	9,991
		59% D	6,888
1966	32	32% R	3,222
		68% D	7,176
1968	33	43% R	9,704
		57% D	8,612
1970	45	44% R	9,256
		56% D	6,525
1972	62	41% R	55,152
		59% D	44,395

was either close to or had a two-thirds majority in the House. The fact that members of this party spent more on the average than members of the minority party might be explained by the fact that a two-thirds majority vote is required on some issues. On the whole, however, the results appear to be consistent with the hypothesis.

Institutional Constraints and the Representative

Because of the relatively small size of legislative assemblies, transaction costs will be low in the legislative choice process. This means that some of the conditions for the Coase Theorem[3] may be met in these bodies. That is, the decisions may more accurately reflect the preferences of the voters than direct voting (remember that the voters are representatives). All of the conditions of the Coase Theorem are not met, however. First, bargaining costs are not zero. Time is a scarce resource, so the bargaining may stop before all gains from trade are realized. Second, and more important, legislators are exchanging things over which they have attenuated ownership rights. That is, they are exchanging votes they cannot legally sell for generalized purchasing power and must, therefore, barter one vote for another. This reduces the degree to which preference intensities can be expressed in the exchange process. With dollar payments, an individual can accurately express intense preferences by a willingness to pay more money. Furthermore, since money is a universal medium of exchange, an individual trying to acquire votes will not have to find someone interested in his or her votes on other issues but only someone who places a lower value on his or her own vote than does the individual who is acquiring the vote. The inablility of legislators to offer more dollars to buy votes on issues about which they feel strongly may be overcome if legislative bodies make a large number of decisions over a period of time. Thus, an individual with intense preferences can agree to trade a single vote on a number of less preferred issues in order to secure votes on a highly preferred issue.

The process of vote trading just described is called *logrolling*. It should be pointed out that, although logrolling allows representatives in legislative bodies to express their preference intensities, these preferences do not necessarily reflect those of their constituents. *Logrolling,* both explicit and implicit, is the topic of the next section.

Logrolling

Implicit logrolling takes place when political candidates put together platforms of many different issues. In elections for the representatives who will make political decisions, candidates will act as political entrepreneurs by putting together platforms of issues in an attempt to win elections. With different platforms to choose from, individuals can vote for the candidate who they believe will vote their way on the issues most important to them, even though

---

[3]See Chapter 3 for a discussion of the Coase Theorem.

the representative may favor some other proposal not especially liked by the individual voter. A voter can, in essence, trade off issues of less importance for issues of more importance by voting for candidates whose platforms include these important issues. Since different individuals have different preferences and consider different issues to be important, the successful candidate can, through his or her platform, attract a large number of voters who hold diverse preferences.

To show how implicit logrolling allows voters to express their preference intensities, consider the following example. Assume we have three voters and two issues that concern them. They must elect a representative who will take part in deciding on these issues in a legislature. Table 6.2 summarizes the options. Voter *A* values "yes" over "no" on Issue (1) by $60. Voters *B* and *C* value "no" over "yes" by $10. Voter *B* values "yes" over "no" on Issue (2) by $70; voters *A* and *C* value "no" over "yes" by $10 and $5, respectively. If simple majority voting were used on these two issues, "no" would win on both issues. This outcome is inefficient since there is a net loss of $40 on Issue (1) and a net loss of $55 on Issue (2). If a candidate puts together a platform of the two issues on which he or she promises to vote "yes," he or she can secure the votes of voters *A* and *B*. This platform allows voter *A* to trade a "no" vote on Issue (2) for a "yes" vote on Issue (1). By giving up a less preferred choice on Issue (2), he or she gets the more intensely preferred choice on Issue (1). Voter *B* gives up a less preferred choice on Issue (1) for the more preferred choice on Issue (2). It is also possible for another candidate to put together a platform that promises a "no" vote on Issue (1) and a "yes" vote on Issue (2). This platform would attract the votes of voters *B* and *C*. Which candidate will win the election? This will be answered in our discussion of explicit logrolling.

Political entrepreneurship, which allows implicit logrolling to take place, permits voters to express their preference intensities when picking their representatives. Note that, for logrolling to take

Table 6.2

		Voter *A*		Voter *B*	Voter *C*
Issue 1	Yes	$60			
	No			$10	$10
Issue 2	Yes			$70	
	No		$10		$ 5

place, more than one issue must be involved. The same is true for the vote-trading form of logrolling, which is more likely to take place in legislative bodies because of the relatively small numbers of voters involved. This type of logrolling involves the actual trading of votes among the voters (representatives in most cases). Like implicit logrolling, vote trading allows voters to express their preference intensities. In the case of *successful* representatives, these preference intensities must, to some extent, reflect the preferences of their constituents.

Table 6.2 also can be used to illustrate direct vote trading (explicit logrolling) for the case in which the voters are elected representatives. As in the previous example, simple majority voting would lead to a "no" vote on Issue (1) as well as on Issue (2). This is true because voters *B* and *C* will vote to reject Issue (1) and voters *A* and *C* will vote to reject Issue (2). If logrolling is employed, however, this result will change. To see why, note that voter *A* would be willing to change his "no" vote to "yes" on Issue (2) in exchange for voter *B*'s agreement to vote "yes" on Issue (1). Voter *A* would be willing to do this because he or she will experience a net gain of $50 ($60 – $10) if both Issue (1) and Issue (2) pass. You can view the position of voter *A* as follows: The price of obtaining $60 in benefits from the success of Issue (1) is the $10 increase in his costs that results from the success of Issue (2). By agreeing to this trade, voter *B* will experience a net gain of $60 ($70 – $10). Voter *B*'s position can be characterized as follows: The price of obtaining $70 in benefits from the success of Issue (2) is the $10 increase in her costs that results from the success of Issue (1). With voter *A* and voter *B* voting in favor of Issues (1) and (2), both issues will pass. The trade leaves both individuals better off and the result is efficient.

You should note, however, that it is possible for voter *C* to change this outcome. Voter *C* would be willing to exchange his "yes" vote on Issue (2) for a "no" vote on Issue (1). Voter *B* would be willing to make this exchange. In fact, voter *B* would prefer this exchange to the exchange offered her by voter *A*. If voter *B* exchanges with voter *C*, voter *B* will experience a net gain of $80 ($70 + $10). Voter *C* experiences a net gain of $5 ($10 – $5). Issue (2) will pass and Issue (1) will fail. This is the solution that will be forthcoming with explicit logrolling. The solution is inefficient, but it will prevail because voter *B* can engage in an exchange with voter *C* that is more advantageous than exchange with voter *A*. Voter *B*'s net benefit when exchanging with voter *C* is $80 rather than $60. The net benefits *to the community,* however, are $15 [($10 + $10 – $60) + ($70 – $10 – $5)]. Explicit logrolling does not result in voters B and C taking account of the costs that their actions impose on voter A. These costs amount to $70. The difference between the costs incurred by voter A, $70, and the sum of the net benefits, $85 ($80+$5), enjoyed by voters B and C is equal to the net community benefits, $15 (calculated above), that result when voters B and C reach an agreement. This can be compared to the net benefits accruing to the community if voters A and B were to reach an agreement [$95 = ($60 − $10 − $10) + ($70 − $10 − $5)].

In this example, explicit logrolling yields a solution that falls short of the most efficient outcome (the outcome that maximizes net community benefits). However, in this case, explicit logrolling results in a more efficient solution than simple majority voting. This result will not always occur, however. Suppose that voter A had valued a "yes" vote on Issue (1) at $30 while voters B and C valued a "no" vote on Issue (1) at $20 each. Suppose, also, that voter B values a "yes" vote on Issue (2) at $30 while voters A and B value a "no" vote on this issue at $20. If this were the case, the most efficient outcome would result if both issues failed. This result would be produced by a simple majority vote on the issues. If explicit logrolling were used, the result would be the passage of either Issue (1) or both Issues (1) and (2). These examples serve to indicate that neither majority voting, implicit logrolling, nor explicit logrolling guarantee that the efficient solution will be selected.

The efficient outcome is only guaranteed if individuals are allowed to buy and sell votes. This result is easily shown. Voter A is willing to pay as much as $60 to insure the success of Issue (1). The compensation required to buy the agreement of both voter B and voter C is only $20. Voter A could insure a unanimous vote on Issue (1) by purchasing the agreement of both voters B and C to vote "yes" on this issue. In regard to Issue (2), voter B is willing to pay as much as $70 to insure the success of this issue. The compensation required to buy the agreement of both voters A and C to vote "yes" on this issue is only $15. The buying and selling of votes will result in both issues passing and will maximize net community benefits.

In summary, logrolling may yield solutions that are more efficient than simple majority voting. However, it is necessary that buying and selling votes take place to guarantee that the most efficient solution results.

Actual logrolling is more complex than these examples suggest. In some instances, the final result may approximate the outcome that occurs when buying and selling votes are allowed. For instance, if more issues were involved, voter A might induce voter B

to trade by trading more than one vote for *B*'s vote on Issue (1). Furthermore, in actual legislative logrolling, dollar appropriations for various issues are decided along with the trading of actual votes. This will affect the benefits individuals associate with the issues. Voter *A* may agree to a smaller expenditure on Issue (1) and an increase in expenditure on Issue (2) in an effort to induce voter *B* to approve Issue (1). The trades, of course, can become very complex. Individuals can be ingenious when it comes to the pursuit of gain.

Pressure Groups

Special interests and pressure groups seem to have a great deal of influence in modern governmental decision making. Elected representatives try to keep track of their constituents' preferences regarding political decisions between elections in order better to assure reelection. They must pay attention to all contacts with the electorate, including the lobbyists and special-interest groups. A problem with this system arises because providing your representative with your opinion has the aspects of a public good. It will benefit all members of the electorate that agree with you on an issue if you induce your representative to vote your way on the issue. Because of the large number of issues voted on and the externalities involved, voters will tend to provide too little information about their preferences between elections (actually, if these costs were low, direct democracy would be possible). What this means is that special-interest groups, which are relatively small in size, may have a great deal of influence with each representative. These groups—such as wheat farmers lobbying for increased price supports on wheat prices—can easily get together and hire a lobbyist to represent their interests. There is an externality here since one farmer successfully lobbying for an increase in the price supports benefits all of them. However, because they are relatively few in number and the potential gains to each farmer are great, they will come to some agreement. They will do this because there will be mutual gains from doing so. On the other hand, the consumers of products made with wheat will be harmed by such a move, and the harm will exceed the benefits to the wheat farmers. Because of the very large number of consumers and the relatively small loss to each consumer, anti-price-support lobbying is underprovided. The public goods nature of this information prevents consumers from mounting a successful anti-price-support campaign. Because of this, the special-interest group is likely to be much more effective in its lobbying campaign. As government gets larger and deals with more complex issues, it becomes more and more costly for the average voter to make his or her wishes known to representatives. Information of this sort becomes more and more of a public good, thus giving presure groups even more power.

Questions and Exercises

1. If individuals would vote for persons of principle to represent them in the legislature, the programs adopted by the government would promote the public good rather than private interests. Comment.

2. Do economists study the preferences of the individual or the constraints that he or she faces in explaining the individual's behavior?

3. Most legislators are lawyers who maintain private law offices while holding public office. Suppose a law were passed that required these legislators to report the sources of income earned in private practice and that restricted such sources to those in which no possible conflict of interest could exist. Do you think this would have any effect on how these legislators might vote in the future? Do you think such a law stands any chance of being passed?

4. If the law mentioned in question 3 were passed, do you think that, over time, there would be more legislators who are lawyers or fewer? Why?

5. Why are political entrepreneurs less likely to weigh the long-term impact of some political action as heavily as private entrepreneurs would in reaching a decision on what action to take, even though they may be confronted with similar alternatives?

6. What are some of the benefits that a legislator will derive from personally associating with a particular political party? What are some of the costs?

7. The franchise owners of chains like Denny's, McDonald's, Vip's and Love's restaurants have an interest in protecting their brand names. They incur costs to insure that individual owners use standard ingredients and processes in preparing the product. Why do they do this? Names like *Republican* and *Democrat* can be viewed as brand names also. Is it in the interest of the representatives of these parties to incur costs to protect their brand name from individual representatives who might take action to depreciate the brand name? Why?

8. Referring to question 7, what type of action by an individual representative would depreciate the value of the brand name? List some of the alternatives that the collective membership of the party may employ in making it costly to any individual member who depreciates the brand name.

9. Provide an economic justification for voters preferring representative democracy over direct democracy. What are the costs to the voter of a representative democracy?

10. If representative assemblies adopted a secret ballot form of voting, would they become less representative? Why?

11. List several similarities and differences between the constraints facing people in the public sector and in the private sector.

12. If you were going to pick the major reason why people working in the public sector behave differently than people working in the private sector, would it be because people in the public sector have different preferences than those in the private sector or because they face different constraints?

13. Simple majority voting does not allow individuals to express the intensity of their preferences. How does logrolling help to overcome this problem?

14. Why do pressure groups pose a threat in democratic societies?

Additional Readings

Buchanan, James, and Tullock, Gordon. *The Calculus of Consent.* Ann Arbor, Mich.: The University of Michigan Press, 1971.

Downs, Anthony. *An Economic Theory of Democracy.* New York: Harper & Row, Publishers, 1957.

Mueller, D. C. "Public Choice: A Survey." *Journal of Economic Literature,* Vol. 14 (June 1976), pp. 395–433.

7

Public Allocation — Bureaucracy

A bureaucracy is an organization of nonelected public officials—bureaucrats—who are responsible for implementing government programs. Examples of bureaucracies at the federal level are the Interstate Commerce Commission and the Departments of Defense and Health, Education, and Welfare. These organizations and others at all levels of government are in the business of providing government services.

The decisions of bureaucrats will have a significant effect on the allocation of resources in the economy. Suppose, for example, the Department of Health, Education, and Welfare (HEW) is given the job of providing tutorial services for economically disadvantaged college students. Individual bureaucrats within HEW will have to decide how much of their appropriation to spend on office space, secretaries, administrators, tutors, equipment, and the like.

In addition to influencing resource allocation within the public sector, the bureaucrat can influence the size of the bureau's budget. This will change the allocation of resources between the public and private sectors.

The power to influence the allocation of resources both within the public sector and between the public and private sectors, combined with the rapid expansion of the public sector, indicates that the bureaucracy has a profound influence on our lives.

Institutional Constraints and the Bureaucrat

In producing public services, we assume the bureaucrat pursues his or her private interests, as opposed to some poorly defined public interest. The bureaucrat is assumed to be a rational utility maximizer in the role of public servant, as in the role of private consumer.

The bureaucrat does not differ from the owner-entrepreneur of a firm in his or her fundamental economic motivations; both seek to maximize utility. A bureaucrat's behavior differs only because he or she faces different constraints. The main objective of the owner-entrepreneur is to maximize utility by maximizing the profits of the firm. The bureaucrat, on the other hand, must maximize utility within the confines of the bureaucracy. The dissimilar outcomes of these two situations result from the differing environments, or constraints, operating on the utility maximizer.

The owner-entrepreneur operates within a system of private property rights, seeking out and engaging in advantageous exchanges. To say that the entrepreneur seeks to maximize profits is another way of saying that he or she seeks to maximize the gains from exchange. The entrepreneur is motivated by the fact that he or she is able to claim a portion of the gain from exchange. In other words, the entrepreneur is a residual claimant. His or her portion of the gain is determined by the difference between revenues and costs. In playing this role, the entrepreneur is subject to the constraints imposed by competition (other entrepreneurs seeking advantageous exchanges) and the fact that individuals cannot be forced to engage in exchanges. That is, both parties to the exchange must receive a share of the gain if an exchange is to take place.

Seeking out and making advantageous exchanges is costly. The entrepreneur will attempt to economize on these costs because, by doing so, profits will increase. This is what is meant when it is said that the market rewards efficiency. In addition, because the entrepreneur is subject to the force of competition, a portion of this cost-saving will be passed to the second party in the exchange.

The constraints faced by the bureaucrat differ from those faced by the entrepreneur in some important respects. First, the bureaucrat does not seek advantageous trades directly with the ultimate consumer. The bureau is provided with a total payment (budget) for performing its entire task. As a consequence, the bureaucrat seeks advantageous exchanges with a third party (the legislature) that more or less (in a gross sense) reflects the desires of its constituency for exchange with the bureau. Second, because the bureaucrat has no direct claim over any portion of the gain from exchange, the incentive to economize on cost is diminished. Likewise, since the bureaucrat cannot benefit from increased profit by providing a better product, the incentive to satisfy those who receive his or her service is also diminished. The bureaucrat is not rewarded for operating efficiently. Third, because he or she is not subject to the force of competition, the bureaucrat is not immediately punished for operating inefficiently by a reduction in individuals willing to exchange with the bureau. As a consequence of these three differences, a bureaucrat will perform any task less well (at higher costs) than a private entrepreneur. Fourth, when the task of the bureaucrat is not well defined—consider as an example regulating monopoly power—[1] he or she will have much more leeway in performing the job. With this increased freedom, the bureaucrat may end up protecting the very monopoly power the bureaucracy was set up to regulate. In this case, the bureaucracy is inefficient because it does not do what it was designed to do and may actively work toward the misallocation of resources.

The kinds of constraints the bureaucrat faces will determine his or her behavior. The most straightforward way of reducing bureaucratic inefficiency is to change the constraints in a way that will induce the bureaucrat to behave in the desired way.

It should be pointed out that the type of efficiency associated with the competitive firm and the owner-entrepreneur can rarely, if ever, be achieved by a bureaucracy. An efficient allocation of resources results directly from the pursuit of self-interest on the part of the owner-entrepreneur. The bureaucrat's pursuit of self-interest, as we have seen, will not generally lead to an efficient outcome. Of course, discovering and imposing the set of constraints that will lead to efficient bureaucratic outcomes is not cost-free. Since the process of finding and enforcing these constraints will use up resources, it will never be desirable to use more resources in the enforcement process than would be saved by reducing bureaucratic inefficiency. In this, as in other problems in economics, we would only want to employ resources in reducing waste up to the point that a dollar spent in waste reduction yields a dollar saved in reduced waste. It is false economy to reduce this type of inefficiency any further.

This discussion points up the fallacy of concentrating on the marginal conditions of the competitive model—that is, on welfare economics—to prescribe outcomes involving public goods. Since the efficiency of the competitive outcome is achieved and maintained without enforcement (in the sense that resources need not be spent on monitoring the entrepreneur), the attainment of the competitive marginal conditions is socially optimal. And since attainment of similar conditions with public allocation by the bureaucracy is not cost-free, these conditions do not provide a guide to public provision of services.

---

[1]This will be examined in greater detail in the discussion of the capture theory in this chapter.

Nonbureaucratic Supply

A frequently overlooked point is that it is not necessary for the state to actually supply public services to assure their provision; it is only necessary to finance them. A great deal of the inefficiency associated with bureaucratic provision of public services can be avoided if, instead, the private sector actually supplies the services. This practice, called privatization, is not new in the provision of public goods such as weapons for defense. It has not, however, been fully exploited in the provision of such services as education and police and fire protection. In some cases, by contracting out the provision of services for specified periods of time to the lowest bidder, these services (fire protection, for example) could probably be provided at a much lower cost. With other goods, such as education, it would be possible to allow large numbers of competing suppliers, both public and private, to operate simultaneously. In this case, financing would be publicly provided, but the user of the service could decide from whom to purchase it. In both of these circumstances, the forces of competition would be effective in assuring significant improvements in efficiency.

Utility Maximization and the Bureaucrat

In Chapter 2 it was shown that goods possessing strong ownership rights will command relatively high market values. Since the market value of property depends upon the strength of the ownership rights attached to it, individuals have an incentive to seek government support in strengthening private property rights. However, public officials (politicians, judges, and bureaucrats) are not always disposed to aid in the attempt to strengthen these rights because a major alternative to private ownership is government ownership, which strengthens the rights of public officials. To illustrate the point, consider the case of public colleges and universities. Students who have been accepted by these schools have the right to attend classes because they have met the standards set by the administration and faculty. Suppose, however, that the right of these students to attend classes was changed to a private property right that could be sold to other people. Clearly, no student would be worse off and those who choose to sell would be better off (they would be more wealthy). In the process, the university administration and faculty would lose the right to decide who is admitted.[2] Since resources were previously employed in reaching decisions regarding admissions, the universities would, under the new system, be able to get along with smaller budgets. The choice set of the administration and faculty would be smaller, which is another way of saying that their wealth would decrease.

It follows from the above discussion that the wealth of the bureaucrat depends, at least in some respects, upon the size of his or her budget. Taking this into consideration, we offer the following simple model of bureaucratic utility maximization.[3] Suppose, for the sake of simplicity, that there are only two goods available in the world. One good, *X,* is privately produced while the public good, *G,* is produced by the bureaucracy. Assume that all individuals exhaust their incomes on the two goods. As above, we assume that the income of the bureaucrat depends upon the size of the budget. Suppose that a fraction of his or her income varies by a proportion, α, of the bureau's budget. The income constraints faced by the nonbureaucrat and bureaucrat are shown below.

$$\text{(nonbureaucrat) } Y_i = P_X X + \gamma P_G G \tag{1}$$

$$\text{(bureaucrat) } \quad \overline{Y}_b = Y_b + \alpha P_G G = P_X X + \gamma P_G G \text{ or} \tag{2}$$

$$Y_b = P_X X + (\gamma - \alpha) P_G G \tag{2a}$$

Y_i is the money income of nonbureaucrats. P_X and P_G are the prices of the goods in the subscript. The tax share of both nonbureaucrats and bureaucrats is given by γ. Note that the bureaucrat's total income, $\overline{Y}_b$, is the sum of his or her salary, Y_b, and the contribution to total income made by the bureau's budget, $\alpha P_G G$. This model is consistent with our previous contention that the bureaucrat faces different constraints. Equation (1) is different from Equation (2). To determine the implications of this, it is necessary to compute the relative price of the public good in terms of the private good. The relative price of the public good to nonbureau-

---

[2]This example is discussed in Armen Alchian and William R. Allen, *University Economics* (Belmont, Calif.: Wadsworth Publishing Co., Inc., 1972), p. 243.

[3]See T. E. Borcherding, ed., *Budgets and Bureaucrats: The Sources of Government Growth* (Durham, N.C.: Duke University Press, 1977).

crats is given by the ratio $\gamma P_G/P_X$ [from Equation (1)]. The relative price of the public good to the bureaucrat is $(\gamma-\alpha)P_G/P_X$ [from Equation (2a)]. If α is greater than zero, the relative price of the public good to the bureaucrat is lower than it is to the nonbureaucrat.[4] As a consequence, an individual who is a bureaucrat will demand relatively more of the public good.

This is shown geometrically in Figure 7.1. Let *uu* represent an indifference curve for the individual. If the individual is a bureaucrat, he will face the constraint given by *bb*. If, on the other hand, he is a nonbureaucrat, he faces the constraint given by *ii*. The slope of *bb* is less than the slope of *ii* because the relative price of the public good is lower if the individual is a bureaucrat. For *the same level of utility,* bureaucrats will prefer a mix that contains more public goods and fewer private goods.

The important point of this discussion is that bureaucrats will want higher levels of government output, not because their preferences are necessarily different but because they face a different constraint; in this case, the relative prices confronting bureaucrats are different from those confronting nonbureaucrats.

Figure 7.1

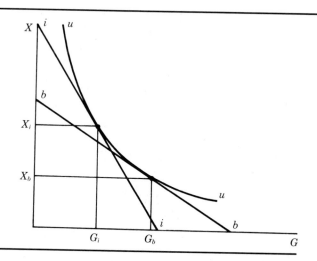

Growth of the Bureaucracy

The growth of the bureaucracy is a measure of the increasing involvement of government in the day-to-day lives of all individuals. This idea can be translated into economic jargon by stating that the government is increasing its control over the composition of output, allocation of resources, and distribution of product by legislative edict and through its tax and expenditure programs. At best, it is difficult to measure the extent of this involvement. However, if we compare real government expenditures to real gross national product over time we see that an increasing percentage of GNP is directly accounted for by government.

With the exception of the Great Depression and World War II, government expenditures have grown smoothly relative to GNP. We should point out, however, that this measure of government involvement may have a significant downward bias. As we note above, the government also exercises control through legislative edict. If a law requires that all autos be equipped with seat belts, the law may cause a change in the composition of output, allocation of resources, and distribution of product. The law will change each of these if, prior to the law, some autos were sold without seat belts. However, except for the additional costs incurred as a result of having to enforce the law, measured government expenditures will not rise. This is true despite the fact that more seat belts are produced after the law, more resources are allocated to seat-belt production, and the resources specific to seat-belt production earn higher returns. In this case, government edict forces individuals to bear costs they would not bear if given a choice. This cost of government action does not show up in the budget.

It has been estimated that the total capital cost of federally mandated pollution control from 1974 to 1983 will be between $175 billion and $263 billion. The annual costs by 1983 are estimated to be between $55 billion and $66 billion. These figures imply that by 1983 between 3 percent and 6 percent of GNP and between 7 percent and 10 percent of gross private domestic investment will be expended to comply with federal clean air and water legislation.[5] This very large cost, though not included in the federal budget, implies a significant shift in resource allocation resulting solely from government edict.

---

[5]These estimates are reported in an article entitled "Ecology's Missing Price Tag," *Wall Street Journal*, August 10, 1976, p. 16.

A Scientific Issue in Political Economics

There have been numerous hypotheses offered as possible explanations for the growth of the government and the attendant growth of the bureaucracy. Generally, these hypotheses fall into two categories. One emphasizes the *voluntary* aspect of a democratic, political decision-making mechanism, and the other emphasizes the *coercive* aspect of any practical, political decision-making mechanism.[6]

The hypotheses that fall within the voluntary category run as follows: First, public goods, in contrast to private goods, have income elasticities exceeding one. Consequently, when real income grows, the demand for public goods grows relative to the demand for private goods. If this hypothesis were correct, we would expect total government expenditures as a percentage of GNP to have dropped from the year 1929 to the year 1933. Did they? (See Table 7.1.)

A second hypothesis, which emphasizes the voluntary approach, argues that, with increasing population and a limited geographical space, individuals impose external costs on one another at an increasing rate. Consequently, there is an increasing demand

Growth of Government   Table 7.1

Year	GNP in 1967 (in Billions of Dollars)	Total Govt. Exp. in 1967 (in Billions of Dollars)	$\dfrac{\text{Total Govt. Exp.}}{\text{GNP}}$ x 100
1929	202.15	20.67	9.9
1933	146.31	27.57	18.8
1940	237.38	43.80	18.5
1945	393.13	180.33	45.9
1950	395.00	84.32	21.3
1955	496.25	121.69	24.5
1960	567.86	153.43	27.0
1965	724.76	197.77	27.3
1970	839.55	268.35	31.9

Source: *Economic Report of the President* (Washington, D.C.: Government Printing Office, 1973).

[6]See J. Hirshleifer, *Price Theory and Its Applications* (Englewood Cliffs, N.J.: Prentice-Hall, Inc., 1976), pp. 486–87.

Table 7.2   **Expenditures on Law Enforcement (in Millions of Dollars)**

	1955	1960	1965	1970	1974
Total of All Governments	2,231	3,349	4,573	7,976	13,550
Police	1,359	2,030	2,792	5,080	8,512
Judicial	409	597	748	1,190	1,798
Corrections	463	722	1,033	1,706	3,240
Total Expenditures in 1976 Dollars	2,781	3,775	4,839	6,858	9,174
Population (Millions)	165	180	194	204	211
Real per Capita Expenditures	16.85	20.97	24.94	33.61	43.47

Source: U.S. Department of Commerce, Bureau of the Census, *Statistical Abstract of the United States,* 97th ed. (Washington, D.C.: Government Printing Office, 1976).

for more government control of what were previously considered private activities in a more widely dispersed society. However, if the problem of external cost is essentially a problem of defining property rights, as we have suggested previously, the large increases in government expenditures would, in the main, be accounted for by increased expenditures on judicial and police services.

The data on law enforcement expenditures seem to be consistent with the hypothesis that external costs rise with increases in population. However, since expenditures on judicial and police services amount to only 1.8 percent of all government expenditures, they cannot by themselves account for the entire increase in government expenditures relative to GNP.

Now let us consider hypotheses that place greater emphasis on the coercive aspects of the political decision-making mechanism. One hypothesis asserts that government bureaucrats have become a relatively powerful political force resisting, in mass, any attempt to reduce the size of the government and actively supporting programs that have the effect of increasing its size. An implication of this hypothesis is that rapid increases in the size of government caused, say, by a national crisis, would not be followed by a reduction in size when the crisis is ended. Was this the case following World War II? (See the figures in Table 7.1.)

A second hypothesis that emphasizes coercive power states that government programs may be adopted in which marginal costs exceed marginal benefits if the benefits are highly visible and accrue to a relatively small group and if the costs are obscure and spread throughout the community. If this is the case, it may pay the benefitting individuals to purchase government support for the program by lobbying. Why don't those individuals who stand to be damaged by the program organize an effort to block it? First, because the costs are obscure, these individuals may not be aware of them prior to adoption of the program. Second, because the costs are spread among many individuals, it may be very expensive for them to organize into an effective political force.

Application

Government Expenditure and the Tax Structure

If the above hypothesis holds, we would expect that the more simple the tax structure, the less costly it will be to gather information concerning the cost of government programs and the easier it will be to organize opposition. Consequently, after controlling for other important variables, the simpler the tax structure, the lower the per capita government expenditures. Richard Wagner constructed an index of tax structure simplicity for 50 sample cities.[7] Phoenix ranked the lowest (had the most complicated tax structure) with a value of .265, and Indianapolis ranked the highest with a value of .815. The mean value for the 50 cities was .44. Wagner found that in those cities with relatively simple tax structures, per capita government expenditures were significantly below those cities with complicated tax structures. Wagner's model predicts that if the 50 sample cities were to adopt tax structures similar to those of Indianapolis, public expenditures in the cities would fall by 22.36 percent. The dollar value of the reduction for these 50 cities alone would be $1.148 billion.

The Equilibrium Size of a Budget-Maximizing Bureau

Certain forces operate to determine a bureau's size and to keep it at that size. These forces can be specified in terms of a set of constraints that face the individual decision makers whom we classify

---

[7]Richard E. Wagner, "Revenue Structure, Fiscal Illusion, and Budgetary Choice," *Public Good*, Vol. 25 (Spring 1976), pp. 45-61.

generally as constituents, legislators, and bureaucrats.[8] Any change in the set of constraints faced by these individuals will cause the equilibrium size of the bureau to change. Our behavioral assumption is that each individual attempts to maximize his or her utility subject to the constraints faced. As before, we assume that there is a direct relationship between the size of the bureau's budget and the income (pecuniary and nonpecuniary) of the bureaucrat. Budget maximization will lead to utility maximization. This assumption seems reasonable since we might expect the bureaucrat's salary and amenities of office to depend upon the size of the bureau's budget. We assume that the force that constrains the bureau in this endeavor is the legislature.

It is important to note again the difference between the constraints faced by the bureaucrat and those of the entrepreneur of a private for-profit firm. Because the entrepreneur is a residual claimant, he or she attempts to maximize profits, which is the difference between total revenue (the value of the output produced) and total cost (the value of output foregone). Because the bureaucrat has no claim on this difference, he or she attempts to maximize the cost (the value of output foregone) of what is produced.

Before proceeding with the analysis, we note that, for all practical purposes, bureaus are monopolies. They are the sole producers of a particular government output. You may think of the Department of Defense or HEW or the FBI. As a consequence, each bureau faces the entire demand curve for its service. The demand for the output is represented by the curve labeled AB in Figure 7.2. The demand curve expresses the preferences of the legislature which must, more or less, reflect the preferences of constituents.

The two questions we wish to discuss are: (1) what is the rate of the bureau's output and (2) what is the size of the bureau's budget? Suppose that CD represents the marginal cost of obtaining units of output. The optimum rate of output is q_p. At this rate, marginal benefits (as reflected by the demand curve) are equal to marginal cost. At q_p the total benefit of obtaining the output is approximated by the area $0AFq_p$, while total cost is the area $0CFq_p$. The difference between these two areas, AFC, is a measure of the net contribution of the output to the welfare of the community. At q_p this difference is maximized. However, q_p will not be the level of output chosen by the bureaucrat. Recall that the bureaucrat

[8]The following analysis can be found in W. A. Niskanen, Jr., "The Peculiar Economics of Bureaucracy," *American Economic Review* (May 1967), pp. 293-305; and A. Breton and R. Wintrobe, "The Equilibrium Size of a Budget Maximizing Bureau: A Note on Niskanen's Theory of Bureaucracy," *Journal of Political Economy* (February 1975), pp. 195-207.

Figure 7.2

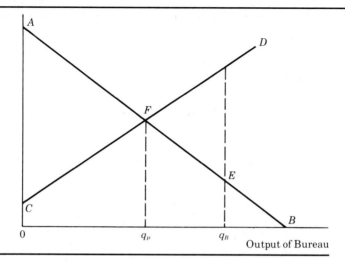

wishes to maximize his or her budget. Suppose the bureau is successful in convincing the legislature that q_B is the quantity that should be produced. At q_B total benefits, $0AEq_B$, may exceed, be equal to, or fall short of total cost, $0CDq_B$.

Another way to look at the problem is to note that the *net* benefit that would accrue to the community, AFC—if the optimum rate of output, q_p, were produced—is, at the very least, partially appropriated by the bureaucracy through higher cost if q_B is produced. ($AFC \leq FED$.) How is the bureaucracy able to extract this net benefit from the community? A somewhat naive answer would be that, since the bureaucracy is a monopoly, it can face the legislature with an all-or-nothing decision. However, while the bureaucracy has a monopoly in the production of the output, individual bureaucrats can be replaced. Consequently, if the legislature knows the marginal cost function, CD, it can force the bureaucracy to produce at q_p with a budget of $0CFq_p$ by threatening to replace the bureau's managers.

Knowledge of the bureaucracy's marginal cost function, however, will be difficult and costly to obtain. (In fact, it is in the interest of the bureaucracy's managers to obscure this information.)[9] Because information regarding the bureaucracy's cost function is expensive to obtain, it will pay the community to acquire,

---

[9]See R. A. Posner, "Theories of Economic Regulation," *Bell Journal of Economics and Management Science,* Autumn 1974, pp. 335–56. (Especially see p. 355.)

through its legislators, an amount of information such that the marginal cost of obtaining the information is equal to the marginal benefits. Under these conditions, the bureaucracy can successfully misrepresent its cost function in order to obtain both a budget higher than $0CFq_p$ and a rate of output exceeding q_p.

Application

Taxicab Markets

One of the implications of the above discussion is that bureaus will choose, when possible, relatively complex cost functions. We expect this because the more complex the function, the more difficult it will be for the legislature to discover the bureau's true marginal cost curve. Thus, the easier it will be for the bureau to obtain larger budgets. Ross Eckert has argued that, for the case of taxicab regulation, monopoly markets are easier to regulate than markets which are more competitive.[10] In the 33 cities he studied, there were essentially two types of agencies responsible for regulating the taxicab markets: regulatory commissions and regulatory bureaus. The salaries of commissioners were generally nominal, and the terms of office were fixed by law. In other words, the size of the commission's budget had nothing to do with the commissioner's salary or term of office. One would expect, then, monopoly taxicab markets to be more prevalent in cities regulated by commissions than in cities regulated by bureaus. The results of Eckert's survey, given in Table 7.3, seem to be consistent with the hypothesis. Of the six markets regulated by commissions, five are monopoly markets. On the other hand, of the twenty-seven markets regulated by the bureaus, only five are monopoly markets. These results would arise by chance less than one percent of the time.

A second implication is that commissions would require uniform rate structures in the markets they are responsible for regulating since a uniform structure would be easier to administer than one which was more complex. Bureaus, on the other hand, would be less likely to require uniform rate structures. The probability that the rate structures, shown in Table 7.4, would arise solely from chance is less than five percent.

---

[10]Based on Ross Eckert, "On the Incentives of Regulators: The Case of Taxicabs," *Public Choice,* Spring 1973, pp. 83–99.

Table 7.3

	Monopoly or Market Division	Neither Monopoly nor Market Division	Total
Commissions	5	1	6
Bureaus	5	22	27
Total	10	23	33

Table 7.4

	Uniform Rates Required	Uniform Rates Not Required	Total
Commissions	6	0	6
Bureaus	15	12	27
Total	21	12	53

The Capture Hypothesis[11]

All governments possess a basic resource which, in principle, is not shared with any of the citizens—the power to coerce. The constitution, if one exists, establishes the limits of this power; that is, it indicates those cases in which the government can employ coercion. A bureau, as the agent of the government policy, may employ this resource to achieve its ends. The fact that this power exists opens the possibility that an industry or occupational group may find it advantageous to use the government's coercive power to increase profits. The Civil Aeronautics Board "protects" us from paying lower air fares that would result from the effects of "unbridled" competition. The board has not allowed a new trunk line to operate since its inception in 1938. The Federal Deposit Insurance Corporation has reduced the rate of entry into commercial banking by 60 percent,[12] and the Food and Drug Administration has succeeded in reducing the rate at which new drugs are developed without appreciably reducing the risk of using drugs.[13]

---

[11]The following analysis was developed by George J. Stigler, "The Theory of Economic Regulation," *Bell Journal of Economics and Management Science,* Spring 1971, pp. 3-21.

[12]Sam Peltzman, "Entry in Commercial Banking," *Journal of Law and Economics,* October 1965, pp. 11-50.

[13]Sam Peltzman, "An Evaluation of Consumer Protection Legislation: The 1962 Drug Amendments," *Journal of Political Economy,* September/October 1973, pp. 1049-91.

There are essentially three benefits that an industry or occupational group may obtain as a result of acquiring the favor of government officials: (1) control over entry into the industry or occupation; (2) regulation of substitute and complementary products; and (3) price maintenance. Each of these will act to frustrate the operation of competitive forces and, as a consequence, industry or occupational profits will be higher than otherwise.

These benefits are not acquired without cost. The coercive power of government is a scarce resource. At a price of zero, the demand for it exceeds its supply. Therefore, any industry or occupation that intends to acquire this power to further its own interests must be prepared to pay with votes, with the resources necessary to acquire votes, and in many cases, with payments to public officials of a more direct nature.

Application

Regulation in the Trucking Industry[14]

Prior to 1925, the trucking industry operated within cities, mainly because highways were very poor and powerful truck motors had not been developed. As these obstacles to trucking were overcome, trucks began to compete seriously with railroads for intercity freight movements. Railroads quickly recognized trucking as a substitute for their own service. By the early 1930s, all states regulated the capacity of trucks through weight limitations. By applying the capture hypothesis, we would expect that weight limitations would be more stringent in states for which trucks were more serious competitors to railroads. Since trucks are relatively efficient for short-haul movements while railroads are relatively efficient for long-haul movements, trucks would be less serious competitors the longer the average railroad haul within a state. In such a case, we would expect the weight limit to be higher. Also, the more individuals within a state that would benefit from freight movements by truck, the greater would be the political resistance to imposing weight limitations, hence, the higher the weight limit. Finally, the better the state highway system, the heavier the trucks that would be permitted. George Stigler estimated the relationship between weight limits and these variables. He looked at the effects of (1) the average length of haul of railroads, (2) a variable to measure the

---

[14]See Stigler, "Theory of Economic Regulation," pp. 8–9.

number of people harmed by weight limitations, and (3) the condition of the state highways, on weight limits in the early 1930s.

Each of these explanatory variables was found to work in the predicted direction and all were statistically significant. The results seem to support the contention that railroads were successful in limiting the ability of trucking to serve as a substitute for short-haul railroad freighting. The railroads were more successful in those states in which the opposition to such limits (and, consequently, the costs to elected officials and bureaucrats) was low.

Public Employee Unions as Pressure Groups

Overall union membership as a percentage of the total labor force has been declining for the past several years. For example, total union membership as a percentage of total nonagricultural employment dropped from 28 percent in 1970 to 26 percent in 1974. Among public employees, however, union membership seems to be increasingly attractive. Union membership among all government employees increased by 26 percent from 1970 to 1974 compared to an increase of 4.2 percent for all types of employees. State and local employee union membership increased by 61 percent in the 1970-74 time period. The percentage of public employee union membership compared to total government employees has increased from 18 percent to 21 percent over the 1970-74 period for all levels of government employees and from 9 percent to 13 percent for state and local employees.[15] Why are public employee unions growing when union membership in the private sector is stagnating? The answer to this question lies in part in the nature of the environment within which the public employee union operates. Public employee unions are actually special-interest groups rather than unions in the traditional sense of the term, and, like other special-interest groups, devote resources to lobbying as well as to campaigning for (and making campaign contributions to) candidates favorable to their causes. Private unions also try to use political power to enhance their market power but, to the extent that they are successful, they can only do this by indirect means such as lobbying for changes in the minimum wage and right to work laws.

---

[15]Sources for these statistics: U.S. Bureau of Labor Statistics, *Handbook of Labor Statistics, Directory of National Unions,* and *Employment and Earnings Monthly.*

Public employee unions lobby directly with the legislature. Since they are a relatively small and well-organized group compared to taxpayers in general, like other pressure groups, they may be able to extract from the legislature special benefits in the form of higher wages, improved working conditions, and so forth. Evidence that the pay of public employees has been increasing over time relative to pay in the private sector lends support to the theory of public employee unions as pressure groups.

James M. Buchanan and Gordon Tullock have shown that government wages and salaries have been increasing relative to nongovernmental pay.[16] For federal civilian employees, pay as a percentage of nongovernment employees' pay increased from 101 percent in 1952 to 129 percent in 1972. For state and local employees the figures were 101 percent for 1952 and 110 percent for 1972. If these increases are compared to those of the workers in the private sector whose jobs are roughly comparable to many public-sector jobs, the increase is even more dramatic. The pay for the private-sector service employees as a percentage of that of all nongovernment employees was 79 percent in 1952 and only 80 percent in 1972. In other words, workers employed in roughly comparable jobs in the private sector experienced only a one-percent relative increase during these years while the relative increase experienced by public employees varied between 9 and 28 percent. Clearly, wages and salaries of government employees have been increasing faster than those of nongovernment employees.

Questions and Exercises

1. What does the theory of bureaucracy imply about the cost of government-supplied goods?

2. It has been suggested by some that the failure of bureaus to provide government services efficiently is a result of appointing the wrong individuals as managers of the bureaus; that is, if the right person were found for the job, bureaus would be run well. Is the theory developed in this chapter consistent with this assertion?

3. What effect does the fact that the control of cost is itself costly have on the marginal welfare conditions for bureaucratic provision of public goods?

---

[16]James Buchanan and Gordon Tullock, "The Expanding Public Sector: Wagner Squared," *Public Choice,* Fall 1977, pp. 147–50.

4. It has been estimated that government workers make up approximately one-third of the voting populace. What impact would you expect this to have on the rate at which government expenditure grows relative to GNP? Why?

5. List some possible motivations that a bureaucrat might have to interpret legislation in favor of the industry he or she is responsible for regulating.

6. Would you expect the costs to a bureaucrat of discriminating by race, sex, religion, or any other non-job-related measure to be higher or lower than the costs of such discrimination to the owner of a private, for-profit firm? Why?

7. How do the opportunities and incentives of bureaucrats differ from those of an entrepreneur?

8. Suppose that the demand for police officers is given by the following relationship:

P	Q
$800	1
700	2
600	3
500	4
400	5
300	6
200	7
100	8

Quantity, Q, is the service of police officers per month. If the marginal cost of obtaining the services of police officers is always $500 per month, what is the optimum quantity? What is the net benefit that accrues to the community? Suppose, now, that a bureaucracy was responsible for providing police services. Assume that the bureaucrat wants to maximize the total budget and that he or she is subject to the constraint that the total budget may not exceed total benefits. What will be the size of the budget request? What quantity of police services will he or she propose? If the budget request is granted, what is the net loss to the community?

9. If you use government expenditures as a percentage of GNP as a guide to the significance of government activity, you can be seriously misled. What types of government activity have a far greater impact than indicated by the cost of such activity?

Additional Readings

Alchian, Armen, and Demsetz, H. "Production, Information Costs, and Economic Organization." *American Economic Review,* December 1972, pp. 777–95.

McKean, Roland. *Public Spending.* New York: McGraw-Hill, 1968.

Niskanen, W. "The Peculiar Economics of the Bureaucracy." *American Economic Review,* May 1967, pp. 293–305.

8

The Distribution of Income and the Structure of Rights

The distribution of income among households has been an important public policy issue for many years. There are few candidates for public office who don't feel obliged to address the topic of income distribution. We have all been treated to the emotionally charged arguments of candidates who urge, coax, cajole, inveigle, and propagandize us to vote for them because they will institute programs that will correct the injustice in the distribution of income. (Inequality in the distribution of income is often mistakenly used interchangeably with injustice in income distribution.) This has been one issue on which successful candidates have stood by their promises. There has been no paucity of social programs offered which are designed to distribute income more equally.

This chapter in part examines the distribution of income in the United States and offers some reasons for why one might expect to observe inequality in the distribution of *money* income. The chapter also discusses private as well as public attempts to alter the distribution of income and offers some evidence suggesting what the effect of these programs has been on the resulting distribution.

The Distribution of Money Income in the United States

One way of measuring the distribution of money income among families is to compare the percentage of aggregate money income received to the percentage of families receiving that income when the families are ranked from poorest to richest. This ranking is given in Table 8.1 for selected years from 1947 through 1974. The families are ranked by fifths from the poorest to the richest.

It is clear from the data presented in Table 8.1 that aggregate money income is distributed unequally in the United States. The lowest 20 percent of the families earn, roughly, 5 percent of aggregate money income while the top 20 percent earn approximately 40 percent. Data on the distribution of money income can also be

Percent of Aggregate Money Income Received by Families   Table 8.1

Families	1947	1950	1960	1964	1965	1967	1968	1972	1974
Lowest fifth	5.0	4.5	4.9	5.2	5.3	5.4	5.7	5.4	5.4
Second fifth	11.8	12.0	12.0	12.0	12.2	12.2	12.4	11.9	12.0
Middle fifth	17.0	17.4	17.6	17.7	17.6	17.5	17.7	17.5	17.6
Fourth fifth	23.1	23.5	23.6	24.0	23.7	23.7	23.7	23.9	24.1
Highest fifth	43.0	42.6	42.0	41.1	41.3	41.2	40.6	41.4	41.0

Source: U.S. Bureau of the Census, *Current Population Reports,* Series P-60, No. 101 (Washington, D.C.: U.S. Government Printing Office, 1976), p. 37.

presented geometrically in the form of a Lorenz curve. Families are again ranked from poorest to richest with the *cumulative* percentage of families compared to the cumulative percentage of income received by those families. If we do this for the data given in Table 8.1 for the year 1974, we obtain Figure 8.1.

If money income were distributed equally among families in the United States during 1974, the Lorenz curve would lie along the diagonal line labeled *aa*. Given the actual distribution of money income among families, the Lorenz curve is the curve labeled *bb*.

Lorenz Curve for 1974   **Figure 8.1**

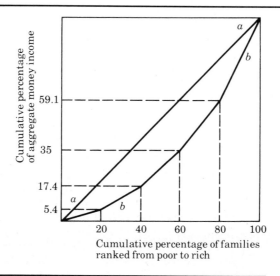

This curve indicates that the poorest 20 percent of the families in the U.S. received 5.4 percent of aggregate money income, the lowest 40 percent of families received 17.4 percent money income (17.4 = 5.4 + 12.0 from Table 8.1), and so on.

The degree of inequality in the distribution of income illustrated by the Lorenz curve can be expressed quantitatively by using the coefficient of inequality. The coefficient of inequality is equal to the area between the diagonal line, *aa*, and the Lorenz curve, *bb*, divided by the area below the diagonal. The coefficient of inequality for the Lorenz curve shown in Figure 8.1 is, roughly, .33.

Reasons for the Observed Inequality in the Distribution of Money Income

What factors explain the observed inequality in the distribution of money income? In examining this question, note that family income is simply the sum of the incomes of the individual members of the family. Consequently, by examining the factors that cause inequality in the distribution of individual income, we begin to understand why we observe this inequality.

Some of the inequality is due to chance. Individuals may be born with good health, superior intelligence, above average physical stature and abilities, an appealing voice, or even with a rich uncle. The different endowments with which individuals come into this world are due to chance. The individual has no control over them. Different endowments clearly account for some of the dispersion that is observed in the distribution of money income. They cannot, however, account for all or even most of it. If all individuals were born with equal endowments, we would still observe an unequal distribution of money income.

Different Choices Regarding the Timing of the Income Stream[1]

One reason why money income may differ among individuals is that they may make different choices regarding the timing of their

---

[1]George J. Stigler, *The Theory of Price* (New York: Macmillan Company, 1966), pp. 289-93, 304.

Figure 8.2

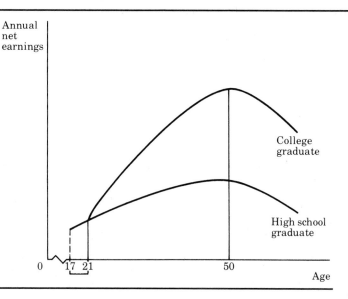

income stream. Consider two individuals with the same endowments who are faced with the choice of whether to attend college or to immediately enter the labor force. If the choice is made to enter the labor force, right out of high school, the individual's income stream will begin at, say, age 17. If the individual decides to attend college, his or her income stream will begin four years hence at age 21. The two alternative income streams are shown in Figure 8.2.

If the individual should choose to go to college, his or her income until age 21 is negative by the expenses of tuition, books, supplies, etc. After age 21, his or her income rises above the income that would have been earned with a high school diploma and then at some age declines. It is possible that the discounted present value of each of these streams will be identical at 17 (in a competitive equilibrium, they would be identical). Yet if one individual chooses to enter the labor force at age 17 and another chooses college, each will be observed to have a different money income at each age thereafter. Table 8.2 presents data regarding the observed distribution of money income to individuals with different levels of education. The reader is cautioned, however, in interpreting Table 8.2 since the data are not adjusted for other factors that affect the distribution of income.

Another reason why money incomes differ among individuals is that income tends to vary with age. The streams in Figure 8.2

Table 8.2

Cumulative Percent Distribution of Families with Head 25 Years Old and Over and Aggregate Money Income by Years of School Completed

1974 Cumulative Percent Distribution of Families Earning	Elementary School 8 Yrs. or Less	High School		College	
		1-3 Yrs.	4 Yrs.	1-3 Yrs.	4 Yrs.
Under $5000	26.5	16.2	8.0	5.5	3.4
Under $10,000	59.9	47.3	27.8	21.5	12.8
Under $15,000	81.0	68.1	56.0	46.7	30.6
Under $25,000	96.6	93.8	89.7	84.0	68.5

Source: U.S. Bureau of the Census, *Current Population Reports,* Series P-60, No. 101 (Washington, D.C.: U.S. Government Printing Office, 1976), p. 17.

are typical. Income tends to be lower when individuals are young, rise until middle age, and then fall again, especially after retirement. Because of this, two individuals with identical lifetime income streams will have different money incomes if one is age 20 and the other 50.

Nominal Differences in the Distribution of Income

Two individuals with the same endowments, same educational level, and of the same age may earn different money incomes because of differences in the cost of living where they are employed. Individuals who live in cities earn higher money incomes than those who live in rural areas. In part, this difference is accounted for by the difference in the cost of living between rural areas and the city. Differences in the cost of living between the Northeast and the South account for some of the difference that is observed in the money income received by individuals living in these two areas.

We should also note that additional money income may be necessary to compensate individuals for living in less satisfactory areas or for accepting jobs that carry a high injury risk or that are particularly unpleasant. These differences, called compensating differentials, are the amounts required to equate, at the margin, the real incomes of individuals who, for example, work in more hazardous employments to the incomes of individuals in relatively safe employments. Two individuals with the same endowments, education, age, and skills may be, in fact, earning the same real income but different money income due to compensating differentials.

Income-Leisure Choices

Another important reason why money incomes differ among individuals is that people value their leisure time differently. College professors may work fewer hours in a year than others with the same level of education. They will also earn less money but they will consume more leisure. Consequently, the observed difference in the money incomes of, say, professors of accounting and practitioners of accounting will overstate any difference in their real incomes by the value of the professors' additional leisure time.

Differences in Real Incomes

An individual's income over any period of time is the sum of the various amounts of services supplied by the individual (one person may supply several different types of service) multiplied by the price of the services. An individual may own and supply the services of capital, land, and the like, as well as labor services. Differences in individual real incomes will occur because different individuals supply different amounts of the various types of services. In general, differences in individual real incomes do not arise because of differences in the price of a particular service obtained by one individual when compared to another. This proposition is not at all obvious. At first glance, it may appear that two clerks, two teachers, two doctors, or two lawyers are paid different prices for doing the same job. If clerk A is paid more than clerk B for doing what appears to be the same job, does this mean that clerk A is overpaid or does it mean that clerk B is underpaid? Usually, neither is true. A profit-seeking entrepreneur would not pay clerk A more than it was worth to have clerk A perform the work. If he were doing so, he would offer clerk A a lower wage and, given clerk A's market opportunities, he would accept. If he did not accept, the entrepreneur could fire him and find some other clerk who could perform the work at the lower market price. On the other hand, if clerk B is being underpaid, he will request a raise from the entrepreneur. If he is underpaid, the entrepreneur will grant the raise. If he does not, clerk B will quit because he knows there are other market opportunities that will pay higher than his current employment for same type of work.

If one observes two different clerks being paid different prices, it is because they are not doing the same job. Clerk A may be more experienced than clerk B. He may make fewer mistakes or have better rapport with customers. He may learn more quickly or present a better appearance. In other words, he may be better at the job than clerk B.

Voluntary Redistribution of Income

Many organizations in the United States are engaged in the voluntary redistribution of income. There are roughly 200,000 voluntary health, welfare, civic, fraternal, and veterans' organizations as well as 300,000 churches that sponsor a variety of charitable activities. The charitable activities of churches alone amount to roughly 800

Table 8.3   Number of Foundations by Size

Type	Number	Total Assets (millions)	Grants (millions)
Small (assets of less than 1 million each)	22,421	$ 2,599	$ 419
Large (assets of more than 1 million each)	2,504	31,497	1,527
Total	24,925	$34,096	$1,946

Source: The Foundation Center, *The Foundation Directory* (New York: Columbia University Press, 1976), pp. XII-XIII.

Table 8.4   Private Philanthropy—Estimated by Source and Allocation (in Millions of Dollars)

	1955	1960	1963	1964	1965	1966	1967	1968	1969
Source									
Individuals	5,100	7,150	8,316	8,926	9,276	10,530	11,144	12,600	13,600
Foundations	450	710	819	834	1,125	1,250	1,268	1,500	1,600
Business Corporations	415	482	657	729	785	805	829	865	900
Bequests	237	570	876	950	1,024	1,309	1,263	1,300	1,500
Allocation									
Religion	3,102	4,545	5,270	5,650	5,983	6,690	6,839	7,500	7,930
Education	682	1,426	1,811	1,960	2,076	2,370	2,500	2,750	2,900
Welfare	1,426	1,337	760	814	855	808	931	1,100	1,200
Health	558	1,070	1,757	1,945	2,076	2,509	2,610	2,740	2,850
Foundations	186	356	x	x	x	x	x	x	x
Civic	x	x	x	x	488	558	621	750	850
Other	248	178	1,070	732	732	959	1,021	1,425	1,870
Total	6,202	8,912	10,668	11,210	12,210	13,894	14,522	16,265	17,600

x = Included in other.

Source: U.S. Department of Commerce, Bureau of the Census, *Statistical Abstract of the United States* (Washington, D.C.: U.S. Government Printing Office, 1971).

million dollars per year.[2] There are approximately 25,000 major foundations with assets in excess of 34 billion dollars which award grants of about 2 billion dollars per year for various purposes (see Tables 8.3 and 8.4).

This private philanthropy accounts for a considerable amount of income redistribution in the United States. The reasons why some, but not all, individuals voluntarily redistribute some of their own income to others can be found by examining Figure 8.3. Tom's income is measured along the horizontal axis and Joe's income is measured along the vertical axis. Suppose that income is initially distributed so that Tom receives the entire amount, say, $1000, and Joe receives none. Assume that it is possible for Tom to redistribute income away from himself to Joe and that his cost of increasing Joe's income by one dollar is one dollar. The possible combinations of Tom's income and Joe's income are given by line *AB* in Figure 8.3. If the dashed vertical lines represent Tom's indifference curves between his income and Joe's income, he will choose to keep the entire $1000 income for himself. Tom's utility does not depend upon Joe's income. Tom's preferences are neutral with respect to Joe's income. Clearly, if everyone's indifference curves were like Tom's, we would not observe charitable contributions.

Figure 8.3

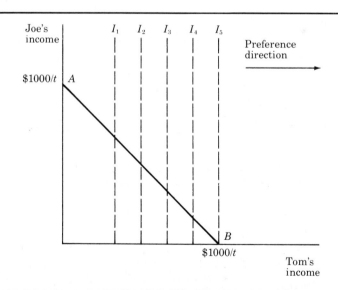

[2]U.S. Department of Commerce, Bureau of the Census, *Statistical Abstract of the United States* (Washington, D.C.: U.S. Government Printing Office, 1971).

Figure 8.4

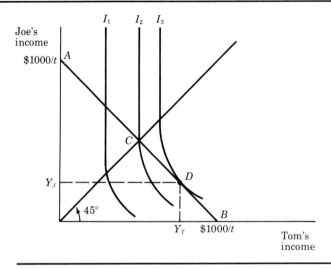

Suppose that Tom's utility is influenced by Joe's income only if Joe's income is lower than Tom's. This case is shown in Figure 8.4. Again, assume that Tom receives all of the income and that he can transfer x dollars to Joe at a cost of x dollars to himself. Since Tom's utility depends upon Joe's income only when Joe's income is less than his own, Tom's indifference curves will have the same shape as those shown in Figure 8.3 for income combinations that lie above the 45-degree line. The points that lie along the 45-degree line indicate income combinations for which Tom's income is equal to Joe's. Any point above the 45-degree line indicates an income combination for which Joe's income exceeds Tom's. The reverse is, of course, true for points that lie below the 45-degree line. Consequently, given the above assumptions concerning Tom's preferences, his indifference curves assume a normal convex shape only after passing through the 45-degree line. In Figure 8.4, Tom will choose to distribute Y_J ($1000 - Y_T) of his income to Joe and keep Y_T for himself. He will choose to do this because no other distribution of the $1000 allows him to reach a higher indifference curve.

Given Tom's constraint (the line AB) and his indifference map, he does not choose an equal distribution of the $1000 between himself and Joe. Tom will, however, choose to distribute more income to Joe if the cost of transferring dollars of income to Joe should fall, that is, if the constraint (line AB) should become more steep (rotate upward around point B). If charitable contributions were tax deductible, line AB would become steeper and more income would be transferred to charity. In the limit, when it costs Tom nothing to increase Joe's income (when Tom's constraint is vertical), Tom will choose an equal distribution.

This observation has application to the programs offered by public officials regarding redistribution of income. If the costs of redistribution are to be spread over the entire community so that the cost *to the public official* is very low, he or she will be inclined to offer a program of redistribution that would result in an equal distribution of income. Put less delicately, if an individual is considering redistributing income other than his or her own, he or she will argue for greater redistribution.

Income Redistribution as a Public Good

There are potential public-good aspects to the redistribution of income. Consider the situation discussed above. A third party (who also has a high income) may benefit when Tom decides to transfer Y_J in income to Joe. The third party benefits but incurs none of the costs of the transfer because she cannot be excluded from enjoying the *knowledge* that Joe has a higher income. When large numbers of individuals are involved as potential donors, the free-rider problem may lead to too little voluntary income redistribution.

If transaction costs are low, free riding can be prevented by forming collective agreements among high-income individuals regarding income distribution to low-income individuals. These collective agreements need not involve the government. When the number of donors is large, however, it might be the case that the transaction costs would be lower if the agreements were handled through the government. These would necessarily involve cases in which *all* high-income individuals *voluntarily* agree to raise their taxes and to distribute the proceeds among low-income individuals. It is, of course, also possible that the cost (measured in terms of the smaller amount of income transferred) of allowing individuals to free ride are lower than the cost of any available alternative that might be adopted to eliminate free riders. If this is the case, the most efficient solution might result from strictly voluntary redistribution. Some individuals in the community may be better off because I choose to use some of my income to feed, clothe, and house my children. In this situation, because those individuals can free ride, too little is spent on my children. The cost, however, of attempting to correct this and similar problems by using the government may far exceed the benefits.

Current Methods of Public Redistribution

Table 8.5 presents a summary of federal, state, and local expenditures on income maintenance in the United States for selected years. Tables 8.6 and 8.7 present a more detailed accounting of public assistance payments presented in Table 8.5. Note that old-age assistance, aid to the blind, and aid to the permanently and totally disabled were superseded by the Supplemental Security Income Program in all 50 states and the District of Columbia beginning in January 1974.

These public income-maintenance programs represent a large portion of total government expenditures. Expenditures on income maintenance rose from approximately 22 percent of all government expenditures in 1950 to 33 percent in 1975. We caution the reader in interpreting the data presented in Tables 8.5–8.7. A portion of the dollar amounts presented in them represents disbursements of retirement benefits. To the extent that current disbursements from the fund reflect the present value of past individual contributions, the disbursements represent present consumption of past savings

Table 8.5	**Public Income Maintenance Programs: Cash Payments (in Millions)**				
			Years		
Type	**1950**	**1960**	**1965**	**1970**	**1975**
Old-Age, Survivors, Disability, and Hospital Insurance (OASDHI)	1,014	11,379	18,512	32,150	67,399
Railroad Retirement	298	942	1,133	1,756	3,282
Public Employee Retirement	784	2,597	4,595	9,165	22,009
Veterans' Pensions	2,223	3,436	4,196	5,480	7,668
Unemployment Benefits	1,559	3,024	2,343	4,221	17,536
Temporary Disability	243	367	465	720	927
Workmen's Compensation	591	860	1,214	1,981	4,420
Public Assistance	2,516	3,262	3,995	8,861	10,433
Supplemental Security Income	x	x	x	x	x
Total	8,676	25,872	36,567	64,470	139,564
As a percentage of all government expenditures	22.8	25.9	26.6	29.4	33.1

x = Included in Public Assistance

Source: Department of Health, Education, and Welfare, Social Security Administration, *Social Security Bulletin,* March 1977, p. 36.

Public Assistance:
Total Money Payments by Program
(in Thousands) Table 8.6

Program	1950	1960	1965	1970	1975
Old-Age Assistance	1,453,917	1,626,021	1,594,183	1,866,087	/
Aid to the Blind	52,567	86,080	77,308	97,087	/
Aid to the Permanently and Totally Disabled	8,042	236,402	416,765	975,504	/
Aid to Families with Dependent Children	547,174	994,425	1,644,096	4,857,178	9,210,104
General Assistance	292,786	319,521	260,612	632,373	1,137,026
Emergency Assistance	—	—	—	16,563	77,515
Institutional Services	—	—	—	415,796	+
Total	2,354,485	3,262,769	3,995,907	8,860,998	10,433,277

+ = Included under medical assistance beginning January 1972.

/ = Superseded by supplemental security income beginning January 1974.

Source: Department of Health, Education, and Welfare, Social Security Administration, *Social Security Bulletin,* March 1977, p. 62.

and not income transfers. Certain other programs are designed to insure against disability and unemployment. Again, to the extent that current disbursements represent the present value of past contributions, these disbursements cannot be considered pure income transfers. Public assistance and supplemental security income programs, on the other hand, represent relatively pure attempts at redistributing income. Expenditures from these two programs amounted to, roughly, $15 billion in 1975.

The public assistance and supplemental security income programs contain very strong incentives for individuals *not* to work. Consider Figure 8.5. Leisure per unit of time is measured along the horizontal axis and income per unit of time is measured along the vertical axis. The individual spends her time at work or at leisure. If she spends zero hours working, she consumes the maximum in leisure, which is T (where T = 24 hours per day or 168 hours per week, etc.). On the other hand, if she spends all of her time at work, she earns income $\overline{Y}$. The rate at which she can transform hours of leisure into dollars of income is given by the hourly wage rate, w, which is equal to the absolute value of the slope of the income/leisure constraint (line $\overline{Y}T$).

Table 8.7

Public Assistance: Recipients of Money Payments and Average Amount per Case, Recipient, or Family— September 1976

Aid to Families with Dependent Children	
Number of Families	3,554,159
Number of Recipients	
Total	11,176,814
Children	7,900,806
Average Money Payment/Month	
Per Family	$235.21
Per Recipient	$74.79
General Assistance	
Number of Cases	665,407
Number of Recipients	888,553
Average Money Payment/Month	
Per Case	$151.65
Per Recipient	$113.57
Emergency Assistance/Month	
Number of Families	22,111
Average Money Payment	$191.51

Source: Department of Health, Education, and Welfare, Social Security Administration, *Social Security Bulletin,* March 1977, p. 63.

Given this budget constraint, the individual will choose a combination of income of $0E$ and leisure of $0L_0$ and will work $0T-0L_0$ hours per unit of time.

Suppose a public assistance program is set up that transfers to the same individual a sum of money equal to $0B$. This type of program takes away one dollar of assistance for each dollar earned by working. Consequently, the individual's constraint becomes the line segments $\overline{Y}CD$. For each dollar earned up to $0B$, a dollar of subsidy is taken away. The individual, by working, moves along CD until she earns $0B$, and then she moves up $C\overline{Y}$. The individual is taxed at a 100-percent rate until she earns $0B$ dollars. After this point, she will receive wage w and thus be on her normal budget line.

Faced with this constraint, this individual will choose a combination of $0B$ income and $0T$ leisure. This combination of income and leisure places her on the highest indifference curve possible given the constraint. With this type of income subsidy, the individual chooses to reduce her work effort to zero.

Figure 8.5

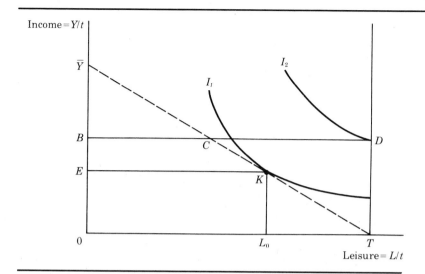

In the above case, an income floor, $0B$, was established so that it exceeded the individual's earnings from work, $0E$. Suppose that the income floor were established below her after-tax earnings. Is it possible that she would still reduce her work effort to zero? Consider Figure 8.6, which is the same as Figure 8.5 except that we assume the income floor is established below the earnings from work, $0E$.

After the income floor is established, the combination of income and leisure yielding the highest utility to the individual is, again, $0B$ income and $0T$ leisure. Her income is less at point D than it is at point K, but the additional leisure consumed at point D is more than enough to compensate for the reduction in income (the individual is on a higher indifference curve at D). In fact, this individual will always choose to reduce work effort to zero as long as the income floor is set above $FT = 0G$.

Gifts and Subsidies

Our present welfare system deals with the problem of low income in two ways: (1) It supplements the individual's income with cash gifts as discussed above, and (2) it subsidizes his or her consumption of particular goods. These subsidies or gifts in kind are transfers of goods or services to individuals at prices below market

Figure 8.6

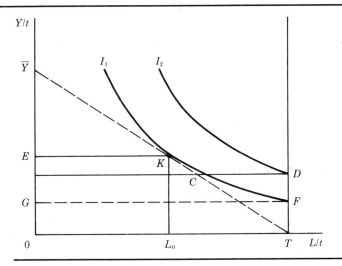

prices. Food stamps, public housing, and Medicare are examples of subsidies or gifts in kind. What impact do these programs have on the individual's utility and consumption basket? Consider Figure 8.7. Along the horizontal axis, units of milk per unit of time are measured. Along the vertical axis, units of some other commodity or basket of commodities, Y, are measured. Given the individual's income constraint and the prices of the two goods, he chooses a combination of M_0 units of milk and Y_0 units of the other good. Suppose, now, that a program is adopted to subsidize milk consumption for individuals whose incomes are below a given amount and that this individual qualifies for the program.[3]

Since he can obtain milk at a lower price after adoption of the program, his budget line will rotate around point A to the right. The relative price of milk to him falls. He consumes more milk, M_1, and he reaches a higher indifference curve at point C'. (See Figure 8.8.)

If P_m is the price of a quart of milk and S is the subsidy, the price of a quart of milk to a subsidized individual will be $P_m - S$. The cost, K, of subsidizing the individual's consumption of milk is the subsidy, S, multiplied by the amount of milk the individual decides to purchase, M_1. Suppose, rather than subsidizing the individual's consumption of milk, this amount ($K = S \cdot M_1$) were, sim-

---

[3]We assume that individuals are prevented from reselling the milk at the market price.

Figure 8.7

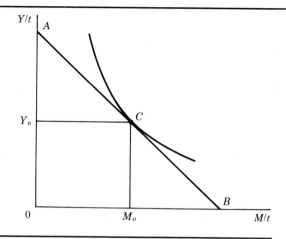

Figure 8.8

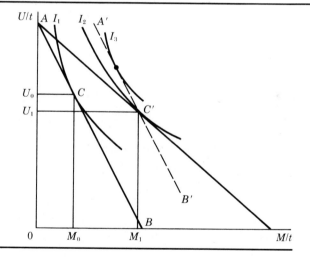

ply, transferred to the individual as a cash gift. Clearly, the individual can continue to purchase M_1 units of milk and Y_1 units of Y if he desires under this new scheme. Consequently, the new budget line must pass through point C'. However, the slope of the budget line, which is given by the ratio of the prices of the two commodities, will be identical to the slope of the original budget line, AB. This new budget line is shown as the dashed line, $A'B'$. Faced with this constraint, the individual will not choose a combination of the two goods equal to Y_1M_1 but will move up $A'B'$ to the higher indifference curve, I_3. The conclusion to draw from this analysis is that cash gifts will allow the individual to reach a higher indifference curve than will the same amount if transferred through a subsidy. We are ignoring the utility that the donor derives from giving the gift. His or her utility may vary not so much with the utility obtained by the recipient as it does with the quantity of milk the recipient consumes. Note that the subsidy induces the recipient to consume more milk than he would if given the cash gift.

The Negative Income Tax

The negative income tax has been proposed as an alternative to the present welfare system. Proponents of the negative income tax propose (1) to eliminate programs that subsidize the consumption of specific goods and (2) build in a work incentive by eliminating the 100-percent tax which is levied on earned income by the present public programs designed to supplement money income. The negative income tax would establish a floor under individual income as does the present system. Instead of the 100-percent tax, however, each dollar earned would be taxed at a rate less than 100 percent. For example, if the negative tax rate were .50, the individual would get to keep 50 cents of each dollar earned. If the individual works $T-L$ hours at wage rate w and if the income floor is DT and the negative tax rate is t, after-tax income, Y_t, will be

$$Y_t = \overline{DT} + w(T-L) - wt(T-L)$$
$$Y_t = \overline{DT} + w(T-L)(1-t).$$

A break-even income level is established when the tax payment $wt(T - L)$ is equal to the income floor $\overline{DT}$. When the individual's income equals this break-even level, her subsidy is reduced to zero. This is shown in Figure 8.9. The line $\overline{Y}NT$ is the constraint indicating the rate at which income and leisure can be traded off in the absence of the negative income tax. The line $0M = TD'$ is the break-even level of income. The line $\overline{Y}ND$ indicates the rate at which income and leisure can be substituted in the presence of the negative income tax.

The impact of replacing the current welfare system with a negative income tax on work effort can be seen in Figure 8.10. Suppose, in the absence of any program to supplement income, the individual would choose a combination of income and leisure given

Figure 8.9

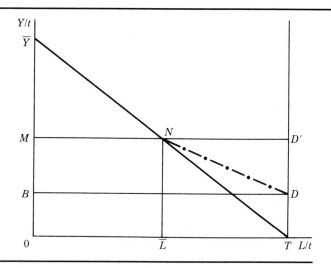

Figure 8.10

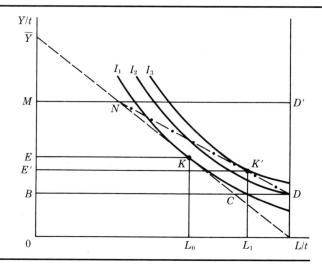

by $0E$ income and $0L_0$ leisure. This combination is given by point
K at which her constraint, $\overline{Y}T$, is tangent to indifference curve I_1.
     If an income floor were imposed equal to $0B = TD$, this indi-
vidual would move from point K to point D. With the income floor,
her constraint becomes the line segments $\overline{Y}NCD$. This constraint
allows her to reach indifference curve I_2 at point D. She reduces her

work effort from L_0T to zero; that is, she spends her entire time at leisure. Her income is equal to the income floor, $0B$.

On the other hand, if a negative income tax were imposed with the same income floor $(0B)$ and a break-even income of $0M$, the individual's constraint would become $\overline{Y}ND$. Faced with this constraint, the individual would choose to be at point K'. She consumes leisure of $0L_1$ and income of $0E'$. Note that her work effort is greater with a negative income tax than it is with a simple income floor but less than it is with no income supplement program.

It is, of course, possible to show that a negative income tax would lower the work effort of some individuals. Suppose that a second individual had an indifference map such that, in the absence of a negative income tax, he reached an optimum at a point along the income/leisure constraint between points $\overline{Y}$ and N. If the indifference curve, which is tangent to $\overline{Y}N$, were to intersect the negative income tax constraint $\overline{Y}ND$ at a point between N and D, the individual would reduce his work effort with the adoption of a negative income tax. Consequently, the effect on total work effort from the adoption of this program is uncertain.

Application

The Trend toward Equality in the Distribution of Net Income[4]

We have shown (see Table 8.1 and Figure 8.1) that money income is distributed unequally in the United States and have listed a number of reasons indicating why we would expect to observe an unequal distribution in money income. A study by Edgar K. Browning has attempted to adjust figures on the distribution of money income to account for *some* of the factors we listed. His adjustment also takes account of the different amounts of taxes paid by individuals who fall within the quintiles as well as the distribution of in-kind income flowing from government expenditure programs. These in-kind benefits include food stamps, public housing, Medicare, and similar programs. Browning's results are presented in Table 8.8. The last two lines of Table 8.8 indicate that net income (adjusted money income) is distributed more equally than money income. The lowest quintile receives only 5.4 percent of unadjusted money income but 12.5 percent of net income; the

[4]Edgar K. Browning, "The Trend toward Equality in the Distribution of Net Income," *Southern Economic Journal,* Vol. 42 (July 1976), pp. 912–923.

Distribution of Net Income in 1972 (in Billions of Dollars)   Table 8.8

Quintile	Lowest	2nd	3rd	4th	5th	Total
Money Income	$37.1	$81.7	$120.1	$164.1	$284.2	$687.2
Plus: Adjustment for Underreporting	6.1	8.0	8.7	11.2	26.8	60.7
Benefits in Kind	22.0	7.0	4.0	3.0	2.0	38.0
Education	8.7	10.4	12.3	13.7	17.5	62.7
Capital Gains	3.3	4.1	4.9	5.5	20.3	38.0
Leisure	18.5	25.3	24.2	17.1	36.3	121.4
Less: Income and Payroll Taxes	1.3	5.8	15.5	26.6	67.5	116.6
Equals: Distribution of Net Income	94.4	130.7	158.7	188.0	319.6	891.4
Per Capita Net Income (dollars)	$2923	$3713	$4210	$4796	$7814	
Percent Distribution	12.5	15.8	17.9	20.4	33.3	100
Unadjusted Percent Distribution	5.4	11.9	17.5	23.9	41.1	100

Source: Edgar K. Browning, "The Trend toward Equality in the Distribution of Net Income," *Southern Economic Journal*, Vol. 42 (July 1976), pp. 912-23. Reprinted by permission.

highest quintile receives 41.4 percent of unadjusted money income but 33.3 percent of net income. Note that Browning's adjustments do not take account of differences in the choices that individuals make regarding the timing of their income streams or of nominal differences in the distribution of money income. As we noted, these are two important factors that give rise to dispersion in the distribution of money income.

Property Rights and the Economy

The assignment and enforcement of property rights are two of the most basic and important functions of government. Without a clear assignment and enforcement of rights, no economy could function. It is important to note that a property right is the right of an individual human being. Once stated, the point seems obvious. However, there appears to be evidence that some rather important people do not understand it. A successful presidential candidate, when questioned on the criteria he would use in appointing justices to the Supreme Court, stated that he would appoint men who would weigh human rights more heavily than property rights when ruling on cases brought before them.

A property right is the individual's expectation that the decisions he or she makes regarding his or her property will be effective. A property right specifies (limits) the rights of an individual in the use of his or her property. Defining and enforcing property rights become more important (there will be a greater demand to do so) as the community becomes more complex, that is, as the interaction among individuals in the community increases. It was not beneficial for Robinson Crusoe to define and enforce property rights prior to the arrival of Friday. By specifying the uses to which an individual may put his or her property and by granting the individual the right to exclusive use of his or her property, individuals are induced to internalize the costs imposed on others when they decide to employ property in particular ways.

In the absence of clearly defined and enforced property rights, exchange would not occur. When an exchange takes place, the two parties agree to transfer the bundle of rights that each has in the two goods. If these rights do not exist, or are not enforced, there is nothing to exchange.

Property Rights, Exchange, and Efficiency

It is not sufficient to define and enforce property rights for an efficient use of resources. Property rights must also be transferable. In other words, individuals must be able to freely exchange what they own. Any restriction on the exchange of resources will prevent individuals from employing resources in their highest valued uses. The owner of a competitive firm, for example, has an incentive to operate the firm efficiently because, by doing so, he will maximize his income (profit). If his right to the profits of the firm were not clearly established and enforced, his incentive to operate the firm efficiently would be diminished.

The voluntary exchange of goods allows both parties to the exchange to obtain preferred combinations of the goods exchanged. The transfer of capital can also lead to gains. Suppose an individual is operating a firm inefficiently. He will be earning a below-normal rate of return on his investment. This will reduce the value of the firm to him. The value of the firm to a competent manager, on the other hand, will be higher. This divergence in values will enable an exchange of the firm to take place at a price mutually beneficial to both parties. Under the new ownership, the firm will be operated efficiently, which is another way of saying that the resources will have moved to their highest valued use. This movement of capital to its highest valued use will take place whenever ownership of capital is transferable.

Another example of how a system of well-defined rights provides economic efficiency is the Law of Contracts. The voluntary exchange process studied in standard microeconomics courses assumes the exchange takes place simultaneously. Individual A trades some amount of good x for some amount of good y (either x or y could be dollars) with individiual B. Since the trade is voluntary, neither party would agree to it unless he or she is made better off. Since trade takes place simultaneously, no outside intervention is necessary to guarantee the satisfaction of both parties. Suppose that individual A agrees to give individual B some amount of good x for the promise of a certain payment in the future. To make the example specific, suppose individual A agrees to sell B an automobile for \$400 with the payments to be spread over a one-year period. This type of agreement can make both parties better off. Individual B may not have the \$400 now, but this agreement allows him to acquire the automobile now and pay later. If only simultaneous exchange were possible, he would have to wait one year to acquire an automobile. Individual A is better off because she can sell the car at a higher price if she is willing to delay collection of the money. Note, however, that individual B can be even better off if he does not pay individual A. In this case, he has the automobile and the \$400. If no recourse were available in this matter, individual A would be very reluctant to agree to exchanges that involve promises of future payments. The Law of Contracts gives individual A this recourse. It creates a means of enforcing collection on agreements to pay in the future. Without the enforcement of contracts, many exchanges would not take place and resources would be allocated less efficiently.

Property Rights and External Effects

When transaction costs are low and rights are transferable, resources will be used efficiently even when external effects are present. This result, known as the Coase Theorem (see Chapter 3), is another reason why well-defined and enforced rights are important. If property rights are not transferable—that is, if the exchange that took place in the farmer-rancher example is prohibited—resource use will not be efficient. If the farmer were not able to buy the rancher's right to allow his cattle to wander in the farmer's corn, the rancher would ignore the damage done to the farmer by the wandering cattle. The external damage would remain too large.

In general, creation and enforcement of laws or rules allow the economy to operate more efficiently by reducing external effects. Traffic laws, for example, are designed to reduce the number of traffic accidents. Although laws such as traffic laws and product safety laws are designed to reduce accidents and facilitate efficient allocation of resources, their purpose is not to *minimize* accidents. Traffic accidents could be reduced to zero by passing a law against driving. Our experience with reducing the maximum speed limit in the United States to 55 miles per hour has resulted in reduced traffic accidents. Why not lower the speed to 35 miles per hour or 25 miles per hour and reduce the accident rate even further? The answer is that there is a cost to reducing the speed limit. It would take individuals longer to get wherever they are going and cost them the additional time, thus raising the total cost of driving at a much reduced speed. Therefore, the benefits of reduced traffic accidents must be balanced against the cost of reduced driving speed.

The Attenuation of Property Rights

Individuals, responding to market-determined prices, will make decisions regarding their property that result in the property being allocated to its highest valued use. For example, we expect individuals responding to market forces to secure the efficient level of product safety. Since safer products will require more costly construction and since some individuals are more averse to risk than others, we expect the market to provide several levels of safety for each product type, with safer products being more expensive. This allows the consumer to pick that combination of expense and safety that he or she considers most desirable. Some individuals, however, do not like the choices that the majority of individuals make regarding safety. These individuals, sometimes called consumerists, believe that the safety level of products chosen by most individuals is too low. These consumerists have employed the legislative and judicial arms of the government as a means to circumvent the market choices made by the average consumer. These changes, by preventing certain exchanges (by attenuating individual rights in property), result in individuals employing property in lower valued, though safer, uses.

The purchase and use of certain products involve risk of injury to the users as well as potential damage to property. These damages can occur as a result of careless use of a product, a defective product, or both. Changes in the rules governing the liability for damages resulting from the use of particular products can promote the efficient allocation of resources. This would be the case if the benefits of the change exceed the costs. In this section, we examine some of the benefits and costs of different liability rules.

First, let us look at the effects of producer liability. Under this rule, producers are liable for damage caused by the use of their products if defects can be proven. When considering the occurrence and extent of damage, remember that it is almost always dependent on the type of use given the product. Very often it is possible for the use of a product, defective or not, to eliminate or minimize the extent of injury. Smashing your thumb with a hammer that has a loose head can be avoided by using a hammer in a proper state of repair. Defects can be worsened by age or by failure to properly maintain a product. Suppose, for example, the steering wheel falls off of your Model A Ford while you are driving it down the highway. Is this a result of a defect or the result of driving a car that is a half a century old? These examples serve to illustrate that one should distinguish between a defective product and a misused product. Further, even when a defect is present, judicious use or nonuse can reduce or eliminate injury.

If producers are liable for all damage done by their products, consumers have less incentive to be careful in the use of the product. The safe use of products is costly. Time must be expended in reading instructions and in learning how to use the product safely. If consumers are compensated for damages that result from the use of products, they will have less incentive to use their valuable time in learning how to use the product safely. Alternatively, under consumer liability (the case in which the consumer bears all of the damage costs), the incentive for careful use is much higher. A system of producer liability will cause the producer (1) to devote resources to making the product safer, (2) to purchase liability insurance, and (3) to shift away from producing some hazardous products. This results in safer, but more expensive, products. These adjustments reduce the choice set available to consumers when compared to consumer liability.

Roland McKean points out in an article on product liability that producer liability may actually lead to more accidents than consumer liability.[5] Even though producers sell fewer risky products, consumers may buy more of those risky products because the relative price of using them is lower and because consumers are compensated for any damage incurred. Furthermore, consumers will have a diminished incentive to avoid accidents by careful use of the products they buy.

Another recent trend has been, through legislation, to restrict or to forbid the sale of certain products. This legislation on product safety reduces the range of choice open to both consumers and producers; it restricts the bundle of rights that they can exchange. Blocking the sale of less safe products (for example, a lawn mower which may cut off a toe if you place your foot under it) will cause the price of these products to rise. The increase in price will reflect the added cost of the safety devices. There may be, however, many consumers who would rather pay more attention to the placement of their toes while enjoying the benefit of cheaper lawn mowers. These consumers are worse off with laws that force them to buy the safe, but more expensive, lawn mower.

Application

The 1962 Drug Amendments[6]

The 1962 Kefauver-Harris Amendments to the Food, Drug, and Cosmetic Act altered the set of rights that existed in the manufacture and purchase of drugs. These amendments were passed to prevent the sale of numerous high-priced, ineffective, and dangerous drugs that were alleged to be flooding the market. Prior to passage of the amendments, the Food and Drug Administration had a 180-day period to deny approval of a new drug and prevent its sale. This could be done if the manufacturer could not demonstrate the drug was safe for its proposed use. The new amendments caused the following restrictions: (1) a requirement was placed on the manufacturer to prove the effectiveness and safety of a new drug (the 180-day limit was also removed so that sale could be held up over an indefinite period); and (2) the FDA placed restrictions on the testing procedures used by drug manufacturers. Apparently

---

[5]Roland McKean, "Products Liability: Implications of Some Changing Property Rights," *Quarterly Journal of Economics,* Vol. 84 (November 1970), pp. 611–26.

[6]Sam Peltzman, "An Evaluation of Consumer Protection Legislation: The 1962 Drug Amendments," *Journal of Political Economy,* Vol. 81 (September/October 1973), pp. 1049–1091.

Congress felt that in passing these amendments, it could improve the situation in the market for drugs. Congress believed that patients and doctors were incompetent to judge what was good for them and that the market did not provide adequate incentives to manufacturers to provide safe and effective drugs. Sam Peltzman estimates that the 1962 amendments kept new drugs off the market which were valued by consumers at about $300–$400 million annually. Also, keeping new drugs off the market made drug firms less competitive. This increased the price of drugs sold. Peltzman estimates the price increase to have cost consumers $50 million annually. The most optimistic estimate of the benefits of the new law is that it saved the consumer $100–$150 million annually. This assumes that the use of new ineffective drugs did not decline as consumers discovered the truth about them. Peltzman found that this was not the case; ineffective drugs were identified by consumers and their use declined. Adjusting for this decline in consumption reduces the benefit of the 1962 amendments to $50–$75 million annually. The total cost of this legislation to consumers amounted to $350–$450 million annually while total benefits amounted to $50–$75 million annually. This is a clear-cut case in which the attenuation of property rights has reduced the wealth of the community.

Questions and Exercises

1. What is the coefficient of inequality in the distribution of money income if 99.99 . . . percent of the families receive no income? What is the coefficient of inequality if income is distributed equally?

2. The Lorenz curve is sensitive to the age distribution of the population. Why?

3. Consider Figure 8.4. Suppose the income tax rate is 25 percent and charitable contributions are not deductible for income tax purposes. Plot the new constraint. How does the tax affect Tom's charitable contributions? Suppose tax laws are changed to allow the entire amount of any charitable contribution to be deducted from income for tax purposes. Draw the new constraint. How does this change alter Tom's charitable contributions? Suppose the tax law is changed again to allow a deduction for charitable contributions of up to but not more than 25 percent of one's income ($1000 in Tom's case). Draw the new constraint. Will this change necessarily alter the amount Tom contributes to charity? Might it change the amount?

4. Consider Figure 8.4. Suppose that you were required to match dollar for dollar Tom's charitable contribution to Joe. Tom knows this and it is up to Tom to decide upon his contribution, which will also determine your contribution. Draw the new constraint that exists between Tom's income and Joe's income. Assume that your income is at least equal to Tom's. What is Tom's charitable contribution? Does it necessarily rise? What is Joe's income? Does it necessarily rise? What is the limit to which Tom would wish to increase Joe's income as additional individuals are required to match Tom's contribution? In the limit, what amount does Tom's charitable contribution approach?

5. Welfare programs that place a floor under money income subsidize the consumption of leisure. In fact, for some individuals, these programs may reduce the relative price of leisure in terms of earned income to zero. Comment.

6. Why might capital be used less efficiently in socialistic countries than in capitalistic ones?

7. Why are well-defined and enforced property rights necessary to the exchange process?

8. Some product safety legislation bans the sale of certain products. Show graphically how this ban can make the consumer worse off.

9. Changes in property rights or laws should only be made when the benefits of the change exceed the costs. With most of these changes, large numbers of individuals are affected. How might this fact complicate the problem of estimating the benefits and costs? How is this problem similar to the problem of public goods?

Additional Readings

Browning, Edgar K. "The Trend toward Equality in the Distribution of Net Income." *Southern Economic Journal,* Vol. 42 (July 1976), pp. 912-23.

Demsetz, H. "The Exchange and Enforcement of Private Property Rights." *Journal of Law and Economics,* Vol. 7 (October 1964), pp. 11-26.

Tullock, Gordon. *The Logic of the Law.* New York: Basic Books, 1971.

9

Personal Income Tax

In this chapter we consider the taxation of personal income. Federal, state, and local governments tax personal income, but it is a much more important source of revenue for the federal government than it is for other levels of government (see Table 9.1 later in the chapter). Before we begin a detailed discussion of the personal income tax, a few general comments concerning taxes will be helpful.

A tax is a compulsory charge levied on an individual. The purpose of a tax is to finance the collective provision of public goods. A tax is necessarily compulsory because of the nature of the problem of supplying public goods.

Recall that when goods that generate significant external effects are supplied, the free-rider problem is likely to arise. If transaction costs were low, it would be possible to reach collective agreements regarding the public good prior to its provision. In this situation, government need play no part in providing the good; no coercion is involved in this process. Each individual willingly engages in the exchange of agreements regarding the provision of the good. These agreements will necessarily include the payments to be made by each individual. However, high transaction costs may provide a rationale for government involvement in the provision of the good, resulting in compulsory, or coercive, tax payments (see Chapter 3). Government involvement through tax finance necessarily implies a separation of the method of finance from the marginal benefits that individuals associate with the goods. Consequently, the efficiency condition for resource allocation in providing public goods (see Chapter 3) loses the predictive content it had under the assumption of low transaction costs.

A second point deserves emphasis. Taxes are levied on individuals. Corporations or business firms cannot pay taxes; only individuals can pay taxes. Furthermore, shifting taxes from local government to state government or from state government to the federal government does not shift taxes from individuals. The federal government does not pay taxes. This process, however, may shift the burden among individuals.

As was noted above, the purpose of taxation is to finance the acquisition of resources necessary to produce public goods. As an alternative, the resources could be acquired by direct expropriation, an example of which is the conscription of military personnel. Direct expropriation of resources, however, places the cost of providing the public good almost entirely on the owners of the expropriated resources, resulting in a wide divergence between the marginal benefits that individuals associate with the provision of public goods and the "prices" that they pay. The presumption is that taxation, by spreading the cost widely among individuals, will result in a more efficient rate of public-good production.

The Elements of Taxation

Every tax scheme is composed of two basic elements, the tax base and the tax rate. The *tax base* is, simply, that quantity against which the tax is levied. The tax base may be anything. Some of the more common tax bases are the values of property, sales, inventory, and income. The *tax rate* is the share of the value of the tax base that the individual must pay per unit of time. The tax rate may be expressed as a marginal rate or as an average rate.

Suppose that the tax base is income and that individuals must pay 10 cents in taxes on each dollar that is earned. If the individual earns $10,000 per year in taxable income, his or her tax liability is $1,000. The average tax rate is computed by dividing the total tax liability by the tax base. In this case the average tax rate is equal to $1,000/$10,000 = .10. If the individual's taxable income should increase to $12,000 per year, his or her tax liability will increase to $1,200 and the average tax rate will remain unchanged. In this case, the marginal tax rate is equal to the average tax rate. The marginal tax rate is computed by dividing the change in tax liability ($1,200 - $1,000 = $200) by the change in the tax base ($12,000 - $10,000 = $2,000), which is $200/$2,000 = .10. When the average tax rate does *not* change as the tax base changes, which is another way of saying that the marginal tax rate is equal to the average tax rate, the tax is defined as a proportional tax.

Let T represent total tax liability and B represent the tax base. The average tax rate is T/B and the marginal tax rate is $\Delta T/\Delta B$. The relationship between the two tax rates and the tax base for a proportional tax is shown in Figure 9.1. Under a proportional tax, the tax liability of the individual and the tax receipts of the taxing authority increase in *proportion* to the tax base.

If the average tax rate rises as the base rises and falls as the base falls (if there is a positive relationship between the average tax rate and the base), the tax is defined as a progressive tax. For example, suppose that an individual's tax liability is one cent on every dollar earned for the first $1,000 in annual income, two cents on every dollar earned in excess of $1,000 but less than $2,000 in

Figure 9.1 **Proportional Tax**

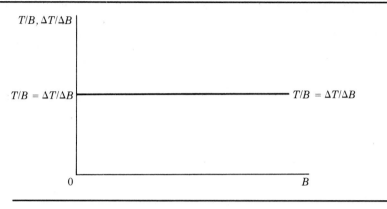

annual income, and so on. Given this tax rate schedule, an individual who earns $10,000 annually in taxable income will have a tax liability of

$$T = .01(\$1,000) + .02(\$1,000) + .03(\$1,000) + \ldots + .10(\$1,000)$$
$$= \$550.$$

The average tax rate paid by this individual is .055. This number is obtained, as before, by dividing the total tax liability by the tax base. If an individual's taxable income should increase to $11,000, his or her tax liability will increase to $660. The average tax rate that he or she pays increases to $.06 (= \$660/\$11,000)$ and the marginal rate that he or she pays is $.11 (= \$110/\$1,000)$. The individual's average tax rate rises with increases in the tax base, and the marginal tax rate exceeds the average tax rate. The relationships are shown in Figure 9.2. With a progressive tax rate, the tax liability of the individual and the revenue of the taxing authority increase more than in proportion to the increase in the tax base.

As you would anticipate, a *regressive* tax is one in which the average tax rate falls as the base rises (the average tax rate and the tax base are inversely related). It follows that the marginal tax rate will be less than the average tax rate. This relationship is shown in Figure 9.3. With a regressive tax, the tax liability of the individual and the revenue of the taxing authority will increase as the base increases up to a base of B_0 in Figure 9.3. It will fall as the base increases beyond B_0.

You should note that defining a tax as progressive, proportional, or regressive depends upon how the average tax rate varies as the base of the tax varies. Sales taxes are sometimes said to be regressive; this is not true. In the U.S., sales taxes are always levied in proportion to the tax base.

Progressive Tax   **Figure 9.2**

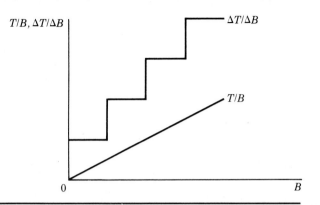

General Taxes and the Concept of Incidence

A tax is truly general if the allocation of resources is not altered when the tax is imposed. This means that a truly general tax must be a tax on individuals that the individuals are unable to escape or avoid paying by altering their behavior. The only truly general tax is a lump-sum tax imposed on the individual, which is unrelated to any economic or social variable subject to the individual's control. Any tax that is a function of variables subject to individual control can be avoided, at least in part. If the tax is a function of income,

Regressive Tax   **Figure 9.3**

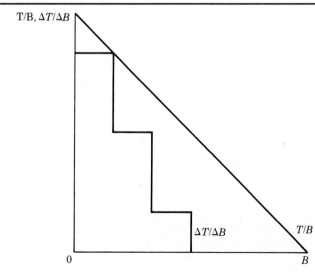

wealth, consumption, marital status, or choice of occupation, the individual can avoid the tax in whole or in part by altering his or her income, wealth, consumption, marital status, or choice of occupation. If the individual upon whom the tax is imposed can avoid all or part of the tax by changing behavior, he or she can shift part of the burden of the tax to other individuals. This means that the individuals who actually pay a tax may be different from those on whom the tax is initially levied. Put another way, the *actual* incidence of a tax may be different from the *legal* incidence. For example, a tax imposed on the sellers of gasoline will in part be borne by the buyers of gas. As we will see in Chapter 11, a tax of this sort will increase the cost of selling gasoline, which will shift up the supply curve and increase the price. Consumers will bear part of the burden of the tax by paying higher prices. The sellers shift part of the burden to consumers by cutting back on their output when confronted with the increase in the cost of doing business caused by the tax.

In part, the analysis of this chapter and the remaining chapters will be devoted to determining who actually bears the burden of the various types of taxes imposed in the United States. As we will see, all taxes can be shifted to a greater or lesser extent by those upon whom they are legally imposed.

Excess Burden

When a tax is imposed, the actual burden of the tax may exceed the dollar value of the taxes collected. This is sometimes called the excess burden, or dead weight loss, of a tax.[1] The excess burden results from the fact that taxes, as stated previously, affect individual behavior. Specifically, taxes tend to affect individuals when the individuals engage in transactions that involve exchange of resources. Taxes drive a wedge between the marginal value in use and the marginal cost of the good or service exchanged. This wedge prevents the individuals involved in the transactions from exploiting all of the potential gains from exchange.

The burden of a tax attributable to the actual tax dollars collected is lost to the taxpayers but not lost to society. Presumably individuals receive, through government acquisition, goods and services that have a market value equal to the taxes collected. The dead weight loss, however, involves no such compensating benefit. It results in an absolute reduction in buyer and seller surplus.

An example will help illustrate this idea of dead weight loss. Suppose a sales tax is placed on the sale of automobiles. The burden of the tax will exceed the amount of tax dollars collected because the tax, by increasing the cost of purchasing automobiles, will tend to cause potential buyers to purchase smaller automobiles

[1]See Chapter 11 for further discussion of the excess burden of a tax.

or forego the purchase altogether. The individuals who forego the purchase of an automobile will pay no tax; however, they will lose consumer surplus since they must shift their expenditures to their next best alternative. The individuals who cut back their expenditures will reduce their tax payments but will also lose consumer surplus as a result of the decrease in their rate of consumption. The losses to consumers of automobiles will exceed the amount of the tax that the consumers pay. As a result of the tax, they shift expenditure to what would be, in the absence of the tax, inferior alternatives. Sellers suffer a reduction in seller surplus since they face a reduction in the size and number of transactions as a result of the tax.

Personal Income Taxation: The Base

Personal income taxation represents an important source of revenue for the government. This is particularly true for the federal government. Data on the personal income tax are given in Table 9.1.

In 1974 the personal income tax generated almost 44 percent of total government tax revenue. The personal income tax collections of the federal government accounted for most (85.9 percent) of total personal income taxes collected. However, the federal government's share has been shrinking since 1955 as state governments have developed the personal income tax as a source of revenue.

Why Tax Personal Income?

It has been argued elsewhere that personal income taxation best meets the criteria of a general tax. A tax is general if it does not alter the *relative* prices of goods and services. If this is the case, the tax will not impose differential burdens on individuals and, as a consequence, individuals will not be able to escape the tax by changing their behavior (for example, by demanding less of a good when its relative price rises and/or supplying less of a good when its relative price falls). If the tax is general, the allocation of resources will not be altered when the tax is imposed.

There is no evidence to support the hypothesis that the personal income tax is truly general. We will argue later that personal income taxes will potentially alter the individual's allocation of time between work and leisure, will reduce the number of market exchanges, and, hence, indirectly alter relative prices and resource allocation through the impact on specialization. Personal income taxes alter the allocation of resources as individuals attempt to escape the tax by taking more of their income in kind rather than in money. The personal income tax also has increased the demand for public accountants and tax lawyers. In fact, the personal in-

Table 9.1   Tax Revenue: Personal Income Taxes by Level of Government

Year	Total Taxes All Governments	Personal Income Tax All Governments	Percent of Total Taxes	Personal Income Tax Federal	Percent of Total Personal Income Tax	Personal Income Tax State	Percent of Total Personal Income Tax	Personal Income Tax Local	Percent of Total Personal Income Tax
1950	51,100	16,533	32.4	15,745	95.2	724	4.3	64	.3
1955	81,072	29,984	37.0	28,747	95.8	1,094	3.6	143	.4
1960	113,120	43,178	38.2	40,715	94.2	2,209	5.1	254	.5
1965	144,953	52,882	36.5	48,792	92.2	3,657	6.9	433	.8
1969	222,708	96,157	43.2	87,249	90.7	7,527	7.8	1,381	1.4
1970	232,877	101,224	43.5	90,412	89.3	9,183	9.0	1,630	1.6
1971	232,252	98,130	42.3	86,230	87.8	10,153	10.3	1,747	1.7
1972	262,534	109,974	41.9	94,737	86.1	12,996	11.8	2,241	2.0
1973	286,595	121,240	42.3	103,246	85.1	15,587	12.8	2,406	1.9
1974	315,547	138,343	43.9	118,952	85.9	17,078	12.3	2,413	1.7

Source: U.S. Department of Commerce, Bureau of the Census, *Statistical Abstract of the United States*, 97th ed. (Washington, D.C.: Government Printing Office, 1976).

come tax seems to be no more general than most others taxes currently employed in the U.S. and other countries.[2] If the rationale for employing personal income as a tax base because it is a general tax is defective, why is it employed? We suggest four reasons. First, when it is coupled with withholding, the personal income tax is a relatively painless way to finance government activity. Second the costs of collection are low relative to the revenue collected. Third, it is a convenient device for redistributing income. Finally if the tax rate is progressive and if it is coupled with withholding, it will allow the government sector to grow (in a somewhat painless way) relative to the private sector. This, of course, is in the interest of the public officials who write and administer the tax laws.

The Definition of Income

An individual's income is his or her total flow of current production that may be consumed without impairing the source of the production. The source of current production is the individual's stock of wealth, which can either be held in physical, nonhuman form (buildings, machines, inventories, land) or in the form of human capital. Human capital consists of the education, experience, and training that the individual has acquired as well as personal characteristics such as his or her punctuality, honesty, diligence, drive, sense of humor and the like.

Income is a flow that is generated by the individual's stock of wealth. There are two methods that can be employed to measure income. The first method attempts to measure the flow of income directly. In other words, an attempt is made to measure the value of the flow of current production less the costs of generating that flow. The second method measures income by calculating the net change in the stock of wealth and adding consumption to that change. This is known as the accretion method.

To illustrate these two methods, suppose that an individual owns 1000 rabbits, A_0, at the beginning of the period over which income is to be measured. The stock of these rabbits grows at a net rate of 10 percent, g, per year. The net growth rate is the birth rate less the death rate. We assume that the cost to the individual of maintaining the rabbits is zero. Under the flow definition of income (Y_f), the income of this individual is

$$Y_f = gA_0 = .10(1,000) = 100 \text{ rabbits per year.} \qquad (1)$$

The 100 rabbits may be saved (added to the stock A_0) or consumed.

---

[2]These are discussed in subsequent chapters.

Of course, the individual may choose to save some (S) and consume some (C). In either case, however, her income is 100 rabbits.

$$Y_f = gA_0 = C + S \tag{2}$$

If we were to employ the accretion method to measure income, we would take the difference between her stock of wealth at the end of the year (A_1) and her stock of wealth at the beginning of the year (A_0) and add consumption to this difference.

$$Y_a = A_1 - A_0 + C \tag{3}$$

Note that her stock of wealth at the end of the year (A_1) will equal the sum of her initial stock (A_0) and the growth in the stock (gA_0) less her consumption (C); that is, $A_1 = A_0 + gA_0 - C$.

$$Y_a = A_0 + gA_0 - A_0 - C + C = gA_0 = C + S \tag{4}$$

Since Y_f in Equation (1) is equal to Y_a in Equation (4), the two methods of measuring income yield the same results.

Suppose something happens to change the net growth rate in the stock of rabbits. Maybe a fox, which was occasionally helping himself to the rabbits, dies so that the death rate decreases and causes the net growth rate to increase to .20. The income flow, expressed as an annual rate, will immediately increase to

$$Y_f = gA_0 = .20(1,000) = 200 \text{ rabbits.} \tag{5}$$

Employing the accretion method of measuring income, we would obtain

$$Y_a = A_1 - A_0 + C = C + S = 200 \text{ rabbits.} \tag{6}$$

Again, both methods yield the same results.

There is another way by which income can be determined. Above, we measured the flow of rabbits produced from a given and unchanged stock of rabbits as the net growth rate changed. On the other hand, we could, conceptually, hold the flow of rabbits unchanged at 100 as the growth rate changes and calculate the stock of rabbits necessary to produce a flow of 100. This is done below.

$$A = Y/g = 100/.20 = 500 \text{ rabbits.}$$

In other words, the flow of 100 rabbits could be produced with a stock of only 500 rabbits after the change in the net growth rate. The individual could consume 500 additional rabbits this year (and this year only) and, with the remaining 500 rabbits, produce an annual flow of 100 rabbits as before.

What is the individual's income? Is it 600 rabbits—the 500 additional that she could consume this year *only* plus the annual flow of 100—or is it 200 rabbits as computed initially? The answer is that both are correct. In one case, we hold the stock of rabbits unchanged at 1,000 and observe the change in the flow that results when g changes. In the other case, we hold the flow fixed at 100 and observe the change in the stock required to produce the flow as g changes. The two answers tell us the same thing (that g has doubled). The fact that it is possible to obtain two different numbers as a result of the same phenomena introduces some problems into the income tax treatment of capital gains, saving, and gifts. We discuss these problems in a subsequent section of this chapter.

Income in Kind

In practice, many problems arise in determining what constitutes income. Wages, salaries, tips, bonuses, dividends, interest receipts, commissions, and other similar money payments are included as taxable income. These are relatively easy to measure. Income, however, is not always received in the form of money and is not always identified as income. Plush executive offices, air-conditioned automobiles for sales representatives, company-financed lunches and dinners, business trips in which the individual travels first class are just some examples of income received in kind (income in the form of goods rather than money) that goes untaxed. To the extent that this type of income is not included as taxable income, the cost to an employee of receiving income in this form will fall relative to receiving income in, say, the form of wages. Entrepreneurs will find that it is cheaper to pay a given amount of real income to an employee by offering more income in kind, which is not identified as such for tax purposes, and less money income. This will cause a change in the allocation of resources as individuals adjust their contractual arrangements to escape the tax.

Homemakers perform many valuable services that otherwise would have to be purchased in a market. The income that would result from these transactions would be subject to the income tax. However, the implicit income that the homemaker receives for the services he or she performs are not subject to tax. The income tax raises the price of household services contracted for in the market relative to the price of the same services when they are produced within the household. Consequently, the income tax encourages do-it-yourself household production. The effect of this is to reduce the gains that individuals would enjoy from specialization and exchange. A few examples of do-it-yourself household production that are encouraged by the income tax are gardening, house painting, growing vegetables, installing a patio, building bookshelves, and refinishing furniture.

Compensating Differentials

Ideally, the base of the income tax should include only real income, not nominal income. Some jobs are particularly hazardous or unpleasant. If individuals are to be attracted to these jobs, they will require additional money income. At the margin, the additional money income earned in, say, relatively hazardous employments when compared to relatively safe employments requiring the same skills is just the amount necessary to compensate workers for accepting the hazardous jobs. The difference in money incomes is a nominal difference, not a real difference. At the margin, the real income of workers employed in safe jobs will equal the real income of workers employed in hazardous jobs. If real incomes were not the same, workers would move to take advantage of the difference and their action would push real incomes towards equality at the margin.

An income tax generally will discriminate in favor of relatively safe or pleasant employments. For example, suppose that, prior to an income tax being levied, employment in a hazardous industry pays $10,000 per year while employment in a safe industry, which requires the same skills, pays $8,000 per year. The $2,000 differential is the amount required to equate real incomes between jobs in the two industries at the margin. Consequently, there is no incentive for individuals to change jobs. If a proportional income tax of 10 percent is levied against money income, the after-tax incomes in these two employments will fall to $9,000 and $7,200 respectively. The after-tax money income differential is now only $1,800 between the two employments and, by assumption, a $2,000 differential is necessary to equate real incomes. Individuals employed in the hazardous industry will quit their jobs and offer their services in the safe industry. This will have the effect of raising before- and after-tax money incomes in the hazardous industry and lowering them in the safe industry. The process will continue; that is, the supply of labor services will continue to fall in the hazardous industry and increase in the safe industry until the after-tax differential in money incomes is returned to $2,000.

Exemptions

The problems discussed above are problems associated with defining and measuring income. Once income has been defined and a method of measurement has been determined, certain deductions and exemptions can be subtracted from measured income (adjusted gross income) to arrive at the final figure (taxable income) upon which the tax will be levied. Federal legislation regarding the personal income tax allows a number of deductions and exemptions from measured income when computing the taxable income base. For our purposes it is enough to list some of the most important ones.

Each taxpayer is allowed personal exemptions equal to the number of dependent individuals in his or her household. Currently, each personal exemption is equal to $750. An individual is defined to be a dependent of the taxpayer if more than 50 percent of the individual's financial support over the course of the year is paid by the taxpayer. An additional personal exemption is allowed for individuals who are blind and/or over the age of 65.

As further deductions from adjusted gross income, individuals may choose to itemize certain allowable deductions or choose the minimum standard deduction, or they may be eligible for the low-income allowance. The low-income allowance exempts the individual from paying any income tax if his or her income is less than $1,700 and the individual is single, or less than $2,100 if the individual is married. However, if the individual is claimed as a dependent by someone else, he or she is ineligible for the low-income allowance. If the taxpayer's income exceeds the limits of the low-income allowance, he or she may choose the minimum standard deduction in computing taxable income. The minimum standard deduction allows the individual to deduct an amount equal to 16 percent of adjusted gross income in computing taxable income. An upper limit, however, is placed upon the amount of the allowable deduction. If the taxpayer is single, the maximum allowable deduction when the minimum standard deduction is employed is $2,400. If the taxpayer is married, the maximum deduction is $2,800.

The third alternative open to the taxpayer is to itemize his or her deductions. The following lists and discusses briefly some of the deductions from adjusted gross income an individual may take in computing taxable income.

1. One half (up to $150) of the annual amount paid for medical care insurance. Actual expenditures on drugs that exceed one percent of adjusted gross income. Actual expenditures for doctors, dentists, nurses, and hospitals that exceed three percent of adjusted gross income.

2. State and local income taxes, gasoline taxes, sales taxes, and property taxes, among others, may be deducted from adjusted gross income.

3. Interest expense on home mortgages, personal bank notes, life insurance loans, bank credit cards, and installment plan purchases may be deducted.

4. Contributions to recognized religious, charitable, educational, scientific, or literary organizations are deductible in computing taxable income.

5. Losses due to casualty or theft that exceed the amount covered by insurance may be deducted from adjusted gross income.

6. Certain miscellaneous deductions are allowed, such as alimony, business use of the home, contributions to political candidates, and union dues, among others.

The above deductions are some of those that are more important in calculating taxable income. Once taxable income has been computed, the individual's tax liability is simply the product of taxable income and the applicable tax rate.

Personal Income Taxation: The Tax Rate

The federal income tax rate, which is applied to the taxable income base, is progressive. This means that the marginal tax rate exceeds the average tax rate. With a progressive tax rate, the individual's

Table 9.2   Rate Schedule

Taxable Income		Tax Rate
Over	But Not Over	Married, Filing Jointly
$ 0	$ 3,000	14.0%
3,000	3,150	15.5
3,150	3,950	17.0
3,950	4,150	18.5
4,150	7,950	19.0
7,950	8,150	21.0
8,150	11,950	22.0
11,950	12,150	23.5
12,150	15,950	25.0
15,950	16,150	27.0
16,150	20,000	28.0
20,000	24,000	32.0
24,000	28,000	36.0
28,000	32,000	39.0
32,000	36,000	42.0
36,000	40,000	45.0
40,000	44,000	48.0
44,000	52,000	50.0
52,000	64,000	53.0
64,000	76,000	55.0
76,000	88,000	58.0
88,000	100,000	60.0
100,000	120,000	62.0
120,000	140,000	64.0
140,000	160,000	66.0
160,000	180,000	68.0
180,000	200,000	69.0
200,000	—	70.0

Source: Department of Treasury, Internal Revenue Service, Package X-Vol. 1, pp. 28-31.

tax liability will increase more than in proportion to increases in taxable income. The tax rate schedule that is applicable to the taxpayer depends upon whether the individual is single, married but filing a separate return, the head of a household, or married and filing a joint return. The tax rate schedule in effect for 1976 and applicable to individuals who were married and filing joint returns appears in Table 9.2. The lowest marginal tax rate is 14 percent and applies to taxable incomes of $3,000 or less. The highest marginal tax rate is 70 percent and applies to taxable incomes in excess of $200,000.

Caution should be employed in interpreting the tax schedule in Table 9.2. Remember that the average tax rate is less than the marginal tax rate under progressive taxes. Also, the rates presented in Table 9.2 apply to taxable income. Deductions drive a wedge between adjusted gross income and taxable income so that the average tax rate on adjusted gross income will be less than on taxable income. The tax, however, *may* be just as progressive against adjusted gross income as against taxable income. Whether it is will depend upon the distribution of deductions among the various income categories. Some data regarding this point are presented in Table 9.3 and Figure 9.4.

The data in Table 9.3 indicate that in 1974 individuals paid, on

Effective Tax Rates, 1974   **Table 9.3**

Taxable Returns (in dollars)	Billions of Dollars			Tax as a Percentage of Adjusted Gross Income	Tax as a Percentage of Taxable Income
	Adjusted Gross Income	Taxable Income	Income Tax	Average Rate	Average Rate
Total	$906.1	$573.3	$123.7	13.65	21.56
Under 2,999	8.5	1.5	.2	2.3	13.3
3,000–4,999	33.1	13.0	2.0	6.0	15.3
5,000–9,999	146.4	80.6	13.6	9.2	16.8
10,000–14,999	192.7	119.1	21.5	11.1	18.0
15,000–24,999	281.9	192.5	37.8	13.4	19.6
25,000–49,999	142.0	105.7	25.0	17.6	23.6
50,000–99,999	46.1	36.5	12.2	26.4	33.4
100,000–499,999	25.1	20.1	9.2	36.6	45.7
500,000–999,999	2.1	1.6	1.0	47.6	62.5
1,000,000 and over	2.2	1.7	1.1	50.0	64.7

Source: U.S. Internal Revenue Service, *Statistics of Income, Individual Income Tax Returns.*

Figure 9.4

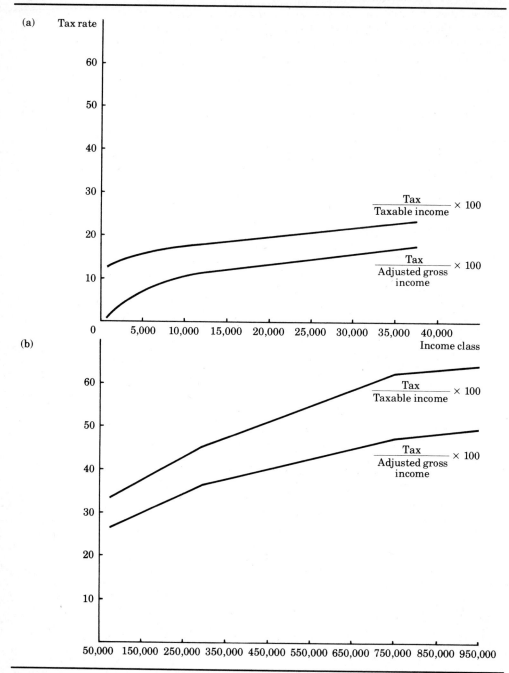

the average, 13.65 percent of total adjusted gross income in federal income taxes. If the average tax rate is computed by using total taxable income, it is equal to 21.56 percent. While the average effective tax rates for each income category are less when adjusted gross income is used as a base rather than taxable income, the average effective rate is progressive with respect to adjusted gross income as it is with respect to taxable income—that is, the average rates rise with income in both cases.

In fact, the federal income tax is somewhat more progressive (the average rate is rising faster) with respect to adjusted gross income than it is with respect to taxable income for income classes up to $15,000 (see Figure 9.4). For income classes from $15,000 through $50,000, the progressivity of the tax appears to be roughly the same with respect to both adjusted gross income and taxable income. For income classes from $50,000 through $750,000, the tax appears to be more progressive with respect to adjusted gross income. For income classes in excess of $750,000, the progressivity of the tax is roughly equal with respect to both taxable and adjusted gross income.

The Timing of the Income Stream

Progressive income taxation introduces a problem with respect to the timing of the income stream. Suppose that an individual's taxable income varies from year to year but that the average annual amount that he earns is $10,000. Let the following represent his taxable income stream:

Year 1 income = $ 2,500
Year 2 income =   17,500
Year 3 income =   15,000
Year 4 income =   5,000

His average income over the four years is $10,000. Suppose the tax rate schedule that applies to him is the following:

Taxable Income	Tax Rate
0–$2,500	10%
2,501–5,000	15%
5,001–10,000	20%
10,001–15,000	25%
15,001–20,000	30%

His total tax payment over the four years is $7,375. If, on the other hand, he had earned exactly $10,000 in each of the four years, his total tax payment over the four years would have been $6,500. Clearly, progressive tax rates discriminate against individuals whose incomes vary a great deal from year to year. On the average, they will pay more in taxes even though they earn no more income than an individual whose income does not vary.

The incomes of professional athletes, real estate brokers, actors, and authors are subject to wide annual fluctuations. For this reason, the Revenue Act of 1964 allowed individuals to average their income when computing their tax liability. The procedures are complicated and we will not discuss them here. It is sufficient to point out that, while the averaging procedures which are currently allowed reduce some of the adverse effect of a progressive tax rate on individuals whose incomes fluctuate, the progressive rate still discriminates against these individuals.

Capital Gains

Capital gains that arise through increase in the net productivity of investment (growth rate of the stock, g) are considered income under our definition and will be measured as such, using either the accretion method of measuring income or the flow method. The increase in the flow generated by the stock will be reflected in an increase in the present value of the stock relative to the value of other stocks and current consumption goods. Taxing the increased value of the stock presently or taxing the increased flow in the future will yield precisely the same results in terms of the individual's flow of consumption and saving.

Capital gains may, however, arise from another source. The rate of interest may decline due to an increase in the preference of individuals for future, as opposed to present, consumption. The decline in the rate of interest will not result in an increase in the future flow of goods from existing stocks although it will cause the present value of existing stocks of long-lived assets to rise relative to the prices of current consumption goods. The existing stocks will now exchange for more current consumption goods than previously. In this sense, the owners of the stocks experience a gain. In terms of our rabbit example, while it is true that the existing stock of 1,000 rabbits will exchange for more current consumption goods than previously, an increase in the rate of consumption of the stock will reduce the rate of future flow generated by the stock below 100 rabbits. This was not the case when the change in the present value of the stock was induced by a change in the stock's net productivity—that is, an increase in g. Under our definition of income, capital gains that arise from a decline in the rate of interest do not represent income.

The situation is analogous to one in which the tastes and preferences of individuals change in favor of ice cream and against candy. The producers of ice cream are now more wealthy, not because they can produce more ice cream with a given amount of resources, but because the price of ice cream will rise relative to that of candy. The producers of ice cream can buy more candy now with a given amount of ice cream. On the other hand, the producers of candy are less wealthy. A given amount of candy will exchange for less ice cream. The same thing happens when the rate of interest changes. The present prices of stocks, which yield future flows, rise relative to the prices of current consumption goods. The owners of the stocks experience a gain. The owners of present consumption goods experience a loss. If a case is made for counting the gains as income when computing tax liability, a case is made also for allowing the owners of present consumption goods to count their loss when computing their tax liability. Roughly speaking, if this were done, the tax receipts of the government would not change with changes in the rate of interest.

In practice, of course, it is very difficult for tax authorities to distinguish between changes in capital values induced by changes in net productivity and changes in capital values that are due to changes in the rate of interest. As a result, all capital gains are treated as income, whether they arise from changes in net productivity or from changes in the preferences for future vs. present goods. The losses to the owners of current consumption goods, however, are ignored.

Capital gains are not taxed as they accrue. They are taxed when realized and have been subject to special treatment. Capital gains on property held less than nine months are taxed as ordinary income. Long-term capital gains (property held over nine months) are taxed at a maximum effective rate of 28 percent. This results from the fact that individuals are allowed to exclude 60 percent of the gain from taxable income and that the maximum marginal tax rate is 70 percent. Up to $3,000 in capital losses may be deducted from other capital gains and other income in any one year. Should an individual's loss exceed $3,000, he or she may carry the residual forward into subsequent years. The 60 percent of the long-term capital gain which is excluded from taxable income is taxed in the following manner: The individual's tax liability is equal to 15 percent of 60 percent of the capital gains minus $10,000 or 15 percent of one-half the capital gains minus one-half of other income tax paid, whichever is greater. This applies to capital gains realized in November and December of 1978. However, for gains realized in 1979 and after, this additional tax on the 60 percent exclusion will not apply.

Allocation Effects of the Income Tax

We now turn to a discussion of the allocative effects of the income tax. Income taxes affect the allocation of resources in the following areas: (1) the work-leisure trade-off, (2) the incentives to save, (3) the incentives to invest in risky assets, and (4) the pecuniary income and income in kind trade-off. To the extent that the income tax affects these and other decisions, it will change the allocation of resources. This change may cause the economy to operate less efficiently. By driving a wedge between social costs (or benefits) and private costs (or benefits), the income tax distorts the allocation of resources. In this sense the income tax and other taxes cause externalities. To see this, consider income earned through labor. An employer pays workers the value of their marginal product (that is, the value of their contribution to production at the margin). This is the marginal benefit to society of the workers' activity. The worker, on the other hand, receives a wage reduced by the amount of the tax. His or her private return or benefit is less than the social return he or she generates. In the process of attempting to correct externality problems caused by the existence of public goods, a government introduces new externalities into the economy through taxation. Another way to look at this is to recall our definition of externalities in Chapter 3. An external effect exists when the activity of one economic unit (in the case of taxes, this unit is the government) damages another economic unit (the taxpayer) outside normal market channels. The coercive nature of taxes clearly imposes nonmarket costs on taxpayers, that is, externalities. The inefficiency caused by these externalities is part of the cost of government activity. The cost of providing a public good will exceed the value of the taxes used to fund that good by an amount at least equal to the inefficiency generated by the tax. Looking at the problem from an economy-wide point of view, the tax system, by reducing the efficiency of the economy, causes fewer goods and services to be available than would be available without that system. The cost to society of the tax, resulting from producing fewer goods and services, is called the welfare cost of the tax.

Application

The Cost of Public Funds

We have argued that the personal income tax is not a truly general tax. It introduces distortions in the allocation of resources (1) by driving a wedge between the relative price of income in terms of leisure, (2) by making receipts of income in kind more attractive at the margin than income in money, (3) by increasing the allocation of resources devoted to tax avoidance, and (4) through its impact on specialization, by making household production more attractive at the margin than market production. These distortions are costly because they reduce the utility that could be acquired by individuals with their scarce resources. Consequently, the cost of financing public goods through income taxation exceeds the dollars collected by the tax. For example, if the government collects $150,000 in taxes and uses this to purchase a military vehicle, the cost of that vehicle, in fact, exceeds $150,000 worth of foregone private goods because of distortions in the allocation of resources introduced by the method of taxing. The cost of the vehicle, measured in terms of the value of private goods foregone, may be $158,000 even though only $150,000 was *collected* in taxes and paid to the producer of the vehicle. The additional $8,000 is sometimes called a welfare cost.

Edgar K. Browning has estimated *some* of these additional costs associated with income taxation.[3] His estimate of the additional cost incurred in 1974 due to distortions in the supply of work effort appears in Table 9.4. Column 5 presents the estimated total

Total Welfare Cost by Marginal Rate Class, 1974   Table 9.4

Marginal Federal Income Tax Rate	Increment Due to Other Income Taxes	Effective Marginal Rate	Income by Income Class[a]	Total Welfare Cost by Income Class[a]
14%	20%	34%	$ 27,603	$ 319.1
15	20	35	17,443	213.7
16	20	36	20,403	264.8
17	19	36	24,485	317.3
18	19	37	5,405	74.0
19	19	38	146,828	2,120.2
21	18	39	21,782	331.2
22	18	40	148,265	2,372.2
23	18	41	3,857	64.8
24	17	41	21,340	358.7
25	17	42	121,023	2,134.9
27	16	43	8,577	158.6
28	16	44	59,426	1,150.5
29	15	44	4,688	90.8
31	15	46	3,853	83.6
32	14	46	32,469	687.0
34	14	48	1,705	39.0
35	13	48	224	5.2
36	13	49	18,884	453.4
38	12	50	936	23.4
39	12	51	10,556	274.6
40	11	51	1,098	28.6
41	10	51	67	1.7
42	9	51	7,066	183.8
45	8	53	5,446	153.0
48	7	55	3,403	103.3
50	6	56	24,842	779.0
Total			$741,706	$12,786.8

[a]Dollar figures in millions.

[3]Edgar K. Browning, "The Marginal Cost of Public Funds," *Journal of Political Economy,* Vol. 84 (April 1976), pp. 283–98.

welfare cost for each tax bracket. Summing these figures gives a total welfare cost over all brackets of about $12.8 billion. If the costs of administration and enforcement are added, the welfare costs of acquiring public funds through personal income taxation are estimated to be $19 billion in 1974. Government expenditure programs financed by the income tax would have had to have been at least $19 billion more productive than the private expenditures foregone in 1974 in order to have improved the allocation of resources, which would have resulted in the absence of the government expenditures.

The Income Tax and Work Effort

To analyze the effects of the income tax on the work-leisure trade-off, we make the simplifying assumption that all income is earned through work effort. Assume the tax is proportional. Consider an individual who must decide how much time to devote to generating income (work) and how much to leisure. The choice is depicted in Figure 9.5, where leisure is measured on the horizontal axis and income on the vertical axis. Both income and leisure are economic goods. The individual's preferences for leisure and income can be represented by an indifference map. In Figure 9.5, I_1, I_2, and I_3 are representative indifference curves. Let $\bar{L}$ be the time period in which the choice is to be made. This could be 24 hours, 1 week (168 hours), 1 month, etc. If the individual chooses not to work, then he can consume $\bar{L}$ leisure. The line $\bar{L}Y$ is the individual's budget constraint, which is determined by the total amount of time available, $\bar{L}$, and his market wage rate, w. The individual's income for period Y is given by

$$Y = w(\bar{L} - L) \qquad (7)$$

where L is the amount of leisure he consumes and $\bar{L} - L$ the amount of time in period $\bar{L}$ that he works. When rewritten as

$$Y = -wL + w\bar{L},$$

we obtain the budget line $\overline{YL}$, which has a slope, $-w$, and a vertical intercept, $w\bar{L}$ ($=\bar{Y}$). If the individual worked for the entire period, his income would be $\bar{Y} = w\bar{L}$. The combination of income and leisure that maximizes the individual's utility in this example is (Y^*, L^*) where $(\bar{L}-L^*)$ is devoted to work effort. If a proportional tax of rate t (where t is a number between 0 and 1) is now placed on income, the individual's disposable or after-tax income, Y^d, will be given by

$$Y^d = Y - tY = (1-t)w(\overline{L}-L) = -(1-t)wL + (1-t)w\overline{L}.$$

The tax rotates the individual's budget line to $\overline{Y^d L}$ (in Figure 9.5). The slope of this line is $-(1-t)w$, which reflects the rate at which the individual can convert leisure into income after the tax. The tax results in an after-tax, or net of tax, wage rate that is less than the before-tax market rate w. The addition of the income tax induces the individual to consume leisure of L' per unit of time. His disposable income is $Y^{d'}$. In this case, the application of the tax induced the individual to increase his consumption of leisure and reduce work effort. He does this to reduce the burden of the tax.

The move from L^* to L' is the result of two effects, an income effect and a substitution effect. To separate these two effects, we give the individual additional income so that he faces a budget line with a slope $-(1-t)w$, which is equal to the negative of the after-tax wage, but tangent to his original indifference curve I_2. The substitution effect that results from the lower price of leisure is given by the move from L^* to L''. The decrease in the relative price of leisure is brought about by the application of the tax. The move from L'' to L' is the income effect. The tax not only reduces the relative price of leisure but also reduces real income. If leisure is a normal good, the reduction in real income brought about by the tax will induce the individual to consume less leisure, that is, to work more. The two effects work in opposite directions in our ex-

Figure 9.5

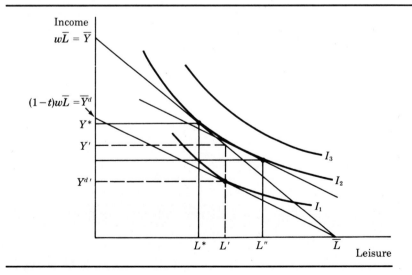

ample. The substitution effect brings about an increase in the consumption of leisure (and less work effort) since the relative price of leisure falls. The income effect results in an increase in work effort (the move from L'' to L'). Since the substitution effect is larger than the income effect, the overall result of the tax is that work effort is reduced (more leisure is consumed) in this example.

It is, of course, possible for the income effect to be larger than the substitution effect. This will cause an increase in work effort. If, on the other hand, leisure is an inferior good, both the income and substitution effects work together to induce a decrease in work effort. No matter what the effect on work effort, the application of the tax by itself lowers the utility of the individual and alters his income-leisure choice.

In Figure 9.5, the tax that the individual pays is $Y' - Y^{d'}$. Presumably, this tax is used to provide public goods and services that yield benefits to the individual. These goods are not considered in our example. They will affect the rate at which the individual is willing to exchange income for leisure and, thus, will alter somewhat the above results. For instance, the provision of public parks may make leisure time more productive, which alone will induce the individual to consume more leisure.

A progressive tax of the same yield will generally augment the results obtained for a proportional tax. In Figure 9.6, the line $\overline{LY}$ again represents the pretax budget line and $\overline{LY^d}$ represents the after-tax budget line with a proportional tax. With this tax, the individual consumes L', which may be more or less than his pretax leisure consumption. The yield of this proportional tax is equal to AB.

Figure 9.6

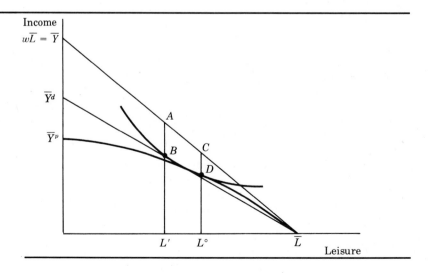

The curved line $\overline{LY^p}$ is the budget constraint with a progressive tax. This tax structure has the same real impact as the proportional tax, since it leaves the individual on the same after-tax indifference curve. With this rate structure, the ratio of the tax payment to pretax income increases as income increases. A progressive rate schedule causes the after-tax wage rate to decrease as income increases. This means that the rate at which leisure can be converted into income decreases as income increases. Note that in this case, the actual tax payment CD is less than the tax paid with the proportional tax AB. However, the amount of leisure consumed is greater with the progressive tax. The marginal tax rate is higher with the progressive tax, meaning that the cost of a marginal hour of leisure time is less. This increases the consumption of leisure. Furthermore, the tax rate increases as income increases. Consequently, the work-disincentive effect of a progressive tax will increase as income increases.

Application

Income Taxes and the Incentive to Work

Assuming leisure is a normal good, we know that the income tax, both progressive and proportional, has two opposing effects on work effort. The income tax shifts the budget line downward; thus, the income effect will result in less leisure being consumed and more work effort. The substitution effect works in the opposite direction. The tax decreases the price of leisure, resulting in the consumption of more leisure. Whether the substitution effect dominates the income effect, causing a decrease in work effort, or whether the income effect dominates the substitution effect, causing an increase in work effort, can only be determined through empirical investigation.

D. B. Fields and W. T. Stanbury[4] set out to measure the extent of the income and substitution effects. They repeated an experiment conducted by G. F. Break.[5] Specifically, both studies examined the effect of the high marginal tax rates resulting from the progressive income tax in the United Kingdom. Both studies used a sample of professionals (accountants and solicitors) who are free to vary their work effort and are knowledgeable about the marginal tax rates. While not giving the magnitudes, Fields and Stanbury

---

[4]D. B. Fields and W. T. Stanbury, "Income and Incentives to Work: Some Additional Empirical Evidence," *American Economic Review,* Vol. 61 (June 1971), pp. 435–43.

[5]G. F. Break, "Income Taxes and Incentives to Work: Some Additional Empirical Evidence," *American Economic Review,* Vol. 47 (September 1957), pp. 529–47.

found that 18.9 percent of their sample experienced net disincentive effects (substitution effects greater than income effects) and 11.2 percent experienced incentive effects (income effects greater than substitution effects). This difference turned out to be statistically significant—more individuals experienced a net disincentive effect than a net incentive effect. Fields and Stanbury also found that the continuation of the high marginal rates seems to be causing an increase in the disincentive effects over time when they compared their results with those of the earlier study by Break.

Effects of the Income Tax on Investment

The income tax will have an effect on investment. At this point we will not make a distinction between financial investment and investment in real assets. That is, we will not distinguish between buying stock or making an economic investment such as building a factory. We will spend more time on this distinction when we discuss the corporate income tax in Chapter 10. For the present, what we are concerned with is the effect of the income tax on an individual's willingness to purchase an asset that will yield a stream of income in the future. Anything that alters this willingness will change the rate of capital accumulation and the growth rate of the economy.

Placing a tax on future income streams will have two effects: (1) the tax will reduce the total income stream, and (2) the tax will change the riskiness of the investment. Since the future is uncertain, investment will always involve an element of risk. When someone invests $100 in the stock market, he or she hopes to come out ahead on the transaction. The individual may, however, lose all or part of the $100. This element of risk affects individuals' investment decisions. For most individuals, riskiness is undesirable and will not be incurred without the prospect of higher gains.

We can demonstrate the effect of the income tax on investment by using a simple numerical example. Let a given investment have a potential gain that we can summarize by using what is called the expected value of the investment. The expected value of an investment is nothing more than the weighted average of all possible returns. The risk can be thought of as the size of the potential variation from this average. Suppose an investment has an average expected return of 10 dollars, consisting of a 50-percent chance that the return is 20 dollars and a 50-percent chance that the return is zero. This investment is riskier than one that has a 10-dollar expected return consisting of a 50-percent chance of a 9-dollar return and a 50-percent chance of an 11-dollar return. The larger the potential variation in the actual return, the more risky the investment. The standard deviation of the return is sometimes used as a measure of risk because it measures the deviation of the average return.

A numerical example can be used to determine the effects of the income tax on the expected gains and riskiness of the investment. Suppose you have the opportunity to invest $4,000 for one year with a 90-percent chance of getting back $5,000 and a 10-percent chance of getting back nothing. Put another way, you have a 90-percent chance of gaining $1,000 and a 10-percent chance of losing $4,000. The expected or average gain is

$$.9(1,000) + .1(-4,000) = 500.$$

The $500 expected gain gives an expected rate of return of 500/4,000, or 12.5 percent. The standard deviation, which measures the risk, equals

$$\sqrt{.9(1,000-500)^2 + .1(-4,000-500)^2} = 1,500.$$

Suppose a 50-percent tax on income from investments is enacted. The effect of this tax depends on the nature of the individual or business firm being taxed. If it is an established business with other income, it can write off or carry forward the loss against these other business earnings. In our example, this means that if the $4,000 is dollars lost, the business can reduce its other taxable income by $4,000 and thus reduce its tax payment by $2,000. In essence, this means it only stands to lose $2,000. However, the potential gains are also cut in half. Given the 50-percent tax with a full write-off possible, the expected earnings of the investment become

$$.9(500) + .1(-2,000) = 250,$$

which reduces the rate of return to 6.25 percent. The tax has reduced the rate of return by 50 percent. This reduction will reduce the supply of investment funds available, which will reduce overall investment activity and will tend to reduce the growth of output in the economy. On the other hand, the riskiness of the investment as given by the standard deviation is now

$$\sqrt{.9(500-250)^2 + .1(-2000-250)^2} = 750.$$

This reduction in the risk of the investment occurs because the potential loss is reduced by the amount of the tax savings the write-off allows. This means that, for firms that can use the write-off, the government will share part of the risk.

The overall effect of the tax in this situation is to cause less overall investment activity, but a relative increase in the number of risky investments out of the total investment that takes place. To the extent that there is some socially efficient level of risk involved in investment, and if this level is the equilibrium level in a competitive economy, the tax on investment income will cause an inefficiently high level of risky investment activity.

If an individual or firm has no other sources of investment income and if failure of the investment causes the firm to fail, the write-off of the tax loss will not be possible. In this situation, any gains will be taxed but all losses will be borne by the investor. The expected return becomes

$$.9(500) + .1(-4,000) = 50.$$

Without the write-off, the expected return is now only $50.

Without the offset of losses, the expected return to risky investments is greatly diminished (from 250 with the offset to 50 without). Furthermore, since the government shares in any potential gain but not in a potential loss, the risk of the investment is not reduced in a significant way by the introduction of the tax.

The necessity of having other investment income to take advantage of the tax write-off places new investors and firms at a relative disadvantage compared to established ones. This makes the establishment of new firms more difficult and expansion of existing firms easier.

The Effect of the Income Tax on the Saving Decision

Under the present income tax laws, there is what is called a double taxation on saving. The double taxation occurs because income is taxed as it is received and then the interest earned on that portion of income saved is also taxed. This tends to reduce the incentive to save (for future consumption) and encourage present consumption.

To see how the income tax distorts the savings decision, consider Figure 9.7. Here we assume that (1) there is a single consumption good; (2) there are two periods, period 0 and period 1; (3) our individual has an initial endowment of income of I_0 in period 0 and I_1 in period 1; (4) for simplicity, the price of the consumption good is constant in both periods; and (5) there are perfect capital markets so that the individual can both borrow and lend at interest rate r. Given these assumptions, the present value (PV) of our individual's income stream is

$$PV = I_0 + \frac{I_1}{1+r}. \tag{8}$$

Figure 9.7

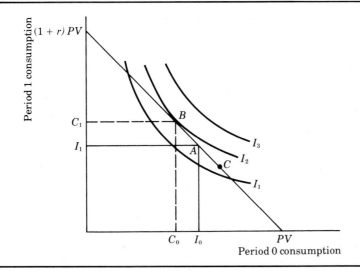

Since prices are constant, the individual's budget constraint indicating his possible consumption choices (in dollar terms) in the two periods is:

$$C_0 + \frac{C_1}{1+r} = PV = I_0 + \frac{I_1}{1+r} \qquad (9)$$

or

$$C_1 = -(1+r)C_0 + (1+r)PV.$$

This budget line (see Figure 9.7) has a vertical intercept of $(1+r)PV$ and a horizontal intercept of PV. Point A is determined by the individual's income endowment (I_1, I_0). The slope of the budget line is determined by the market interest rate r. The indifference curves (I_1, I_2, I_3) indicate our individual's preferences for present vs. future consumption. The individual maximizes his utility by picking point B and consuming C_0 in period 0 and C_1 in period 1. At point B the individual is saving $I_0 - C_0$ of his income in period 0 so that he can consume $C_1 - I_1$ more than his endowment in period 1. Since the interest rate, r, is positive, the increased consumption in period 1 $(C_1 - I_1)$ exceeds the savings in period 0 $(I_0 - C_0)$. If the individual had picked a point like C below A, he would, instead of saving, be borrowing and would consume more than I_0 in period 0 and less than I_1 in period 1.

Let's assume that a tax of rate t is placed on income but that interest income is exempt from the tax. The tax shifts our individual's endowment point down to D (see Figure 9.8). His disposable endowment income in the two periods is $(1-t)I_0$ and $(1-t)I_1$, exclusive of any interest income, respectively. If both C_0 and C_1 are normal goods, the tax will reduce the individual's consumption of both goods.

However, since interest income is exempt from the tax, the tax causes a parallel shift in the budget line and does not distort the relative price facing the individual of present vs. future consumption. If, as is presently the case, interest income is not exempt, an individual who saved would pay tax on the interest from savings. If the individual saved s dollars in period 0, the interest on that would be $r{\cdot}s$ and the tax would be $t{\cdot}r{\cdot}s$, leaving him $(1-t)r{\cdot}s$ after taxes. This would cause his budget line to rotate downward around point D so that the new after-tax budget line would be $FD(1-t)PV$. The slope of that part of the line between D and F would be $-[1+(1-t)r]$. The rate at which the individual can substitute future for present consumption is decreased by the tax on interest income, since $1+r > 1+(1-t)r$. The price of future consumption has increased; that is, the return to saving has decreased. This will tend to discourage savings and encourage present consumption. When the tax is placed on interest income, our individual increases his present consumption and decreases his savings (see Figure 9.8).

As can be seen from Figure 9.8, the tax on income, including a tax on interest income, tends to reduce savings. When savings are

Figure 9.8

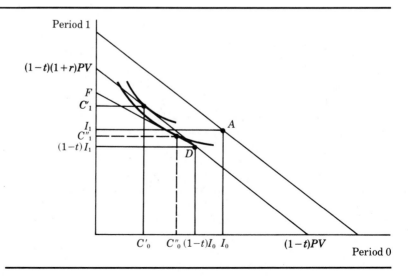

reduced, capital formation and growth will be reduced. When the income tax is progressive, the effect on savings will be more pronounced. This is because the proportion of current income saved increases as current income increases. Since individuals with higher incomes save proportionally more out of their incomes than do individuals with low incomes and since the progressive tax will decrease their savings relatively more than it decreases low-income savings, total savings will fall by more than under a proportional tax of equal yield.

The Trade-off between Money Income and Income in Kind

Not only does the income tax discriminate in favor of leisure and against money income, it discriminates in favor of all other forms of income in kind. Since the income tax base includes money income only, the tax tends to encourage individuals to take their income in the form of employer contributions to medical insurance, life insurance, retirement funds, company cars, and expense accounts. Since a dollar's worth of these items is untaxed whereas a dollar's worth of money income is taxed, the individual will end up better off by taking some of his or her income in untaxed employer-provided health insurance than by taking it in dollars and buying the health insurance independently.

The Income Tax and Efficient Allocation of Resources

In Chapter 2 we examined the conditions for an efficient allocation of resources. One of these conditions is that the marginal value in use of a good, say x, equals the marginal cost of x.

$$MV_x = MC_x$$

Consider the income-leisure example. Before the tax, the individual will equate the marginal value of leisure to the wage rate ($MV_L = w$), which is the price of leisure. The firm employing this worker equates the value of the marginal product of labor to the wage rate. Note that the value of the marginal product of labor is what can be produced by giving up leisure. It is the marginal cost of leisure. Since both the MC_L and MV_L equal the wage rate, we know that

$$MC_L = MV_L$$

and our condition for the efficient allocation of resources is satisfied. When income is taxed, the worker faces a wage equal to $(1 - t)w$. He or she will equate the marginal value of leisure to the after-tax wage $(1 - t)w$. The firm employing the worker still pays the full wage w, so it continues to equate MC_L to the wage rate w. Since the worker sets $MV_L = (1 - t)w$ and the firm sets $MC_L = w$, and since $-t < 0$, we know that

$$MV_L < MC_L.$$

The worker converts too little leisure time into income; that is, time is not allocated efficiently between work and leisure. The private rate at which individuals can convert leisure into income is less than the social rate as a result of the tax.

The Progressive Income Tax: Two Final Issues

A common justification for the progressive income tax is that an individual's taxes should be based on his or her ability to pay. More specifically, taxes should go up if income goes up. This occurs with proportional taxes as well as with progressive taxes and may occur with a regressive tax structure. Actually, what many have in mind when they use the ability-to-pay argument is that taxes should be used to redistribute incomes. Specifically, the income tax should be used to make the distribution of income more equal.

Even if the majority of individuals desire some redistribution of income, the progressive tax is probably not the best means that could be employed in accomplishing this objective. Direct transfers of cash accompanied by a proportional tax would result in less economic distortion. As we have seen in the case of the labor-leisure trade-off and the saving-consumption trade-off, a progressive tax causes more distortion than a proportional income tax. Another problem is that it leads individuals to invest resources in tax avoidance. Most of the resources devoted to various tax shelters do nothing to increase the output or efficiency of the economy.

Another serious problem with the progressive income tax is that *real* income tax payments go up as a result of inflation. Inflation causes an individual's real tax payments to go up even if his or her real income is unchanged. This results from the fact that as money income increases, the individual moves up to a higher marginal tax bracket. If his or her money income goes up by 10 percent solely as a result of monetary inflation, taxes will go up by more than 10 percent and his or her real after-tax income will go down.

Actually, the problem that inflation causes is twofold. By raising real tax rates, it increases the distortion in the economy caused by taxes and, since real tax receipts can be increased simply by printing money without the need of legislation, governments are tempted to use inflation to increase tax receipts. To the extent that the links between inflation, taxes, and deliberate government action are not recognized, raising taxes by inflation may bring about less public outcry than the more traditional legislative approach.

Questions and Exercises

1. Show graphically the income and substitution effects of a progressive income tax that results in an increase in work effort.

2. Explain the differing effects of the income tax on investment risk.

3. Under what conditions will an income tax distort the savings-consumption decision?

4. Why, in the presence of an income tax, would we expect an inefficiently high level of income to be taken in nonpecuniary form?

5. In our analysis of the distortion effects of the income tax on the work-leisure choice, the worker paid the tax. If the employer paid the tax, would the results be different? Why or why not?

6. Why does a progressive income tax lower the cost of inflation to politicians?

7. How could one distinguish between a capital gain caused by an increase in the net productivity of investment and one caused by a decrease in the rate of interest? Hint: An examination of the bond market might help you.

8. A change in the rate of interest will result in some individuals experiencing capital gains and others experiencing capital losses. Why is this the case?

9. Suppose you wanted to construct a tax that would yield a constant stream of revenue regardless of the size of the tax base. Would this tax be a progressive, proportional, or regressive tax? Substantiate your answer.

10. What two methods are employed to measure income?

11. The income tax will tend to make individuals more self-sufficient. Why? Is that an advantage in the sense that it improves resource allocation?

12. The income tax will result in more individuals being employed in relatively safe jobs. Why? Is this an advantage in the sense that it improves resource allocation?

13. The income tax is more progressive with respect to taxable income than it is with respect to adjusted gross income. Comment. What is your evidence?

14. Suppose you believe that the income tax paid by an individual should rise with his income. Would this necessarily cause you to prefer a progressive rate schedule? Would you necessarily reject a regressive rate schedule?

Additional Readings

Blum, Walter J. and Kalven, Harry, Jr. *The Uneasy Case for Progressive Taxation.* Chicago: The University of Chicago Press, 1963.

Goode, Richard. *The Individual Income Tax.* Washington, D.C.: The Brookings Institution, 1964.

Peckman, Joseph A. *Federal Tax Policy.* Washington, D.C.: The Brookings Institution, 1971.

10

Corporate Income Tax

The corporation income tax, in addition to the personal income tax discussed in the previous chapter, is an important source of revenue for the federal government. Table 10.1 compares the amount of revenue produced by the corporate income tax at the federal level to the total amount of revenue produced from all other sources. Even though the corporate income tax produced over forty billion dollars in revenue for the federal government in 1976, corporate income taxes have been declining in importance as a source of revenue. This is the result of the decline in the tax base (corporate profits) *relative* to other bases against which federal taxes are levied. Table 10.2 compares corporate profit, which is the base against which the corporate income tax is levied, to the compensation of employees, which roughly comprises the base against which personal income taxes and social security taxes are levied, and to na-

Table 10.1   **Corporation Income Tax**

Years	Total Federal Revenue (in millions of dollars)	Corporation Income Tax (in millions of dollars)	Corporation Income Tax as a Percent of Total Federal Revenue
1950	$ 35,186	$10,488	29.8%
1955	57,589	17,861	31.0
1960	92,500	21,494	23.2
1965	116,800	25,461	21.7
1969	187,800	36,678	19.5
1970	193,700	32,829	16.9
1971	188,400	26,785	14.2
1972	208,600	32,166	15.4
1973	232,200	36,153	15.5
1974	264,900	38,620	14.5
1975	281,000	40,600	14.4
1976	297,500	40,100	13.4

Source: U.S. Office of Management and Budget, *The Budget of the United States Government, Annual.*

**Comparison of Corporate Profits
to National Income (Figures in Billions)**   **Table 10.2**

Years	1950	1955	1960	1965	1970	1972	1974	1975
Corporate Profits	32.7	43.0	44.7	73.8	64.1	87.2	73.7	85.4
Compensation of Employees	148.4	216.0	281.2	377.3	577.4	677.8	831.0	879.0
Originating in:								
Corporate Business	98.8	144.9	190.8	259.7	399.3	470.6	587.3	612.7
Proprietorships	25.0	31.7	36.2	40.0	47.4	50.6	58.2	61.3
Other Private Business	1.0	1.3	1.5	2.2	3.3	4.1	4.9	5.3
Government	23.6	38.1	52.7	75.4	127.4	152.5	180.6	199.7
National Income	236.2	328.0	412.0	566.0	798.4	951.9	1,135.7	1,207.6
$\frac{\text{Corp. Profits}}{\text{Compensation of Employees}} \times 100$	22.0	19.9	15.8	19.5	11.1	12.8	8.8	9.7
$\frac{\text{Corp. Profits}}{\text{National Income}} \times 100$	13.8	13.1	10.8	13.0	8.0	9.1	6.4	7.0

Source: U.S. Bureau of Economic Analysis, *The National Income and Product Accounts of the U.S., 1929-74;* and *Survey of Current Business,* January and July 1976.

tional income. As Table 10.2 indicates, corporate profits have declined relative to both national income (from 13.8 percent to 7.0 percent) and compensation of employees (from 22 percent to 9.7 percent) for the years 1950–1975.

The Tax Base

For tax purposes, a corporation is treated as a legal person, capable of paying taxes, as are individuals. This, however, is a legal fiction. Corporations cannot pay taxes; only individuals pay taxes. Consequently, taxing corporations does not shift taxes away from individuals. As we will argue later, the corporation income tax is paid by the stockholders, who are the owners of the corporation; the consumers of the firm's products; and/or by the owners of the resources employed in producing the product of the corporation.

The base of the corporation income tax is the accounting profit of the corporation, which is computed by deducting expenses from receipts. Expenses include such things as depreciation of plant and equipment, interest paid on loans, state and local taxes, contributions to charity, as well as wages and salaries, the purchase of raw materials, and the like.

It is important to keep in mind that the accounting concept of cost is employed when calculating the corporation's expenses. This concept considers only historical out-of-pocket costs in computing expenses. This is distinguished from the economic concept of cost, which defines the cost of any act as the most valuable alternative necessarily forsaken as a result of engaging in that act. Choice implies cost and a cost is only incurred when a choice must be made. When you choose to buy a pair of shoes for $30, you release, or forsake, claims on other goods worth $30 in the market. The cost of the pair of shoes to you is not the money but the highest valued alternative forsaken that you could have obtained with $30.

What does this have to do with the measurement of a corporation's expenses, profit, and tax liability? In some cases, both the economist and the accountant would reach the same answers when computing an expense. There is, however, at least one exception that has important consequences for corporate income taxation. When you buy the pair of shoes, your net benefit per period of time is the difference between the value of the flow of services yielded by the shoes (the gross benefit) and the value of the flow of services that would have resulted had you purchased your next highest valued alternative (the expense of owning shoes). In a sense, this difference (the net benefit) is the profit that results from owning the shoes. You will, of course, increase your purchases of shoes up to the quantity such that the net benefits *at the margin* vanish. By doing so, you will maximize your profits from shoe ownership. Suppose that the government begins to tax the owners of shoes but not the owners of other goods, and the base that is employed in computing the tax is the *gross* per period benefit of shoe ownership. This will reduce marginal net benefits to something less than zero with the result that you will reduce your ownerhsip of shoes and increase your ownership of other goods. The tax will change the allocation of resources because it is levied on gross benefits rather than on net benefits.

The corporation income tax works in a way which is similar to the above example of a shoe tax. When an individual buys shares of stock in a corporation, he or she, like the purchaser of shoes, is saying that the value of the flow (his or her share of the profits of the corporation) yielded by the stock exceeds the value of the flow that would result from purchasing the next best alternative. Consequently, the net benefit to the stockholder is not the share of the profits of the corporation, but this share less the alternative cost of

stock ownership. The corporate income tax does not take this alternative cost into account when computing the corporation's tax liability. Hence, the corporate income tax is levied on gross benefits
in a way which is analogous to the above shoe tax example. The
result is that individuals will choose to own less corporate stock
and more other goods. Since the corporate tax alters the allocation
of resources, it is not considered a general tax.

Because the tax does not allow the owners of the corporation to
expense the alternative cost of capital acquired through equity finance (sales of stock) but does allow them to expense the alternative cost of capital acquired through debt finance (sales of bonds),
debt finance will be more attractive to the owners than will equity
finance. Corporations will be more highly levered (have a greater
ratio of debt to equity) than they would be in the absence of the
tax.

The Tax Rate

Prior to 1975, the basic tax rate on corporation income was 22
percent on the first $25,000 plus a surcharge of 26 percent on in-
come in excess of $25,000, so that the combined rate was 48 percent
on all income in excess of $25,000. The tax rates that were effective
for the years 1975 through 1977 were 20 percent on the first $25,000
of income, 22 percent on the second $25,000 of income, and 48
percent on income in excess of $50,000. Effective January 1, 1979,
the following rates are applicable. The first $25,000 in earnings is
taxed at a rate of 17 percent, the second $25,000 at a rate of 20
percent, the third at 30 percent, and the fourth at 40 percent.
Earnings over $100,000 are taxed at 46 percent.

The corporation income tax is progressive under both the
1975-79 rates and the rates that existed prior to 1975. Table 10.3
presents data concerning the distribution of the tax burden by the
asset size of the corporation. The data indicate that, while most of
the tax returns filed are from relatively small corporations, the
bulk of the corporation income tax is collected from a few large
firms.

The data in Table 10.3 indicate that the corporation income
tax is progressive and that in 1973 the bulk of the tax (64 percent)
was collected from the owners of corporations that had assets in
excess of 100 million dollars. These corporations, however, represented less than two-tenths of one percent of the corporations filing
tax returns. It is of some interest to note that 58 percent of the
corporations filing tax returns had average annual incomes of
$2,365 and that 93 percent of those filing returns had average in-
comes of less than $40,000.

Table 10.3   Corporation Income Tax Returns, 1973

	Total	Under $100 Thousand	$100–499.9 Thousand	$500–999.1 Thousand	$1–4.9 Million	$5–9.9 Million	$10–49.9 Million	$50–99.9 Million	Over $100 Million
Number of Returns in Thousands	1,905	1,099	560	114	94	15	17	3	4
Income in Billions of Dollars	115.5	2.6	7.0	4.5	11.1	4.6	10.0	4.7	71.0
Tax in Billions of Dollars[a]	52.4	.8	2.2	1.8	5.0	2.1	4.7	2.2	33.7
Average Income	$60,629	$2,365	$12,500	$39,473	$118,085	$306,666	$588,235	$1,566,666	$17,750,000
Tax Rate (percentage)	45.3	30.7	31.4	40.0	45.0	45.6	47.0	46.8	47.4

Asset Size Class

[a]Tax liability is before deduction for foreign tax credit, for investment credit, and for 1973 work incentive credit.

Source: U.S. Internal Revenue Service, *Statistics of Income 1973, Corporation Income Tax Returns.*

The Double Taxation of Corporation Income

We mentioned at the beginning of this chapter that corporations are treated as legal persons capable of paying taxes. We emphasize that this is at odds with reality. Only individuals can pay taxes. Consequently, since the earnings of individuals generated through corporate business activity are taxed once by the corporation income tax and once again by the personal income tax when the earnings are distributed in the form of dividends, the corporate income tax results in a double tax on the earnings of stockholders.

To illustrate, suppose that an individual's share in the earnings of a corporation is $1,000. This income will be subject to a 48-percent tax. If the remainder ($520 = $1,000 − $480) is distributed in the form of dividends, and if we assume that the individual's personal income tax bracket is 35 percent, he will pay an additional tax of $182. Thus, the total tax on his earnings of $1,000 is $662. If, on the other hand, the $1,000 had been from a source other than corporate earnings, the total tax that the individual would have paid would be $350 ($1,000 × .35).[1] The additional tax that he pays on the $1,000 in corporate earnings is $312.

Most corporations do not pay out all of their earnings as dividends. Roughly one-half of corporate earnings are paid out as dividends. The earnings that are retained by the corporation will not be immediately subject to the personal income tax. Presumably, the earnings are retained because the owners of the corporation believe that there are profitable investment opportunities open to the corporation. If they prove correct, the market value of stockholder shares in the corporation will rise by approximately the amount of retained earnings. The owners may, then, choose to sell off some of their shares. Any gains made on these sales will be taxed at a capital gains rate that is lower than the rate paid on ordinary income. Corporate retention of earnings will result in those earnings being taxed at a lower rate than they would be if paid out in dividends. However, as long as capital gains are taxed, the tax rate on corporate earnings will exceed the tax rate on earnings from other sources. In the above example, retention of a portion of the $520 in after-tax earnings will result in the individual paying less than $662 in taxes on before-tax corporate earnings of $1,000. Recall that $662 is the amount the individual would pay if the entire $520 in after-tax earnings were paid in dividends. However, as long as he realizes a gain on the retained earnings, he will pay more than the $350 he would pay if the $1,000 in earnings were from another source.

Retention of corporate earnings does not allow the stockholder

---

[1]We are assuming that the additional $480 received by the individual under this alternative does not change his or her marginal tax rate.

to escape the double tax on corporate earnings as long as the reinvestment of earnings is successful and the individual realizes the gain. The retention of corporate earnings does mitigate the impact of the double tax and does provide an incentive to retain a greater portion of earnings than otherwise.

Integrating the Corporate and Personal Income Taxes

The double taxation of corporate earnings could be eliminated if the corporate and personal income tax were integrated. This could be accomplished by eliminating the tax on corporate earnings at the level of the corporation and by imputing the earnings to individual stockholders. Thus, the taxable income of the stockholders would reflect the earnings of the corporation regardless of whether the earnings were paid out in the form of dividends or retained by the corporation. The earnings of individuals received from corporate business activity would be taxed as personal income as is income from other sources. This method of taxing individuals' profits earned from ownership of corporate stock is called the partnership method because it treats the earnings of stockholders in essentially the same way as it does the earnings of partnerships.

It would be possible to couple the partnership method of taxing corporate earnings with income tax withholding. The corporation acts as an agent to withhold taxes on the earnings of its employees, and it could also act as an agent to withhold taxes on the earnings of its stockholders. To illustrate, suppose that an individual stockholder's share in the profit of a corporation is $1,000. Suppose the corporation is required to withhold taxes at the rate of 30 percent on earnings. The corporation would pay the Treasury an amount equal to 30 percent of its earnings. It would notify this stockholder that her share of the earnings was $1,000 and that $300 has been withheld for tax purposes. The notification may be accompanied by a dividend check, but the amount of this check will be of no importance to the stockholder in computing her tax liability. She will report earnings of $1,000. If her marginal tax rate is 25 percent, she will owe $250 in personal income taxes on the earnings of $1,000. At the same time, she will note on her income tax return that $300 in tax has been withheld. Since her tax liability is less than the amount withheld, she will receive a refund of $50. Had her marginal tax rate exceeded the withholding rate, she would have paid the Treasury the difference upon submission of her tax return.

Because the partnership method of taxing corporate earnings eliminates double taxation, it results in a revenue loss to the federal government. The revenue loss cannot be calculated by computing the reduction in tax revenues using the present base. In fact, eliminating the corporate tax and using only the income tax to collect revenues as they accrue to the individual would result in an increase in the tax base. The corporate income tax retards capital formation, slows economic growth, and results in a lower level of national income than would exist without the tax. Consequently, part of the lost revenues from the corporate tax would be recovered through increased personal income tax revenues.

Depreciation of Assets

Whenever individuals generate taxable income streams with assets whose lives span the tax computation period, a problem arises in defining and computing the amount by which the value of the long-lived assets decline during the tax period. If this amount were not deducted from receipts in computing the income stream, the result would overstate the income earned during the period. Some allowance must be made for the portion of long-lived assets used up in generating the income stream. While this problem is not unique to the computation of corporate income, it is convenient to discuss it at this point.

Recall that income is defined as the maximum amount of the flow of current production that may be consumed without impairing the source of the production. If no allowance were made for the long-lived assets used up in the production process, production in future periods would fall and computed income for the current period would be overstated.

The allowance that is made for the value of long-lived assets consumed in the production process is called depreciation. Normally, all long-lived assets decline in value as they are used. This is true of physical assets as well as human assets. The knowledge possessed by doctors, lawyers, engineers, teachers, or plumbers will depreciate in value unless it is maintained through further study and communication with others in the field. The rate at which human assets depreciate is very difficult, if not impossible, to determine. Human assets are embodied in individuals and are not sold in markets as are physical assets. Consequently, it is difficult to determine the value of the human asset subject to depreciation. The tax laws, however, have made some provision for costs associated with maintaining human assets. The costs of professional publications, attendance at professional meetings, and additional schooling required by the job may be deducted in computing tax liability. Also, the personal income tax exemption may be viewed as a concession to the fact that human assets depreciate.

Since physical assets are sold in markets, it is much easier (less costly) to determine the value of the asset subject to depreciation. A question arises, however, as to the rate at which these assets depreciate. For tax purposes, there are three methods of depreciating long-lived physical assets that may be employed in computing tax liability: (1) the straight line method, (2) the double declining balance method, and (3) the sum-of-the-years digits method. The straight line method allows the individual to expense the initial cost of the asset evenly over the anticipated life of the asset. If the initial cost of the asset is $10,000 and its anticipated life is 10 years, the individual may expense $1,000 ($10,000/10 years) each year for 10 years. The double declining balance method of depreciation allows the individual to expense the initial cost of the asset at twice the rate of the straight line method; however, the rate is applied to the undepreciated cost of the asset. Thus, if the asset is the same as discussed above, 20 percent of the undepreciated cost may be deducted each year. The first year's depreciation expense would be $2,000 (.2 × $10,000). The second year's depreciation expense would be $1,600 (.2[$10,000 − $2,000]), and so on. The sum-of-the-years digits method allows the individual each year to expense a portion of the initial cost of the asset equal to the ratio of the remaining life of the asset to the sum of the years over the anticipated life of the asset. In the above example, the sum of the years over the anticipated life is 55(10 + 9 + 8 + . . . + 1). The depreciation expense allowed in the first year is $1,818.18 (10/55 × $10,000). The second year's depreciation is $1,636.36 (9/55 × $10,000), and so on.

Reduction in the individual's tax liability each year due to depreciation is the applicable tax rate times the depreciation expense. Since the three methods yield different streams of expenses, they will result in different tax streams. The double declining balance and sum-of-the-years digits methods result in high depreciation expenses and low tax liabilities in the initial years of the asset's life when compared to the straight line method. This situation reverses itself as the asset becomes older. Because the timing of the tax liability is different depending upon which method is used, the impact on the individual's net present wealth of choosing one method over the other will be different. Only if the rate of interest were zero would the individual be indifferent in choosing among the three methods. The higher the rate of interest, the greater will be the incentive to employ more accelerated rates of depreciation (double declining balance and sum-of-the-years digits). Suppose, for example, that the annual income stream net of all costs other than depreciation and taxes, which is generated by our $10,000 asset, is $2,500 and that the tax rate is 50 percent.

Given the assumptions used to construct Table 10.4, the individual would choose to employ the sum-of-the-years digits method when the rate of interest is 5 percent and when it is 10 percent. (Try shortening the life of the asset to 5 years. Do you get the same answer?) Note that the individual's incentive to employ an accelerated method of depreciation is greater the higher the rate of inter-

**Present Cost of Tax Stream
under Different Methods of Depreciation**   **Table 10.4**

				Tax Payment					
Year	Tax *DDB*	*PC* *r*=.05	*PC* *r*=.10	Tax *SOYD*	*PC* *r*=.05	*PC* *r*=.10	Tax *SL*	*PC* *r*=.05	*PC* *r*=.10
1	250	238	227	341	324	309	750	714	681
2	450	408	371	432	391	355	750	680	619
3	610	527	458	522	451	392	750	648	563
4	738	607	504	613	504	418	750	617	512
5	840	658	520	704	551	436	750	588	465
6	922	687	520	795	593	448	750	559	423
7	988	702	506	886	629	454	750	533	384
8	1,004.28	679	467	977	661	455	750	507	349
9	1,082.23	698	458	1,068	688	452	750	483	318
10	578.91	355	222	1,159	711	446	750	460	288
Total		5,559	4,253		5,503	4,165		5,788	4,602

DDB = Double declining balance.
SOYD = Sum-of-the-years digits.
SL = Straight line.
PC = Present cost.

est. The difference between the present cost of the tax liability between the *SOYD* method and the *SL* method when the interest rate is 5 percent is $285 ($5,788 – $5,503). In other words, the net present wealth of the individual would be $285 lower if he uses the *SL* method to calculate depreciation expense than if he were to use the *SOYD* method. On the other hand, if the rate of interest is 10 percent, the difference is $437. It is more costly to employ slower rates of depreciation as the rate of interest rises.

Incidence of the Corporation Income Tax

Short-Run Incidence

If a tax is placed on the returns to capital in the corporate sector, the owners of capital in that sector will bear the full burden of the tax in the short run. In the short run, since capital is fixed, the return on capital is a rent. (Because it is a rent only in the short run, it is sometimes called quasi-rent.)[2] Since the amount of capital

---

[2] An economic rent is said to be earned on an asset if an increase in its price does not result in an increase in the amount of the asset supplied.

is fixed in the short run, the owners of capital will be unable to make any adjustments to shift the burden of the tax elsewhere. This is true even if the owner of a capital asset sells the asset because the price he or she will be able to obtain will fall to reflect the capitalized present and future amount of the tax. The purchasers of the asset will not bear the tax since the price is reduced by the capitalized value of the tax. Since the purchaser of an asset has the opportunity to buy from the untaxed noncorporate sector, he or she would only buy in the corporate sector if the after-tax rates of return are greater than, or at least equal to, those in the noncorporate sector.

In the short run, the corporate income tax will not affect output. The tax is levied against profits. Revenues are taxed only after costs are deducted. In this situation, marginal cost will shift down since costs are deductible when calculating the tax. However, marginal revenue will shift down by the same percentage. Since marginal revenue and marginal cost were equal at the quantity produced prior to the tax, each curve will shift down by the same amount at this quantity after the tax is levied. As a result, the two curves will intersect at the same quantity as they did prior to the tax being levied. The profit-maximizing rate of output will remain unchanged.

Figure 10.1 depicts a competitive firm in the corporate sector. Before the application of the tax, the firm faces price P and produces Q. The tax shifts the firm's short-run (marginal) cost curve down to SMC $(1-t)$ and the marginal revenue curve to $P(1-t)$.

Figure 10.1

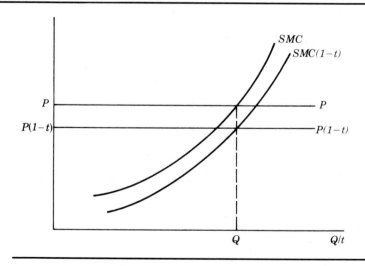

Since the tax shifts both curves down by the same amount, the output of the firm is not affected by the tax.[3]

Long-Run Incidence

The long-run effects of the corporate income tax depend upon the nature of the tax base. As the tax is applied in the United States, it is not a tax on economic profits; it does not allow deduction of the opportunity cost of capital from gross receipts. The corporate income tax allows for the deduction of explicit cost only; it does not allow the corporation to deduct a normal return on its capital.

If the tax was on economic profits only, it could not be shifted and its burden would fall on the owners of capital. In the long-run competitive equilibrium, the marginal firms in each industry earn zero economic profits. These firms would pay no tax at all. The inframarginal firms may earn positive economic profits in the nature of rents to nonreplaceable and/or nontransferable inputs such as favorable locations near transportation facilities or natural resources. Since these returns are economic rents, the tax would have no effect on the behavior of the firm. The situation is analogous to the short-run analysis in that the tax, since it is a tax on an economic rent, is actually a tax on a fixed factor and will not affect either the long-run marginal cost or the marginal revenue of the firm.

Since the corporate income tax is not a tax on economic profits but rather a tax on accounting profits, long-run shifting of the tax will occur. The owners of corporate capital will not bear the full burden of the tax. They will, by altering their behavior, shift some of the tax to other individuals. The corporate income tax may be shifted away from the owners of corporate capital to three groups of individuals: (1) owners of capital in the noncorporate sector, (2) owners of other resource inputs in all sectors (labor is a significant group here), and (3) consumers of the output of the corporate sector.

Owners of Noncorporate Capital. In Figure 10.2, the markets for both corporate and noncorporate capital are presented. In long-run equilibrium, before the application of the tax, the rates of return in both sectors are equal. If this were not the case, capital would move from the sector with the lower rate of return to the sector with the higher rate.

Figure 10.2(c) presents the market for capital. The demand for capital, D_T, is the horizontal sum of the demand in the corporate sector, D_C (the line AB), and the demand in the noncorporate sec-

---

[3]Although this discussion concerns purely competitive firms, the result applies to any profit-maximizing firm.

Figure 10.2

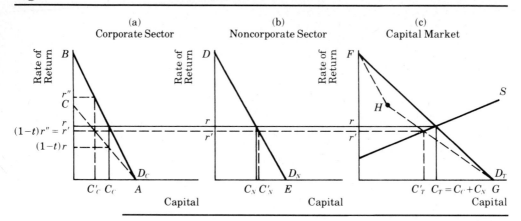

(a)
Corporate Sector

(b)
Noncorporate Sector

(c)
Capital Market

tor, D_N (the line ED). Given the supply curve of capital, the total quantity of capital employed is C_T and the marginal return earned by capital in both sectors is r. The quantity of capital employed in the corporate sector is C_C and the quantity employed in the non-corporate sector is $C_{N.}$

If a proportional tax[4] is imposed on returns to capital employed in the corporate sector, the after-tax demand curve in the corporate sector will rotate around point A down to AC. Initially, prior to any adjustment in the total quantity of capital employed and the quantities employed in each sector, the after-tax return in the corporate sector falls to $(1-t)r$. The return in the noncorporate sector is unchanged at r. The return to capital employed in the noncorporate sector exceeds the return to capital employed in the corporate sector. This difference will not persist in the long run. Individuals will allocate capital away from the corporate sector to the noncorporate sector in an effort to capture the higher returns earned in that sector. This reduces the amount of capital employed in the corporate sector and increases the amount employed in the noncorporate sector. There is *not* a one-for-one substitution, however. The reduction in capital employed in the corporate sector exceeds the increase in capital employed in the noncorporate sector. This occurs because the tax causes a reduction in the aggregate demand for capital. The relevant demand curve for capital in the corporate sector after the tax is AC. The demand curve in the noncorporate sector remains unchanged at DE. Summing these two curves horizontally yields an aggregate demand curve for capital given by the line segments FHG in Figure 10.2(c). The total quantity of capital employed falls to C'_T. The rate of return earned on capital falls to r'.

---

[4]For simplicity, the analysis deals with a proportional tax. The results would be the same, though more difficult to demonstrate, with a progressive tax.

Note that the after-tax return in the corporate sector, r', will equal the return on capital employed in the noncorporate sector after all adjustments have taken place. The after-tax return in the corporate sector is equal to the before-tax return, r'', less the tax, that is, $r' = r'' (1-t)$. This return, r', is lower than the return earned in the absence of the tax, r, but higher than the return earned prior to any adjustment after the tax is levied, $(1-t)r$.

The adjustment induced by the tax results in a reduction in the rate of return in the noncorporate sector. In other words, a portion of the tax is shifted to the noncorporate sector. In fact, the burden of this tax is shared equally by both sectors. The tax has reduced the after-tax rates of return in both sectors from r to r'. This is true even though the tax is levied only on the returns to capital employed in the corporate sector.

A further point is important. The tax results in a smaller quantity of capital employed, C'_T rather than C_T. The tax drives a wedge between the marginal social returns yielded by the employment of capital and the returns earned by the owners of capital. The marginal social returns yielded by capital are given by the height of the demand curve at different rates of capital employment. These returns are measured in terms of the increase in the amount of future consumption goods that can be obtained as a result of employing additional capital. The marginal cost of acquiring these returns is measured by the height of the supply curve. At C'_T, the marginal social benefit that results from employing additional capital exceeds the marginal cost. This indicates that the net social dividend would increase if additional capital were employed up to a quantity of C_T. Individuals, however, will not increase the employment of capital beyond C'_T because the tax prevents them from reaping the benefits that would result from doing so.

Shifting to Labor. Part of the burden of the corporate income tax may be borne by the owners of other resource inputs. We consider the possiblity of the burden being shifted to labor, though the same argument would apply to other inputs as well.

Just as the burden of the tax is borne by all owners of capital, the part of the burden of a corporate tax that is shifted to labor (or owners of other inputs) must be borne equally by labor in all sectors, not just the taxed sector. This occurs because, if the wage in one sector is higher than the wage in another, labor will move from the low-wage to the high-wage sector. This will drive down the wage rate in the one sector and bring up the wage rate in the other sector. This adjustment will continue until the wages in all sectors are equal for homogeneous types of labor.

As capital shifts from the taxed to the nontaxed sector, the total demand for labor may be reduced relative to that of capital. This will tend to reduce the real wage and reduce the share of national income that goes to labor. Thus, labor may share part of the burden of the tax. This effect depends upon the relative intensities with which capital and labor are employed in the two sectors and upon the elasticities of demand for the final output in the two sectors. It is possible, however, under certain conditions, for labor to gain as a result of the tax if the relative demand of labor increases.

Effects on Consumers. The corporate income tax, by increasing the amount of capital used in the noncorporate sector, can cause an increase in output and a decrease in prices of goods produced in that sector. This would be accompanied by a decrease in output and an increase in prices in the corporate sector. This means that consumers of corporate output would pay higher prices for that output and consumers of noncorporate output would pay lower prices. The tax will also tend to decrease the total amount of capital formation and lead to an inefficiently large level of investment in the noncorporate sector.

Application

The Incidence of the Corporate Income Tax

The implicit model used in our discussion of the incidence of the corporate income tax was developed by Arnold Harberger.[5] In the Harberger model, as in our discussion, the burden of the tax could fall on the owners of capital, labor, and/or consumers. Who in fact bears the burden can only be determined by empirical investigation. Using rather crude methods and assumptions, Harberger came to the conclusion that the entire burden of the tax is borne by the owners of capital in both the taxed and untaxed sectors.

Monopoly

We now examine the effects of the corporate income tax on a monopoly. The impact of the corporate income tax on a firm that has a monopoly position in a market depends upon the nature of the tax base. If the tax is placed on economic profits, it will have no effect on resource allocation. As in the competitive case, the tax will shift down the firm's marginal revenue and marginal cost by the same amount and leave output unchanged. If the tax is propor-

---

[5]Arnold C. Harberger, "The Incidence of the Corporation Income Tax," *Journal of Political Economy,* Vol. 70 (June 1962), pp. 215–40.

tional at rate *t*, after-tax monopoly profits are given by the following equation.

$$(1-t)\pi = (1-t)TR - (1-t)TC, \tag{1}$$

where π is the profit rate, *TR* is total revenue, and *TC* is total cost. The profit-maximizing condition for the monopoly is

$$(1-t)MR = (1-t)MC; \tag{2}$$

$$MR = MC.$$

The $(1-t)$ can be canceled from both sides of Equation (2), leaving the marginal conditions unchanged by the tax. Furthermore, when economic profits are zero, the tax will be zero and the monopoly will continue operation since it would be doing as well as it could in its next best alternative.

Figure 10.3 demonstrates what happens to the economic profits of the monopoly as a result of the tax. The solid line represents profits before the application of the tax, and Q' represents the before-tax output of the firm. The tax on monopoly profits decreases the economic profit of the monopoly without affecting the output rate.

If the tax is based on accounting profits and not on economic profits (as it is in the United States), it will affect the behavior of the firm. The tax will affect the output rate of the monopoly if it

Figure 10.3

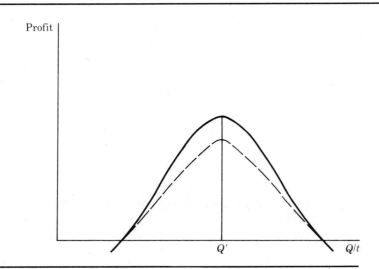

remains in operation, and it may induce the firm to shut down. Since the tax base is accounting profits, the tax payment will not be zero when economic profits are zero. Under these circumstances, the monopoly's after-tax economic profit will be negative. When pretax economic profits are zero the following holds:

$$\pi = TR - (EC + IC) = 0. \tag{3}$$

In Equation (3), π and TR are once again profits and total revenue. Explicit costs are EC and the implicit *economic* costs of capital are IC. The expressions in Equation (3) and in the following equations should be thought of as the present values of future streams of revenues and costs. This is necessary since we will be concerned primarily with the long-run or planning horizon where the firm will be choosing a firm size as well as an output level. The tax payment of the firm will be: Tax $= t(TR-EC) - tDep$. *Dep* is the allowance for depreciation. The deduction for depreciation can be viewed as the taxing authority's recognition that the implicit costs of capital are positive. If the depreciation allowance granted by the taxing authority is such that it equals the implicit costs of capital, the corporation tax will be equivalent to a tax on economic profits. In this case, the long-run impact of the tax will be equivalent to the short-run impact previously discussed. There is no reason to expect, however, that this will be the case. If it is not, the corporate tax will change the long-run output rate of the firm. This is shown in the following analysis.

The depreciation allowance reduces the firm's present and future tax payments and should be thought of as a present value. The term t is the tax rate. Since IC is positive, $TR - EC$ will be positive when economic profits are zero. The after-tax profits of the firm when before-tax economic profits are zero will equal

$$\pi - \text{Tax} = TR - (EC + IC) - t(TR - EC) + tDep$$

$$= -t(TR - EC) + tDep. \tag{4}$$

Equation (4) indicates that the firm's after-tax profits may be negative when the monopoly's before-tax economic profits are zero if the absolute value of the term $-t(TR-EC)$ exceeds the term *tDep*. If this occurs, the tax will cause the monopoly to close down in the long run.

In this situation, the owners of the monopoly corporation might try to convert their firm into a partnership or other type of noncorporate entity in order to avoid the tax.

The tax will also affect the output rate of the monopoly in the long run even if the firm continues to operate. The after-tax profits of the monopoly again are

$$\pi - \text{Tax} = TR - (EC + IC) - t(TR - EC) + tDep$$

$$= (1-t)TR - (1-t)EC - IC + tDep. \tag{5}$$

In the short run, implicit costs (*IC*) are fixed, as is the depreciation allowance (*Dep*), so that maximizing after-tax profits results in

$$(1-t)MR = (1-t)MEC$$

$$MR = MEC,$$

where *MEC* is marginal explicit cost, more traditionally referred to as short-run marginal cost. The tax does not enter into the output decision in the short run since *IC* and *Dep* are fixed. In the long run, however, implicit costs are not fixed. The firm can vary its capital costs because it can vary its capital. Consequently, the profit-maximizing condition in the long run will include marginal implicit costs and the marginal effect of changing firm size on the depreciation allowance. The firm will set its output and, thus, its firm size so that the following equation, which can be derived from Equation (5), holds.

$$MR = MEC + \frac{1}{1-t}(MIC - tMDep). \tag{6}$$

In Equation (6), *MIC* is the marginal implicit cost of capital. This term is not zero since changing output in the long run involves changing firm size and, thus, the capital stock. The term *MDep* is the marginal effect on the depreciation allowance that results from the change in the capital stock of the firm.

If the depreciation allowance was set equal to *MIC*, then the tax on accounting profits plus depreciation would equal the tax on monopoly economic profits. To see this, substitute *MIC* for *MDep* in Equation (6). Equation (6) would then become

$$MR = MEC + \frac{1}{1-t}(MIC - tMIC)$$

$$= MEC + \frac{1}{1-t}(1-t)MIC$$

$$= MEC + MIC.$$

In this case, the tax would not affect the firm's output decision. The depreciation allowance would allow the firm to subtract from the tax base the implicit cost of capital. Hence, it would pay tax only on economic profits. In this situation, the depreciation allowance allows the firm to expense implicit costs exactly as if the tax base were economic profit. In general, the depreciation does not reduce the tax base by the full amount of implicit cost. If the *MDep* term is less than *MIC,* the tax will induce the firm to alter its output behavior. Suppose, for example, $tMDep = tMIC - \gamma$ where γ is some positive value. Substituting $tMIC - \gamma$, which is less than *tMIC,* into Equation (6) we get

$$MR = MEC + MIC + \frac{\gamma}{1-t}. \qquad (7)$$

Since $1-t$ and γ are positive, the effect of the tax will be to increase the right-hand side of Equation (6) over what it would be if there were no corporate tax or what it would be if the tax were based on economic profits. In Equation (7), the tax increases the long-run marginal cost of the firm and, among other things, will cause the firm to reduce its output and firm size. The effect of the tax is shown in Figure 10.4. The tax shifts up the long-run average cost, *LAC,* and long-run marginal cost, *LMC,* to the levels indicated by the dashed *LAC'* and *LMC'* curves. This will lower the firm's profit-maximizing output to Q' from Q and increase the price charged for that output to p' from $p.$[6]

The corporate tax increases the marginal cost of capital rela-

Figure 10.4

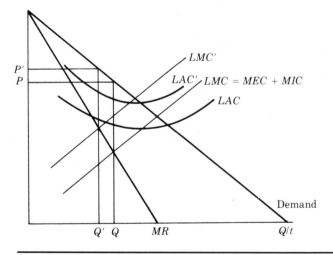

---

[6]The results of this analysis hold for competitive firms as well.

tive to that of labor for both competitive and monopoly firms. This causes the firm to reduce its capital and, thus, its firm size. The reduced output has the effect of raising the price of output so that the firm places part of the burden of the tax on the consumers of its output.

An economic justification for allowing accelerated depreciation can be drawn from this example. Accelerated depreciation increases the present value of the *tMDep* term and may bring it more closely in line with *tMIC* (the amount the accounting profits tax base must be reduced to convert the tax base to economic profits). Under these circumstances, the tax would tend to leave the output decision of the firm unchanged.

Application

The Effect of Nonneutral Taxation on the Use of Capital by Sector

The analysis in this chapter implies that the corporate tax structure results in a smaller amount of capital being employed in the corporate sector than would result if the tax structure were neutral between sectors. David J. Ott and Ahiat F. Ott[7] have estimated the effect of different tax structures on the allocation of capital among the corporate, agricultural and housing sectors for the year 1969. Their results appear in Table 10.5.

The results indicate that the present tax law has caused considerably less capital ($222.0 billion) to be allocated to the corporate sector than would have been the case under a neutral tax structure. Furthermore, they estimate that this distortion in the

Capital Stocks by Sector,
Present Law, Neutral Taxation, 1969 (in Billions of Dollars)   **Table 10.5**

Sector	Present Law	Neutral Taxation
Corporate	$ 923.0	$1,145.0
Agriculture	259.0	253.0
Housing	558.0	342.0
Total	$1,740.0	1,740.0

Source: David J. and Ahiat F. Ott, "The Effect of Nonneutral Taxation on the Use of Capital by Sector," *Journal of Political Economy,* Vol. 81 (July/August 1973), pp. 972–81. Copyright © 1973 by The University of Chicago Press. Reprinted by permission of The University of Chicago Press.

[7]David J. Ott and Ahiat F. Ott, "The Effect of Nonneutral Taxation on the Use of Capital by Sector," *Journal of Political Economy,* Vol. 81 (July/August 1973), pp. 972–81.

allocation of capital caused by the present law resulted in a net loss of $11.7 billion in 1969.

Questions and Exercises

1. Increasing corporation income taxes and reducing personal income taxes will reduce the tax burden of individuals. Comment.

2. A tax levied on economic profits will not alter the allocation of resources. Since the corporate tax is levied on profits, this tax will not alter resource allocation. Comment.

3. To incur a cost is to sacrifice an opportunity. Do you agree? Explain.

4. Why can't money expenditures be identified with costs?

5. Why might you expect corporations to be more highly levered in the presence of the corporation income tax than in its absence?

6. "Most corporations are large firms and, because of their market power, are able to earn millions of dollars in profits." There are a number of errors in this statement. Point them out.

7. How could integration of the corporate and personal income taxes eliminate the double taxation of income earned through corporate activity?

8. Discuss the long-run incidence of the corporate income tax in the competitive sector of the economy. How does this differ from the short-run incidence?

9. Since the owners of a corporate monopoly may earn a long-run return on capital which, given their opportunities, cannot be duplicated elsewhere, the corporation income tax will not induce them to reduce the quantity of capital employed in producing the good in which they have a monopoly. Comment.

10. "Recently a number of steelmaking organizations in Western Europe and the USSR have eliminated several costly steps in the manufacture of steel by advancing the technique known as continuous casting. U.S. steel firms, which account for about a third of the world's output, were for the most part content to observe these developments. They were inhibited by a paradox of industrial supremacy; the huge sums already invested in established methods made experimentation with the new technique seem impractical. The smaller producers, whose competitive position might have been enhanced by continuous casting, could least afford to build the pilot plants." Comment on this explanation of the behavior of U.S. firms. Assuming that the statement concerning their behavior is true, can you think of some alternative explanation(s)?

11. If a tax is levied on labor income in the corporate sector only, will labor in the noncorporate sector be affected? If so, show this effect graphically.

12. In an untaxed competitive economy, firms that continue to incorporate will do so because it is economically_____. If the implementation of the corporate income tax halts this continued incorporation, what can we say about the effects on the economic efficiency of the tax?

13. The ability of an economic unit to shift a tax to some other unit depends upon its ability to_____.

14. Elimination of the corporate income tax would result in increased capital formation and economic growth. Comment.

15. Some states as well as cities use the corporate income tax to raise revenues. If the tax rates vary across states and cities, corporations in high-tax areas will be able to lower their tax payments by moving to low-tax areas. How is this movement similar to "shifting" as discussed in this chapter?

16. If corporations are not really legal individuals that can pay taxes, are there any economic reasons why corporations should be taxed?

17. In Table 10.2, we saw that corporate profits have been decreasing over time. How might the corporate income tax be affecting this trend?

18. Corporate taxes may be favored by politicians because their impact on the voters is not well understood. What effect might this have on the size of government expenditures?

Additional Readings

Aranson, Peter. *The Multiple Tax on Corporate Income.* Los Angeles: International Institute for Economic Research, 1977.

Goode, Richard. *The Corporation Income Tax.* New York: John Wiley and Sons, Inc., 1951.

Harberger, Arnold C. "The Incidence of the Corporation Income Tax." *Journal of Political Economy,* Vol. 70 (June 1962), pp. 215–40.

Krzyzaniak, M., and Musgrave, R. M. *The Shifting of the Corporation Income Tax.* Baltimore: Johns Hopkins University Press, 1963.

11

Taxation of Consumer Expenditure

Taxes on commodities are called excise taxes. Excise taxes may be placed on the sale of goods and services at any level of the production and distribution chain—manufacturing, wholesale, or retail—but, in the United States, most are placed at the retail level. Taxes levied at the retail level are called sales taxes.

There are two methods used to levy a sales tax: (1) an ad valorem tax, assessed as a percentage of the sales price of the item and (2) a unit tax, assessed as a dollar amount per unit of the item. Sales taxes may be levied on a selective basis (that is, applied to some goods but not others), or the tax may be levied as a general tax that is applied uniformly to all goods and services sold.

At the federal level, sales taxes are levied on a selective basis. The products taxed at the federal level are a relatively small group consisting of motor fuel, alcoholic beverages, tobacco products, and services provided by public utilities such as the telephone. Some of these taxes are actually substitutes for direct user fees. The motor fuel tax, for example, is used as a substitute for tolls in financing the provision of roads and highways.

At the state level, the retail sales tax is an important source of revenue. Every state levies selective taxes on motor fuels, alcoholic beverages, and tobacco products, and all but five states have a general sales tax as well. Altogether, in 1975, the states collected 54.1 percent of their total revenues in the form of general and selective sales taxes, with 23.5 percent coming from the individual income tax, 8.3 percent from state corporate income taxes, and 4.9 percent from motor vehicle and operators' licenses.

At the local level, sales taxes are not as important a source of revenue as the property tax, but they do play a role.[1] In 1974, 7.4 percent of city government revenue came from sales taxes. At the same time, cities received 19.8 percent of their revenues as inter-government transfers from states, and much of this state-collected revenue was generated by sales taxes.

---

[1]The property tax will be discussed in Chapter 12.

Selective Sales Taxes

In this section, we examine the economic effects of the selective sales tax. First it must be noted that the effects of levying the tax on the buyer are equivalent to levying the tax on the seller of a good. This point can be easily demonstrated graphically. In Figure 11.1, we depict the market for ice cream. The pretax demand and supply curves are given by D and S, respectively. P and Q are the pretax equilibrium price and quantity.

Suppose a unit tax of t is levied on the seller side of the market. The tax raises the cost to each firm by t for each unit sold. The tax causes a parallel upward shift in the supply curve by the amount of the tax. The supply curve, S, gives the quantity suppliers are willing to provide at each price. The imposition of the tax does not alter the quantities that will be forthcoming at a given net price received by the suppliers. Consequently, to induce suppliers to offer the same quantity as they would at a pretax price, a posttax price, which is t dollars higher, must be paid by consumers. The posttax equilibrium quantity in the ice cream market is Q'. The price suppliers receive for supplying Q' is P°. Consumers pay P' after the imposition of the tax (where $P' = P^\circ + t$). The revenue collected from the tax is tQ' or $(P' - P^\circ)Q'$—the area $P'abP^\circ$ in Figure 11.1.

The tax results in a decrease in the equilibrium quantity of ice cream, an increase in the price paid by consumers, and a decrease in the price received by sellers.

Figure 11.1

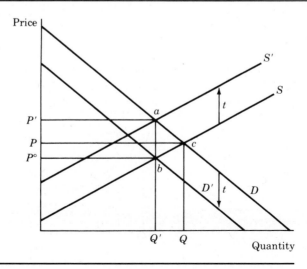

If the tax were placed on the buyer, the net demand curve shifts down by t to D'. The gross price consumers are willing to pay for each quantity is still given by D. This means that the net price received by the sellers for each quantity sold will be given by D'. (The supply curve in this situation is S.) The equilibrium quantity when the tax is imposed on the buyer side is Q'. The price paid by consumers is P'. The price received by sellers is P° and the revenue collected from the tax is tQ'. This is the same result that was obtained when the tax was imposed on sellers.

You should note that the incidence of the tax (meaning, who *actually* pays the tax) is the same whether the tax is levied on consumers or producers. In both cases, the price to the consumer rises from P to P' while the price received by the producer falls from P to P°. The difference between P' (the price paid by consumers) and P° (the price received by producers) is equal to the tax per unit. Since the price paid by consumers rises from P to P', the incidence of the tax on consumers (the consumers' share in the tax payment) is equal to this difference. The producers' share in the tax payment per unit is the difference between P and P°. These shares are the same whether the tax is levied on consumers or producers.

Ad Valorem Taxes

An ad valorem tax is assessed as a percentage of per dollar sales rather than as a fixed dollar amount per unit. The effect of an ad

Figure 11.2

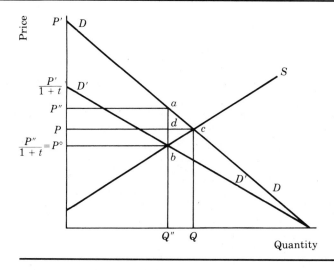

valorem tax levied on the sale of ice cream is shown in Figure 11.2. The pretax equilibrium price and quantity are given by P and Q, respectively. The tax may be levied on either the buyer or seller side of the market. Once again, the results would be the same in either case. We will look at what happens when the tax is levied on the buyers' side. Ad valorem taxes are assessed on the net or before-tax price of an item. If an ad valorem tax of rate t is levied on buyers of ice cream, the net demand curve as perceived by sellers will rotate downward around point a. The demand curve as viewed by sellers rotates down to point $P'/(1+t)$ on the vertical axis, from point P'.

With an ad valorem tax, the tax per unit goes up as the price goes up since the tax is actually a fixed percentage of the per unit price. With the imposition of the tax, the gross price (including the tax) consumers are willing to pay is still given by D. The supply side of the market will now confront the after-tax demand given by D'. Buyers now pay a gross or after-tax price of P'' for quantity Q''; sellers receive a price of $P°$ for quantity Q''. The total amount paid by buyers, $P''Q''$, will equal the amount received by sellers, $P°Q''$, plus the amount paid in taxes, $tP°Q''$ (that is, $P°Q'' + tP°Q'' = P''Q''$). Manipulation of this relationship yields the relationship between gross price and net price, $P° = P''/(1+t)$.[2]

It is relatively easy to show that, for a given market, an ad valorem tax that collected the same revenue as a unit tax would yield the same results in terms of output and prices. To see this, note that a unit tax which would yield the same revenue as that collected in Figure 11.2 would result in an after-tax demand curve that passes through point a and is parallel to D.

Excess Burden

When a sales tax is imposed as in Figure 11.2, the burden of the tax for the individuals in the market exceeds the dollar value of the taxes actually collected. This additional burden, which we call the excess burden or dead weight loss, is given by the area abc in Figure 11.2. This area is the amount by which the loss in consumer and producer or seller surplus attributable to the tax exceeds the revenue collected from the tax. The portion of the loss ($P''abP°$) that is collected in taxes is lost to the consumers and producers in this particular market but not to society as a whole. Presumably, individuals receive, through government acquisition, goods and services that have a market value equal to the taxes collected. The

---

[2]The fact that actual ad valorem taxes are based upon the net price paid as opposed to the gross price, as has been assumed elsewhere, has been pointed out by Norman Van Cott.

dead weight loss (*abc*) results from the fact that the tax drives a wedge between the marginal value in use (measured in terms of other goods that individuals would willingly forego) of the good to consumers and the marginal cost (measured in terms of other goods that are necessarily forsaken) of the good to producers. This wedge prevents consumers and producers from exploiting the entire potential gain from exchange. The gain from exchange, which is foregone as a result of the tax, is equivalent to the area *abc*. This will be discussed later in greater detail.

The Burden of the Selective Sales Tax

The burden of the selective sales tax in a competitive economy depends upon the elasticities of the supply and demand curves of

Figure 11.3

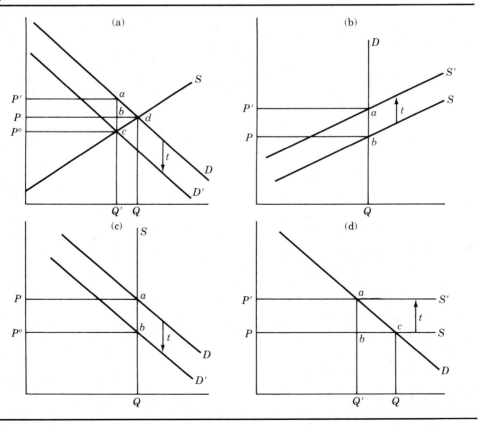

the taxed good. Figures 11.3(a)–(d) depict four possible cases for a selective unit sales tax.

Figure 11.3(a) illustrates the standard case. The tax shifts the demand curve down to D'. The burden to consumers, given by the loss in consumer surplus, is $P'adbP$. This burden consists of a tax payment of $P'abP$ and an excess burden of abd. The consumers, however, do not bear the full burden of the tax even though the tax is levied directly on them. By altering their behavior, consumers can pass part of the burden on to the seller. By cutting back their consumption of the good in response to the tax, the consumer forces the seller to share part of the burden. The seller's burden is $PbdcP°$, which is the loss of producer surplus resulting from the change in the consumer's behavior.

If the tax were placed on the seller side of the market, the results would be the same. In that case, by cutting production the sellers would force the consumer to share the burden. Again it makes no difference whether the tax is levied on the buyers or on the sellers.

In Figure 11.3(b), the market demand curve for the taxed good is perfectly inelastic. In this case, the entire burden of the tax is borne by consumers. The before-tax price and output are P and Q, respectively. The tax leaves the equilibrium output unchanged, but consumers now pay P' per unit. Producers face the before-tax price P even after the tax is imposed. Since buyers do not alter their behavior as a result of the tax, they bear the entire burden of the tax, which is $P'abP$. Note that, in this case, there is no dead weight loss. Since output remains unchanged as a result of the tax, the tax results in no net welfare loss to society. The tax results in a transfer of resources from the taxpayer to those who receive the benefits of the public expenditure financed by the tax.

In Figure 11.3(c), the supply curve is perfectly inelastic. In this case, the sellers bear the full burden of the tax $PabP°$. As in the previous case, output does not change as a result of the tax. This time, however, since the sellers do not alter their behavior when confronted with the tax, they bear the full burden of the tax. Here again, there is no excess burden since the tax does not result in a reallocation of resources.

When the supply curve is perfectly elastic, as in Figure 11.3(d), the consumer bears the entire burden of the tax.

A general principle is revealed in these four examples. The more inelastic the demand curve (supply curve) the larger the share of the burden borne by buyers (sellers). This is because the elasticity of the demand curve (supply curve) reflects the willingness of buyers (sellers) to alter their behavior by cutting back consumption (production) when the tax is imposed. The more elastic the curve on a given side of the market, the larger the share of the burden that will be passed on to the other side (other things being equal).

Effects on an Untaxed Good

Imposing a sales tax on some goods in the economy will result in an economic impact on untaxed goods. Suppose, for simplicity, that two goods are produced in the economy. When a tax is placed on one of the goods, the price of that good will increase to the buyer and decrease to the seller (see Figure 11.4). Consumers will tend to switch their consumption from the taxed good to the untaxed good. This will cause the demand for the untaxed good to increase (shift to the right at each price). Some producers will move their resources from production of the taxed good to that of the untaxed good. It is likely that the long-run supply curve in the untaxed industry is upward-sloping as in Figure 11.4. This means that as the demand curve shifts outward in the untaxed industry, prices will increase in that industry and consumers of the untaxed good will bear part of the burden of the tax. The amount of the burden that is shifted to consumers of the untaxed good depends upon two factors: (1) the elasticity of substitution in consumption of the untaxed good for the taxed good and (2) the elasticity of substitution in production of the untaxed good for the taxed good.

If consumers can easily substitute the untaxed good for the taxed good, the rightward shift in demand for the untaxed good will be greater. This will mean that consumers of the untaxed good will bear more of the burden than they would if it was more difficult to substitute the untaxed good for the good which is taxed.

If the two goods are easily substituted in production, the long-run supply curves of both goods will be more elastic. This means that consumers of the taxed good will bear more of the burden than they would if substitution were more difficult.

Figure 11.4

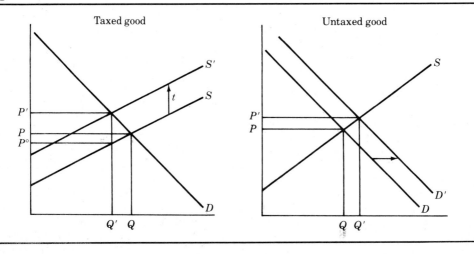

Selective Sales Tax under Monopoly

If an ad valorem tax is imposed on the output of a monopoly, there will be a further distortion in the allocation of resources over and above that caused by the monopoly alone. Figure 11.5 depicts the situation in which an ad valorem sales tax is imposed on a monopoly. The tax shifts the demand and marginal revenue curves, respectively, from D and MR to D' and MR'. This causes the price paid by the consumer to increase from P to P' and the output to fall from Q to Q'. The tax will decrease monopoly profit and, thus, the monopolist will bear part of the burden of the tax.

Examination of Figure 11.5 reveals that the tax increases the divergence between price and marginal cost for the monopoly. This means that the tax increases the distortion in the allocation of resources that results from the monopoly. As we will see in the next section, a selective sales tax distorts the allocation of resources under competition as well.

The Selective Excise Tax and Economic Efficiency

In Chapter 2, we examined several conditions necessary for an efficient allocation of resources. One of these conditions is given in Equation (1).

$$MV_{xy} = MC_{xy} \qquad (1)$$

Figure 11.5

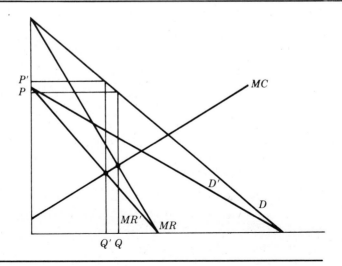

MV_{xy} is the marginal evaluation or marginal value in use of good x in terms of good y. MC_{xy} is the marginal cost of good x in terms of good y. Equation (1) must be satisfied for all individuals consuming goods x and y and for all firms producing x and y if resource allocation is to be efficient. That is, if the socially efficient levels of x relative to y are going to be produced, the marginal value in use of good x in terms of good y for all individuals must equal the marginal cost of good x in terms of good y for all firms as specified by Equation (1). A selective excise tax drives a wedge between the marginal value in use and the marginal cost, causing an inefficient allocation of resources.

Individuals maximize their utility by equating marginal value in use to the ratio of the prices of x and y as in Equation (2).

$$MV_{xy} = \frac{P_x}{P_y} \tag{2}$$

Each individual adjusts his or her consumption of x and y so that Equation (2) is satisfied. All consumers face the same prices in a competitive economy. Consequently, each consumer equates his or her MV_{xy} to the same value.

Since profit-maximizing firms will equate marginal cost to price in a competitive economy, Equation (3) will be satisfied.

$$MC_{xy} = \frac{P_x}{P_y} \tag{3}$$

If a selective unit tax equal to t is placed on good x, consumers would face a price equal to $P_x + t$ and make their consumption decision by setting:

$$MV_{xy} = \frac{P_x + t}{P_y}. \tag{4}$$

If consumers face a gross price of $P_x + t$, the price producers will receive will be P_x. The production decisions will result in Equation (5) being satisfied.

$$MC_{xy} = \frac{P_x}{P_y} \tag{5}$$

Equations (4) and (5) imply that:

$$MV_{xy} > MC_{xy}. \tag{6}$$

Equation (6) indicates that a selective excise tax will cause the marginal value in use of the taxed good to exceed the marginal cost of the taxed good.

The MV_{xy} for each consumer is the value of an additional unit of x in terms of y for that consumer. The MC_{xy} is the cost of an additional unit of x in terms of y to society. Equation (6) implies that a selective excise tax causes the value of an additional unit of x in terms of y for each consumer to exceed the cost of x in terms of y. In other words, the value of producing more x exceeds the cost. For an efficient allocation of resources, more x and less y should be produced.

Application

Legal and Illegal Markets for Taxed Goods

In our discussion of the selective sales tax we argue that, by reducing consumption of a taxed good, consumers can place some of the burden on others. Another type of response to taxation is to employ illegal means to avoid the tax. Since tax avoidance involves some use of resources and results in resources being used in tax enforcement, tax avoidance is costly.

Rodney Smith has examined the effects of excise taxes on illegal markets for distilled spirits.[3] Specifically, he looks at the incentive of wholesalers to underreport sales of distilled spirits in order to avoid paying state excise taxes. Using statistical techniques, Smith finds evidence of a significant illegal market in distilled spirits resulting directly from excise taxation. The size of this market (underreporting on the part of wholesalers) increases with the tax rate. The market decreases, however, when additional resources are devoted to tax enforcement.

General Sales Tax

With specific sales taxes—because they are levied only on certain goods—it is possible for the owners of resources that are employed

[3]Rodney T. Smith, "The Legal and Illegal Markets for Taxed Goods: Pure Theory and Application to State Government Taxation of Distilled Spirits," *Journal of Law and Economics,* Vol. 19 (August 1976), pp. 393–429.

in producing the goods to escape part of the burden of the tax by reallocating their resources away from the taxed industry to industries that are not taxed. The effect of this is to shift a portion of the burden away from themselves to others with the result that the relative prices of goods are altered. The observed change in relative prices reflects the fact that a portion of the burden has been shifted.

In this section, we consider general sales taxation. Under a general sales tax, many commodities are taxed rather than a few, as in the case of a specific sales tax. For a tax to be truly general, all of the goods and services produced in the economy must be subject to the tax. If any one good or service is untaxed, the tax is not general and the owners of resources in the taxed industries will attempt to escape the tax by reallocating their resources to the production of nontaxed goods, as in the case of specific taxes. A general tax has not as yet been implemented; all real-world taxes are specific. Consequently, all real-world taxes will result in the reallocation of resources and in a welfare loss.

The retail sales tax, however, is sufficiently broad in coverage to have many of the characteristics of a general sales tax. Although the tax is not a general tax, since many goods and services are excluded from taxation, we will treat it as though it were general.

The retail sales tax, as the name suggests, is imposed at the point when a retail sales transaction occurs, that is, when the good is sold to the final consumer. As Table 11.1 indicates, this tax contributes a significant amount to total tax revenues collected by state governments.

The Base and Rate of the Tax

The base of the retail sales tax is the retail price of the good subject to tax. The tax is levied as a percentage of this base. In other

Table 11.1 — **State Government Revenue, 1960–1974 (in Millions of Dollars)**

	1960	1965	1970	1971	1972	1973	1974
Total Tax Collections	32,838	48,827	88,939	97,233	112,309	129,808	140,815
General Sales Taxes	4,302	6,711	14,177	15,473	17,619	19,793	22,612
General Sales Taxes as a Percentage of Total Revenue	13.1%	13.7%	15.9%	15.9%	15.6%	15.2%	16.0%

Source: U.S. Department of Commerce, Bureau of the Census, *Statistical Abstract of the United States,* 97th ed. (Washington, D.C.: Government Printing Office, 1976).

words, the tax is an ad valorem tax. If the retail price of the item being taxed is two dollars and the tax rate is five percent, the tax paid will be ten cents. Tax rates vary among the states from two to six percent.

While the general sales tax is levied at the retail level, it could be levied at any stage in the distribution process. A sales tax which is levied at each level of the distribution process is called a turnover tax. The effective tax rate on a turnover tax is much higher than the specified rate. If the specified rate is one percent and if the good changes hands four times—passes through four stages of production and distribution—before reaching the final consumer, the effective rate of the tax will be about four percent. Turnover taxes provide firms with an incentive to integrate vertically because by doing so they can lower the effective tax rate.

The value-added tax is another method of applying a general sales tax to each stage of the production and distribution process. Since the base of this tax is only the value added by the particular production or distribution stage in question (that is, the value added in previous stages of production and distribution are excluded from the base), a three-percent, value-added tax will be equivalent to a three-percent sales tax that is levied on the final sales price of the good. This is true because the sum of value added at each stage of the production process must equal the final price of the good. Value-added taxes are not employed in the United States. Congress, however, has considered the tax from time to time in its continuous search for new methods of raising revenues.

Tax Progression and the General Sales Tax

There seems to be some confusion among journalists and public officials over whether the general sales taxes employed by state governments in the United States are proportional or regressive. Remember, the progression of a tax is determined on the basis of how the tax rate varies with respect to the base. Since general sales taxes apply a fixed rate to the base of the tax, these taxes are proportional taxes.

Of course, if one arbitrarily selects some base other than the base against which the tax is actually levied to determine its progression, it may be possible to show that the tax is regressive or progressive with respect to the arbitrarily selected base. For example, a base that is sometimes selected is income. The total sales tax paid by individuals during a particular time period is divided by their income in that time period. If it is true that individuals with low income spend a greater fraction of measured current income (as opposed to lifetime permanent income) than do individuals with high measured current income, the computation will show that the sales tax is regressive with respect to measured current income. Suppose, for example, that a general sales tax equal to 10 percent of the sales price on all items purchased is in effect. Suppose, also, that the income of individual A is $15,000 in year one and $5,000 in year two. Assume that he will spend the entire amount that he earns over the two-year period but that he prefers to maintain a constant rate of consumption. If this is the case, individual A will spend $10,000 on consumption in each year. The first year he spends $10,000 out of his income of $15,000 and saves $5,000 so that, when this amount is added to his income for the second year, he can spend $10,000 on consumption. Individual A spends 100 percent of his permanent income (in this example we take permanent income to be the average over two years) but the fraction that he spends out of measured current income varies. The tax that he will pay in each year is $1,000 (.10 × $10,000). The tax expressed as a percentage of his permanent income is 10 percent ($1,000/$10,000). However, the tax expressed as a percentage of his measured current income in the first year is 6.67 percent ($1,000/$15,000), while his tax expressed as a percentage of his measured current income the second year is 20 percent ($1,000/$5,000).

When measured current income is used to determine the progression of the tax, the tax appears to be regressive. The tax rate is higher (20 percent rather than 6.67 percent) when the individual's income is lower ($5,000 rather than $15,000). However, this occurs simply because the individual decides to consume $10,000 worth of goods and services in each year rather than $15,000 worth the first year and $5,000 worth the second. In either case, he would pay the same amount in taxes over the two-year period ($2,000) and the tax rate for the two-year period would be the same, 10 percent ($2,000/$20,000). However, if he consumes $10,000 in each year and if measured current income is employed to determine the progression of the tax, the tax will appear to be regressive when, in fact, it is proportional.

Apart from the fact that employing measured current income to determine the progression of a tax violates standard practice and yields arbitrary results, the above method assumes that the incidence of the tax falls on consumers, that is, that the burden of the tax is borne by consumers. This may not be the case; the burden of the tax may fall on the owners of resources.

The Incidence of the General Sales Tax

If the sales tax is general, that is, if the tax falls on the sales of all final goods and there is no nonmarket production, the owners of resources employed in the production of these goods will not be able to escape the tax by reallocating their resources to the production of nontaxed goods. The situation is analogous to one in which a specific tax is levied on a good for which the supply curve is perfectly inelastic with respect to price. To the first approximation, the tax will not cause the quantity of these goods supplied to change. As far as consumers are concerned, the tax initially causes all money prices to rise proportionally while leaving relative prices unchanged. With relative prices unchanged, consumers will wish to purchase the same mix of commodities as they did prior to the tax.

However, with unchanged money incomes, their total expenditures must remain unchanged. This means that the amount received by the producers' net of the tax must fall. The result is that consumers obtain the same quantities of goods after the tax as they do prior to the tax for the same total expenditure but that producers' revenue falls. The difference between the expenditures of consumers and the net revenue of producers is the government revenue from the tax. At this point it is crucial to specify what the government does with the proceeds of the tax.

If the government does not spend the proceeds, that is, if it does not return them to the expenditure stream by acquiring real resources, the price level will fall in each period because the payments to factors of production are falling. In other words, the money incomes of all individuals in the community are falling each period by the amount of the tax. In this case, the tax has no real effect. Individuals consume the same quantities of goods as they consumed prior to the tax. Hence, there is no incidence or tax burden.[4]

If the government uses the proceeds to purchase goods in the same mix that private individuals would have purchased them and distributes the goods to private individuals in proportion to the taxes they paid, the tax, again, has no real effects (ignoring administrative costs). In this case, as in the previous case, there is no incidence or burden to the tax. There can only be a tax burden if the tax results in a reduced flow of goods to at least some individuals.

On the other hand, if the government uses the proceeds to purchase goods in a different mix or distributes the goods in a proportion that differs from the proportion in which taxes are paid, the tax has a real effect. Some individuals will gain and some will lose. Since consumers and producers are just different names that we assign to the same individuals (in general, consumers must also be producers), it is not particularly useful to attempt to determine whether the consumers or the producers suffer. Some consumers

---

[4]This discussion assumes a constantly declining money supply and price level induced by the government's sterilization of the tax proceeds.

will be net gainers and some will be net losers, and the same can be said for producers. The owners of relatively unique resources who experience an increase in demand for those resources will gain while others will lose. Those consumers who receive goods from the government that they value more highly than the goods they could have purchased with the taxes they paid gain, while others for whom the reverse is true lose.

We have mentioned previously that there is no truly general sales tax. Individual states exclude many types of goods from the tax base. Some states exclude food. Medicine and services are not normally subject to the tax. The owners of resources will allocate a greater quantity of resources to these industries than they would otherwise in an attempt to escape a portion of the tax.

Corrective Excise Taxation: A Numerical Example

Sales taxes are sometimes used to correct external effects. To illustrate the problem of corrective excise taxation, we return to the example of the cattle rancher and the corn farmer discussed in Chapter 3. You will recall that a problem arose because the rancher's cattle wander into the farmer's corn field and destroy part of his crop. The damage to the farmer's corn depends upon the number of cattle that the rancher raises above a particular amount. When the rancher does not bear the cost that his wandering cattle impose on the farmer, he will raise too many cattle. ("Too many" means that the sum of the net benefits of cattle ranching and corn farming are not maximized.) We argued that this problem could be solved if private property rights were assigned. Further, it made no difference in terms of the final allocation of resources whether the property right to be free of wandering cattle was assigned to the farmer or whether the property right to allow cattle to wander was assigned to the rancher. Mutual gains from trade would push the final outcome to the same result under either assignment of rights. The outcome that is established by this process is the one which maximizes the sum of the net benefits of cattle ranching and corn farming. This result holds as long as information and transaction costs are zero. Suppose, on the other hand, that these costs are so high that they preclude trade between the farmer and the rancher. In this case it *may* be possible for the government to impose a corrective tax on the cattle rancher, which will induce him to raise the same quantity of cattle he would raise if high transaction and information costs did not preclude trade between him and the farmer (the amount that maximizes net benefits). Of course, if information and transaction costs are high for the farmer and the rancher, there is no a priori reason to presume they will be lower for the government officials responsible for administering the tax (see the discussion in Chapter 3). For the present, we will assume that government officials can acquire accurate information at low costs.

Table 11.2 reproduces Table 3.2 except that we now assume that a tax of three dollars per head is imposed on the cattle rancher for each head in excess of nine that he raises. In the absence of the tax and given the assumption that exchange between the rancher and farmer will not occur due to high information and transaction costs, the rancher will choose to raise 14 head of cattle because this is the number that maximizes his profits. Note that net benefits are not maximized when the rancher raises 14 cattle. If the tax is imposed on the rancher, his after-tax profits will fall to the amounts presented in column three. His after-tax profits are maximized at 12 head, and this will be the number that he decides to raise. Note, also, that net benefits are maximized at this quantity and this is the quantity he would choose to raise if trade were possible.

It is, of course, important that the proper tax rate be chosen. Had the taxing authority imposed a tax of $4.50 per head, the rancher would have chosen to raise 11 head of cattle rather than 12 head. The net benefits of cattle ranching and corn farming would have been lower. In order to determine the proper tax rate, the taxing authority must know the farmer's loss as additional cattle are raised. Accurate information regarding the farmer's loss may be difficult to acquire. Note that the farmer has an incentive to overstate his loss; his profits are highest if the rancher raises only 9 cattle. If he can convince the taxing authority that he suffers a $7 loss when the rancher raises the tenth head and if the taxing authority imposes a $7 tax on the tenth head, the rancher will raise only 9 head of cattle. Net benefits are not maximized, but the farmer's profits are higher than they would be if 12 head were raised. The farmer's profits are higher by $6 (the reduction in his loss) if only 9 head are raised, and he would be willing to spend up to this amount in an attempt to convince the taxing authority to tax the tenth head at $7.

Table 11.2

Cattle	Profit of Rancher before Tax	Profit of Rancher after Tax	Loss to Farmer	Net Benefit
9	$ 94	$ 94	$ 0	$ 94
10	100	97	2	98
11	105	99	3	102
12	109	100	6	103
13	111	99	10	101
14	112	97	15	97
15	111	93	21	90

Why does it pay the farmer to misstate his loss in this situation but not in the situation when property rights are assigned and the farmer and rancher exchange agreements? Assume that the property right to be free of wandering cattle is assigned to the farmer so that the rancher must buy the farmer's agreement before he can increase the size of the herd. The rancher would be willing to pay up to $6 for the farmer's permission to raise the tenth head. Note that the farmer's loss is only $2. If the farmer obtains, say, $5 from the rancher as payment for permission to raise the tenth head, the farmer's profit will increase by $3 ($5 – $2). If, however, the farmer overstated his loss at $7, the rancher would not exchange. The farmer would lose the profit of $3 on this first exchange and all subsequent exchanges. In this case, it is costly for the farmer to be dishonest. When property rights are not assigned and the government employs its taxing power to attempt to achieve the outcome that maximizes net benefits, it pays the farmer to overstate his loss because he is not forced to bear the costs of the misinformation he provides.

There is another important difference between the results obtained when a corrective tax rather than property right assignment is employed to solve an externality problem. When a corrective tax is employed, a portion of the income of the community accrues to the taxing authority. In our example, this amounts to nine dollars per period. If a property right assignment were employed, the net that results from allocating resources more efficiently would accrue to the farmer and rancher.

Recall that the motivation for employing a corrective tax to solve the problem of wandering cattle was the assumption that the cost of exchanging agreements between the rancher and the farmer are prohibitive. Suppose a corrective tax of $3 per head is imposed. We have shown previously that this tax will maximize net benefits if trade is not possible. The rancher will produce 12 head. His after-tax profits are $100, and the total damage to the corn farmer is $6. However, once this has been achieved, the farmer's profits would increase by $3 (the reduction in his loss) if the herd size were reduced to 11. The rancher's after-tax profit would fall by $1 if he reduced the herd size to 11. The potential gain from an exchange of agreements to reduce herd size by one is $2—the difference between the farmer's increase in profits and the rancher's reduction in profits.

As long as information and transaction costs are less than this potential gain from exchange, it will pay the two to exchange agreements that will alter the herd size. In this case, however, the exchange will move the solution away from the efficient outcome. To illustrate, suppose that the information and transaction costs are 50 cents and that they must be paid by the farmer. The farmer would be willing to offer the rancher $2.50 (the difference between the farmer's loss reduction and transaction and information costs) for his agreement to reduce the herd size by one. The rancher will accept anything over $1. The exchange will be made and herd size will be 11 head of cattle. This is less than the efficient quantity. Further trades will not occur because the potential gain less the information and transaction costs is negative. The result is that if corrective taxes are imposed when information and transaction costs are positive but not prohibitive, a less than efficient quantity of cattle will be raised.

To summarize, corrective taxes may be employed to improve resource allocation when transaction and information costs are high for private individuals but low for the taxing authority. The tax will motivate some individuals to misstate the damages that they experience from the externality-generating activity. The tax will result in a different distribution of the net gain than would result if trade in agreements were possible. If transaction and information costs are positive but not prohibitive for the private parties, the tax may not achieve the desired outcome. The following application discusses a particular case in which a corrective excise tax has been imposed on the owners of firms that discharge pollutants into the sewer system.

Application

Sewer Surcharges and Pollution Control

Don Ethridge has estimated the impact of charging the owners of firms for the pollutants that their firms discharge into the sewer system.[5] The charge is based on the strength of the wastes disposed of in this way. The types of firms examined were beet and poultry processing firms. These firms discharge wastes that deplete the oxygen content of the water into which they are dumped, thus affecting certain aquatic organisms that require oxygen and imposing external costs on people who fish. Ethridge estimated that charging $.02 per pound of strong wastes disposed of through the sewer system would decrease the amount of the wastes disposed of in this way by 75 percent in beet processing firms and by 25 percent in poultry processing firms. Furthermore, he estimated that increasing the charge by 1 percent would reduce the amount of strong wastes disposed of through the sewer system by more than 6.5 percent in beet processing plants and by more than .5 percent in poultry processing plants.

Note that increasing these charges does not necessarily reduce the amount of waste generated by firms to the extent indicated by the reported percentages. It reduces the wastes *disposed of through*

[5]Don Ethridge, "User Charges as a Means of Pollution Control: The Case of Sewer Surcharges," *Bell Journal of Economics and Management Science,* Vol. 3 (Spring 1972), pp. 346–54.

the sewer system by the reported percentages. Charging firms for the wastes disposed of through the sewer system will induce them to find less costly ways of waste disposal. It is hoped that they will discover methods of waste disposal in which the social cost of disposal more closely approximates the private costs of disposal than was the case prior to the charge being levied.

Questions and Exercises

1. Imposing corrective taxation on an externality-generating activity when transaction and information costs are positive will always bring about an efficient outcome. Comment.

2. The free exchange of private property rights will induce the parties that benefit and those that are damaged by an externality-generating act to more honestly reflect their benefits and damages than would be the case if the activity were taxed. Comment.

3. When a decision is made to correct for an externality-generating activity through taxation rather than the assignment of private property rights, does the property right to decide the rate of externality-generating activity vanish? If not, to whom does it accrue? Does this right have value; that is, can it be exchanged for rights in other goods? What is your evidence?

4. Gasoline is produced in two grades, premium and regular. The price of premium is higher than the price of regular. If a 5-cent unit tax is levied on gasoline to discourage its consumption, the quantity of premium gasoline demanded will rise relative to the quantity of regular gasoline demanded. Why?

5. Raising the excise tax imposed on tobacco products will increase the revenue that the government collects from this tax. Comment.

6. As a consequence of imposing a unit tax of T dollars on good Q, the quantity produced falls from Q_0 to Q_1. (See the following figure.) Area $ABCE$ is equal to \$90,000,000. The share of labor in variable cost is one-third. The annual wage rate is \$6,000. How many workers will have to seek employment elsewhere as a result of the tax?

7. In this chapter, a selective sales tax was shown to distort the allocation of resources. Would this result hold for a general sales tax? Show why.

8. In the same discussion, the selective sales tax was placed on the buyer side of the market. Show the effects of placing the tax on the seller side. Are the results the same in both cases?

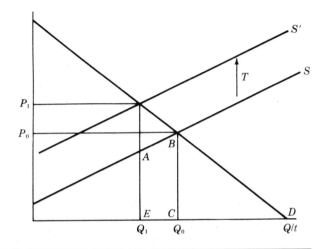

9. When the demand curve for a taxed product is elastic, consumers are better able to shift the burden of the tax elsewhere than when it is inelastic. Does this mean that consumers are made worse off by a tax of equal rates when the demand is inelastic than when it is elastic?

10. What are some of the major problems encountered in implementing a truly general sales tax?

11. If the supply curve of a taxed good is perfectly inelastic, the sellers will bear the entire burden of the tax. Explain why this is the case.

12. Explain why a 5-percent value-added tax and a 5-percent turnover tax yield different results.

Additional Readings

Barzel, Yoram. "An Alternative Approach to the Analysis of Taxation." *Journal of Political Economy,* Vol. 84 (December 1976), pp. 1177-97.

Buchanan, J. M., and Stubblebine, W. C. "Externality." *Economica,* Vol. 29 (November 1962), pp. 371-84.

Due, John F. "Sales Taxation and the Consumer." *American Economic Review,* Vol. LIII (December 1963), pp. 1078-83.

12

Wealth Taxation

In the United States, the taxes that fall under the general category of wealth taxation are the property tax and the estate and gift taxes. The property tax, though it is not employed by the federal government, is important because it is a major source of revenue for local governments and is used to some extent by state governments. Estate and gift taxes are employed by both federal and state governments but do not contribute significantly to total government revenue. (See Table 12.1.)

The property tax accounts for more than 32 percent of local government revenue and amounts to almost 10 percent of the revenue collected by all levels of government. This tax is the major form of wealth taxation in the United States. Since this is the case, estate and gift taxes will be treated only briefly in this chapter. Most of our effort will be devoted to a discussion of the property tax.

While the property tax is an important source of revenue for local governments (that is, cities, counties, school districts, and spe-

Table 12.1 **Wealth Taxes for All Governments, 1974 (in Millions of Dollars)**

| | All Governments | Federal | State and Local | | |
			Total	State	Local
Total Revenue	$484,650	$289,059	$237,916	$140,815	$143,193
Property Taxes	47,754	—	47,754	1,301	46,452
Estate & Gift Taxes	6,465	5,035	1,430	1,430	—
Property Taxes as a Percentage of Total	9.8%	—	20.1%	.9%	32.4%
Estate & Gift Taxes as a Percentage of Total	1.3%	1.7%	.6%	1.0%	—

Source: U.S. Bureau of the Census, Governmental Finances.

cial districts), it recently has declined as a percentage of total city government revenue collected. In 1960, the property tax accounted for almost 35 percent of total revenue collected by cities. In 1974, however, this had fallen to 23 percent while intergovernmental revenue (transfers from the state and federal government to the cities) increased substantially. It appears that local government officials have used the increased revenue received from the federal and state governments to finance new expenditures while "holding the line" on property taxes.

Although the property tax has declined somewhat in importance when compared to the total revenue collected by cities, it accounts for more than 50 percent of the *tax* revenue collected by cities and seems to be a more important source of total revenue *and* tax revenue for smaller cities than it is for larger cities. (See Table 12.2.) The property tax increases from 68 percent of the *tax* revenue collected for cities of 50,000 or fewer in population to 74 percent for cities of about 200,000 in population, and then declines to 54 percent for cities with populations in excess of 1,000,000.

The Equivalence of Income and Wealth Taxation

We define the contribution of an asset to the wealth of an individual as the present price (present value or capitalized value) of the stream of net future income that the asset is expected to yield. An individual's total net present wealth is computed by summing all the present prices of his or her assets and subtracting his or her

**Property Taxes as a Percent
of Other Revenue by City Size, 1974**   **Table 12.2**

Property Taxes as a Percent of:	Population						
	Less than 50,000	50,000 to 99,000	100,000 to 199,000	200,000 to 299,000	300,000 to 499,000	500,000 to 999,000	1,000,000 or more
Total Local Government Revenue	30.2	35.0	34.9	27.1	23.3	24.4	24.1
Local Government Tax Revenue	68.8	73.3	74.4	65.4	59.3	56.9	54.8

Source: U.S. Bureau of the Census, *City Government Finances.*

liabilities, which are the present prices of expected future expenses. There is no time dimension associated with the individual's net present wealth. In other words, an individual's wealth is a stock not a flow; it is not wealth per year or per month but as of this moment. An individual's wealth exists uniquely in time. It reflects, given current information, an estimate of what the future holds. Consequently, it is subject to change as perceptions of the future change, that is, as estimates of future income and expense flows change.

Income, on the other hand, is a flow. We speak of income per month or per quarter or per year. There is always a time dimension associated with income. The stream of expected future income yielded per unit of time by an asset is called the net productivity of investment. It is this income stream, or net productivity, which is used to compute the contribution of an asset to the individual's net present wealth. Of course, since individuals prefer income now to income in the future, future income is worth less than the same amount of income received today. Consequently, expected future income must be discounted by the rate of interest in computing its present value or price. Specifically, suppose you could purchase a property that would yield a perpetual stream of net income equal to $500 annually. If the interest rate is 10 percent, the most you would be willing to pay for that property is $5,000. This is true because $5,000 invested at 10 percent would yield a perpetual stream of income of precisely $500. You would not be willing to pay more than $5,000 for this property, say, $5,100, because $5,100 invested alternatively at 10 percent would yield a perpetual income stream of $510 annually, which is more than you could earn owning the property in question. You would, of course, be more than happy to pay less than $5,000 for the property. If you were able to obtain it for less, your net present wealth would rise by the difference between what you pay and $5,000. The most you would be willing to pay for the property (its present price or value) is, in this case, computed by dividing the income stream by the interest rate ($5,000 = $500/.10).[1] This illustrates that the value of any asset may be expressed in terms of the stream of income that it yields or, alternatively, in terms of its present price.

It should be clear from this discussion that it would be a matter of indifference to the individual if the government should levy a 20-percent annual tax on the $500 income stream (.20 × $500 = $100), a 2-percent annual tax on the $5,000 value of the property

---

[1]For income streams of finite maturity the appropriate equation is:

$$P = \frac{F}{r}\left[1 - \frac{1}{(1+r)^n}\right]$$

where P is the present price, r is the rate of interest, and n is the number of years over which F (the annual income) is earned.

(.02 × \$5,000 = \$100), or a one-time \$1,000 tax on the \$5,000 property value. Each of these taxes reduces the present price or value of the property from \$5,000 to \$4,000. In other words, each of these taxes will reduce the individual's net present wealth by the same amount. It is possible, then, to levy wealth taxes that are equivalent to income taxes in terms of the impact of the tax on the individual.

Any income stream, no matter how short or long its duration, can be converted into a present value. If, in levying wealth taxes, the capitalized value of *all* income streams (in the broadest sense) were included in the base of the tax, no individual could escape the tax by altering the forms in which he or she holds wealth. In practice, however, wealth taxes discriminate among different forms of wealth. As a rule, only relatively long-lived assets such as real estate, autos, and, in some states, furniture and household appliances are taxed. This has, as you would expect, certain implications for the analysis of the incidence of the tax and will be discussed later in this chapter.

The Property Tax Base and Rates

The most important tax on wealth levied in the United States is the property tax, particularly the real estate tax. Roughly 50 percent of the revenue produced by this tax is collected from the owners of residential property. About 40 percent of the tax revenue is collected from levies on the property of commercial business enterprises and the remaining 10 percent is collected from levies on agricultural property.

The property tax is levied as a percentage (the nominal rate of the tax) of the assessed value (the tax base) of the property. The property tax rate is, generally, only applied to a fraction of assessed value in computing the tax liability. The assessment is an attempt to estimate indirectly the market value of the property. Consequently, the base of the property tax is some fraction of the estimated market value of the property.

Since property taxes are, for the most part, levied by local governments, tax rates vary among localities. Real estate tax rates for certain selected cities appear in Table 12.3. Since the fraction of assessed value subject to tax differs among cities, the nominal rate of the tax must be adjusted to reflect the effective tax rate on the estimated market value of the property when comparing the tax rates among different cities.

The first column of Table 12.3 presents the effective tax rate per \$100 of assessed market value. The effective tax rate varies between about 1 and 4 percent for these cities. The effective tax rate is computed by multiplying the normal tax rate (third column) by the fraction of assessed value subject to tax (second column).

Table 12.3   Real Estate Tax Rates in Selected Cities

City	Effective Tax Rate per $100 of Assessed Market Value	Percent of Assessed Value Subject to Tax	Normal Tax Rate
Buffalo	$4.31	$40.6	$10.61
Los Angeles	3.43	24.4	14.04
Indianapolis	3.29	26.5	12.40
Philadelphia	2.80	62.5	4.48
Chicago	2.75	32.3	8.51
Detroit	2.73	42.4	6.45
Houston	2.38	41.0	5.81
New York	2.18	29.6	7.35
San Francisco	2.13	16.7	12.75
Seattle	1.82	46.3	3.93
Denver	1.71	21.6	7.93
New Orleans	1.69	20.6	8.19
Phoenix	1.55	13.2	11.72
Columbus	1.17	27.4	4.76

Source: U.S. Department of Commerce, Bureau of the Census, *Statistical Abstract of the United States,* 97th ed. (Washington, D.C.: Government Printing Office, 1976).

One of the most difficult problems in computing property tax liability is assessing the market value of the property. If all of the property subject to this tax were relatively homogeneous and changed hands frequently in unrestricted markets, assessment of market value would not be a problem. However, particular parcels of real estate, which comprise the largest portion of the property tax base, are somewhat unique. Each parcel is different with respect to its location and other attributes. Furthermore, there may be considerable periods of time during which the parcel is held by a single owner and not subject to a market valuation. Tax assessors take into consideration the price at which the parcel sold in its most recent exchange. But real estate prices, like all other prices, are subject to change over time. If it has been a long time since the exchange occurred, this price is not likely to reflect the current market price of the parcel accurately. Another source of information for the tax assessor is the price at which different properties with similar attributes were recently exchanged. This method has its limitations, however, because a particular location is often an important variable affecting the value of any parcel of real estate.

Another way the assessor may estimate the market value of a particular parcel is by capitalizing the future stream of net earnings that ownership of the parcel is expected to yield. We have shown that the present market price of any long-lived asset will reflect the expected future stream of earnings yielded by that asset when employed in its highest valued use. If the tax assessor has accurate information concerning expected future earnings, capitalizing these earnings at the appropriate interest rate will yield an accurate estimate of current market price. In some cases, it may be easier for the assessor to obtain an accurate estimate of the future yield of the property than it would be to estimate its present market price directly. This may be true in situations where the property is leased for a specified period of time and for a given annual fee. In other cases, however, the expected future yield may be difficult to estimate. A particular piece of agricultural property may be located on the edge of a growing town. Its present market price will reflect the probability that it will be converted to residential or commercial use in the future. Consequently, capitalizing the property's expected future returns if employed in agriculture will not yield an accurate estimate of its market value.

This brief discussion illustrates that estimating the base of the property tax is a difficult problem. There is no doubt that many mistakes are made in the estimation of the tax base. If these mistakes occur randomly, the mistakes will not affect resource allocation. If, on the other hand, there is some bias in the incidence of mistakes, the mistakes themselves will result in a different allocation of resources than would be the case in the absence of mistakes.

The property tax rate is determined by the revenue requirements of the local government and by the tax base (total assessed value of all property within the jurisdiction). The revenue requirement is, of course, determined by the planned expenditures of the local government. For example, if planned expenditures on schools are $50,000 and the total assessed value of property is $1,000,000, the rate levied for school finance would be 5 cents per dollar of assessed value.[2] If planned expenditures on schools should rise with an unchanged total assessment, the tax rate will rise so that the product of the new rate and old base will yield an amount equal to the new increased expenditures.

Local government expenditures, of course, comprise more than expenditures on schools; therefore, a separate levy is made for each different type of expenditure. If planned expenditure for police protection is $20,000, an additional levy of 2 cents per dollar of assessed value would be added to the levy for schools. When the property owner receives his tax bill, each of these rates will appear separately. This provides him with information concerning *his share* of the cost of local government programs. As a consequence, he is better able to make a judgment concerning whether the benefits he receives from these programs exceed his cost. This method of billing for taxes is unique to local government.

---

[2] In practice, property taxes are generally levied in terms of mills per $100 of assessed value. One mill = 1/1000 of a dollar.

Estate and Gift Taxes

Estate and gift taxes are taxes imposed on the transfer of wealth from one individual to another. As we noted earlier (Table 12.1), these taxes do not contribute significantly to government revenue. The base of the estate tax is the estimated market value of the decedent's net worth (assets less liabilities) less an exemption of $60,000, which is not subject to the tax. Tax rates vary from 5 percent on the first $5,000 subject to tax up to 77 percent on amounts in excess of $10,000,000.

The incidence of the estate tax falls on both the donor and the recipient. Clearly, the recipient bears part of the burden of the tax because he or she obtains command over fewer resources than he or she would in the absence of the tax. However, the donor bears a portion of the burden, also. This statement may appear to imply that a dead person can pay taxes. That, however, is not what we intend. Obviously, a positive relationship exists between the donor's utility and the wealth of the recipient prior to the donor's death. The donor's utility is higher today because he or she knows that the wealth of the recipient will be greater in the future by the amount of the bequest. The knowledge that the estate tax will reduce the amount transferred reduces the donor's utility today. The estate tax will alter the relative prices confronted by the donor. It will raise the price of transferring wealth in the future relative to the price of consuming it today. Consequently, the donor will choose to consume more today and transfer less in the future. Second, the donor will attempt to avoid part of the tax by employing the services of a professional estate planner, accountant, or lawyer. The demand for the services of these professionals by testators attests to the statement that a portion of the tax is borne by the donor.

Transfers of wealth prior to death are subject to the gift tax. The donor is allowed to transfer $3,000 per year per recipient without being subject to the gift tax. However, should this transfer to any recipient exceed $3,000 in any year, the difference will be accumulated with other gifts exceeding $3,000 in the computation of the tax base. The donor is allowed one exemption of $30,000 during his or her lifetime. Once the above differences exceed this amount, the residual is subject to tax, the rates of which vary from about 2 percent to about 58 percent.

Wealth Taxes and the Accumulation of Wealth

The rate at which the wealth of individuals grows depends upon the rate at which the present value of their net assets grows. We use the term assets in a broad sense to include human assets (education and skills), nonhuman physical assets, and the stability of political institutions (in particular, the laws protecting private property). The present value of the net assets owned by individuals may grow over time either because the quality of these assets is improved (an individual acquires a skill) or because the individual acquires more net assets of the same quality. The increase in the present value of net assets over time is largely accounted for by saving and investing, that is, foregoing present consumption (saving) in order to convert present goods into goods that will yield increased consumption in the future (investing).

The rate at which individuals desire to increase wealth will depend upon their preferences and their opportunities. That is, the rate at which wealth is increased will depend upon the rate at which individuals are willing to trade off present for future consumption and the opportunities they confront in doing so. This is summarized in Figure 12.1. Along the horizontal axis, the quantity of saving and investment per unit of time is measured. Along the vertical axis, we measure the rate at which individuals are *willing* to trade off future consumption for present consumption (the rate of interest, r) at various savings rates and the rate at which they *can* make this trade-off (the net productivity of investment, g) at various rates of investment. The equilibrium rate of saving and investing is given by I_0 and S_0 in Figure 12.1. At any lower rate of saving and investing, the net productivity of investment exceeds the rate of interest. Individuals will find that they will be better off (able to obtain more future consumption than is necessary to compensate for foregone present consumption) by moving to S_0 and I_0.

Figure 12.1

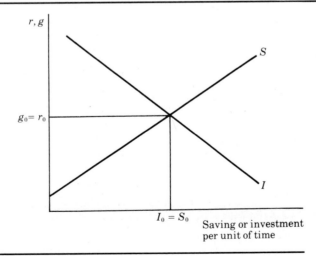

The reverse is true for rates of saving and investing in excess of S_0 and I_0. In equilibrium the net productivity of investment, g, is equal to the rate of interest, r, at the margin. Consequently, the rate of interest reflects the relative price of present consumption in terms of future consumption at the margin. The rate of interest reflects the quantity of future goods that must be foregone to increase consumption of goods now.

Suppose that a general tax is levied on wealth. It has been shown that a tax levied on the income flow generated by an asset can be equivalent to a tax levied on the present price or capital value of the asset. Suppose that a one-time tax is levied on the capital values of all assets. The tax will not affect the net productivity of investment because it does not affect the technical relationship that gives the rate at which individuals *can* trade present for future consumption. If it was possible, prior to the tax, to obtain two consumption goods one year from now by saving and investing one consumption good today, it will continue to be possible after the tax is imposed. Consequently, the tax does not affect the investment function (I) in Figure 12.1. The tax, however, does reduce the total amount of wealth owned by private individuals. Since consumption and saving are positively related to the individuals' wealth, both present consumption and saving will decline at each rate of interest. This is reflected by a leftward shift in the saving function (S) as shown in Figure 12.2. The tax will cause the rate of saving and investing to decline. Put another way, the rate at which the stock of wealth is augmented will decline. The rate of interest and net productivity of investment rise from g_0 and r_0 to g_1 and r_1.

Figure 12.2

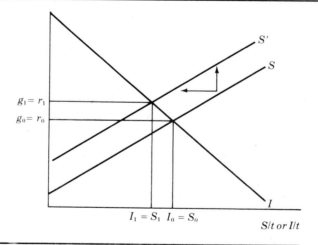

As we have mentioned, the wealth taxes that are levied in the United States are not general wealth taxes; they are levied only on particular classes of assets. However, they are sufficiently broad so that the effects discussed above concerning a general tax are qualitatively correct in a total or overall sense.

On the other hand, wealth taxes (real estate taxes in particular) are levied at different effective rates in different local government jurisdictions. These differences will affect the after-tax rate of return (net productivity of investment) within these jurisdictions, other things being equal. Investment in jurisdictions with relatively high tax rates will decline while investment in jurisdictions with relatively low tax rates will rise. Reallocation of investment will continue until after-tax rates of return are equal among jurisdictions. This will cause the relative prices of assets that are tied to particular jurisdictions to change. Real estate is one of these assets. Consequently, the price of real estate in jurisdictions that have high tax rates will fall relative to the price of real estate in jurisdictions with low tax rates; that is, the tax will be capitalized. It is important to note that the above discussion assumes that the benefits financed by the tax are held constant among jurisdictions. If benefits vary positively with taxes, the above results may not be observed. Consequently, if real estate tax capitalization is to be observed in any particular case, an adjustment must be made for different benefit levels among jurisdictions.

Application

Local Tax Rates, Public Benefit Levels, and Property Values

Harvey Rosen and David Fullerton have estimated the extent to which property tax differentials were capitalized in 53 northeastern New Jersey communities for the year 1970.[3] Since the proceeds of the property tax are used mainly to finance public schools, Rosen and Fullerton used student achievement test scores as a measure of the benefits financed by the property tax. The hypothesis is that average real estate property values are inversely related to the average effective tax rate within the jurisdiction and positively related to average student achievement test scores within the jurisdiction. The value of real estate and improvements will, of course, depend upon many things other than tax rates and test scores. One might expect it to vary with the number of rooms per home, the

[3]Harvey S. Rosen and David J. Fullerton, "A Note on Local Tax Rates, Public Benefit Levels, and Property Values," *Journal of Political Economy*, Vol. 85 (April 1977), pp. 433–40.

distance to the work center, the age of the home, and the quality of the home for which the income of the owner may act as a proxy. Rosen and Fullerton adjust their estimate for each of these variables. Their results indicate that, once these adjustments are made, about 88 percent of the tax differential among jurisdictions is capitalized. Further, according to their estimates, as average achievement test scores rise, property values rise. Median property values rise by about $4,300 as the average achievement in reading increases from the bottom decile to the top decile.

Incidence of the Property Tax

Short Run

To begin, assume, as is actually the case, that property tax rates vary across localities. In the short run, if a local government increases its property tax rate relative to tax rates in other areas, the owners of property in that locality will bear the full burden of the tax. This is because all real property, including the structures, is fixed in the short run. Since the supply curve for all real property is vertical in the short run, holders of real property are unable to alter their behavior when confronted with the tax and will bear the full burden of the tax rate increase. Owners of property cannot escape the tax by selling that property because the higher rate is capitalized into the price. Purchasers of real property will not buy property in the relatively higher tax rate areas unless the rate of return is at least equal to that in relatively lower tax rate areas. This means that the price of real property in high tax rate areas will be lower than that in the low tax areas. The difference in price will equal the capitalized value of the difference in tax rates between the high and low tax areas. The lower price of high tax rate property will just allow the new purchaser of the highly taxed property to earn the same rate of return as if he or she had bought the low tax rate property.

Long Run

In the long run, since land is fixed, the owners of the land at the time when the new tax rate is applied will bear the full burden of the tax. As in the short run, the relatively higher tax rate will be capitalized. This lowers the price of land and results in equal rates of return to holding land in high and low tax rate areas.

In the long run, however, improvements to land are not fixed. Capital investment in improvements will tend to move from the high tax rate areas to low tax rate areas. Residential, commercial, and industrial construction will tend to concentrate in the low tax rate areas. This will increase the demand for land in the low tax rate areas and at the same time will decrease the demand in the high tax rate areas. The movement will continue until the rates of return on investing in improvements to real estate net of taxes are equalized. The equilibrating, or balancing, factor here is the price of land, which will decrease in the high tax rate jurisdiction and increase in the low tax rate jurisdiction so that the net rates of return in all jurisdictions are equal.

Since maintenance and repair of existing structures are a form of investment, the rate of return on this activity will decrease in high rate areas as opposed to low rate areas. This will tend to cause the existing structures in high rate areas to deteriorate relative to those in the low rate jurisdictions. As in the case of the corporate income tax, the overall result of increasing tax rates will be to lower the rate of return on investment. It should be pointed out that, when this movement in investment takes place, the price of land in the low rate jurisdictions will increase.

The burden of an increase in property tax in one jurisdiction will be borne by the landowners in that jurisdiction. That portion of the tax on improvements to land (for example, buildings and other structures) will be borne by all investors in this type of capital because investors in high tax areas can alter their behavior in the long run and shift part of the burden to investors in low tax jurisdictions. Finally, owners of land in low rate jurisdictions benefit from rate increases in the high rate jurisdictions since this increases the value of their land.

Tiebout Model

An assumption of the previous discussion was that the per capita benefits—resulting from government expenditure on goods and services—provided by high and low tax rate jurisdictions were the same. If this assumption is relaxed, the results with regard to the burden of the tax and capitalization of the tax may be entirely different. If benefits in different jurisdictions or cities vary along with property taxes, the benefit differentials may be capitalized into the value of land. Actually, what one might expect is that the net benefits (the value of the benefits minus taxes) would be capitalized. High net benefit jurisdictions would have higher land prices for equivalent property than low net benefit areas, so that the rates of return, including the value of net benefits, are equalized.

Charles M. Tiebout has hypothesized that, under certain conditions, the provision of local government services may be much more efficient than provision of public goods at the federal level.[4] Essentially, Tiebout asserts that there is a market for public goods and services at the local level which will lead to optimal public expenditure at this level. Rather than relying on the political mechanisms we have discussed in previous chapters, provision of local public goods may take place in a market similar to normal competitive markets.

Tiebout begins with a set of seven assumptions that he uses to develop his hypothesis. Tiebout shows that it is possible for public provision at the local level "(1) to force the voter (resident) to reveal his preferences; (2) to be able to satisfy them in the same sense that a private goods market does, and (3) to tax him accordingly."[5] Tiebout's seven assumptions are:

1. Individuals are mobile, so that they are able to move to the community that has an expenditure pattern (expenditure levels for the various local public goods) and accompanying tax rate that maximize the individuals' utility.

2. Individuals are assumed to know the expenditure patterns and tax structure of all communities.

3. There are a large number of communities among which individuals can choose.

4. Restrictions due to differences in employment opportunities among communities do not exist.

5. The public goods and services provided by communities do not exhibit intercommunity externalities.

6. There is an optimum size for each community. That is, each community has a U-shaped, long-run average cost curve for the provision of public goods and services to individuals. The optimum size would be at the minimum of that curve.

7. Communities below optimum size seek to attract new residents, and those above optimum size seek to reduce their populations. This last assumption implies that the individuals who govern communities attempt in some sense to maximize profits.

If a community is below its optimum size, it is possible to lower the costs per individual to the existing residents by attracting new residents. It is assumed that it is politically expedient to do so. Politicians who are successful at doing this will be rewarded by being

---

[4]Charles M. Tiebout, "A Pure Theory of Local Expenditure," *Journal of Political Economy,* Vol. 65 (October 1956), 416–24.

[5]Tiebout, pp. 417–18.

reelected. However, when communities become too large, per capita taxes increase, causing some individuals to move to lower cost areas.

In the Tiebout model, individuals shop around for the community that has the public expenditure and tax rate package best suited to their preferences. This "voting with one's feet," or moving to the utility-maximizing community, provides information to local politicians about the tastes and preferences of actual and potential residents. Preferences are much more likely to be revealed in this context than in the more traditional voting context. If a city provides a generally unsatisfactory bundle of public goods and/or provides them at a high tax rate, individuals will leave that city. As the population drops below the optimum size, there will be upward pressure on per capita costs and taxes. Under these circumstances, the remaining residents can vote for a more effective set of politicians.

The fact that individuals have many alternatives not only generates more information about preferences but also breaks the monopoly of the governmental unit providing the goods and services. Since there are alternative providers of public goods, no one provider has the monopoly power that the government has at the federal level.[6] The competition among local governments provides the incentive for local politicians to satisfy the preferences of their constituents for public goods and tax rates.

In the Tiebout model, no capitalization of differential tax rates would be observed in the long run. This is because, in a long-run equilibrium, differences in tax rates among communities would result only from different levels of expenditure on public goods. These different expenditure levels would be determined by the preferences of the residents in the various communities. Each community would tend to be populated by individuals with similar tastes and preferences. Because of the large number of communities, each individual can find a community whose taxation and expenditure patterns match his or her preferences. For example, older individuals, single individuals, and childless couples would tend to live in communities in which the level of expenditure on public education is low. Individuals with children would live in other communities where the level of expenditure on public schools is higher. They will be willing to pay higher tax rates to maintain a quantity and quality of education that maximizes their utility.

---

[6]Actually, government at the national level does not enjoy a complete monopoly because individuals can emigrate to other countries. This international "voting with your feet" is the only way citizens of many countries can alter the government under which they live; that is, by emigrating to a country with a more satisfactory political system. This is why the Soviets are so reluctant to allow their citizens to leave. Many desire to do so, and this clearly signals the failure of their political system.

The higher tax rate in communities that spend more on education will not be accompanied by lower property prices since the higher tax rates result in an education expenditure preferred by that community. Land prices will not fall as a result of the higher tax; that is, the tax will not be capitalized.

In the real world, as might be expected, local public goods are not always provided at their optimum levels as predicted by the Tiebout model. Many of Tiebout's assumptions are not satisfied in the real world. First, localities use other taxes as well as the property tax. Some of these taxes, such as corporate income taxes and inventory taxes, are hidden, so that it is difficult for individuals to know the full cost of the government in a given community. Second, job locations and commuting time tend to restrict mobility.

Despite these problems, provision of goods and services at local levels is probably more efficient than at the national level. "Voting with your feet" and competition from other communities place a constraint on local government that does not exist at the federal government level.

Competition among government entities plays a role at the state level as well as at the local level. Evidence for this can be found in the fact that many individuals and businesses are leaving the New Jersey, New York, and New England areas, where taxes are higher than the national average and are not accompanied by satisfactory levels of public goods and services. The population tends to be moving to the South and Southwest where taxes are much lower.[7]

Application

The Tiebout Model and Capitalization

In the Tiebout model, local governments adjust their level of public expenditure and tax rates in response to the revealed preferences of individuals. Under certain conditions (Tiebout's seven assumptions), this adjustment will lead to an optimal allocation of public goods with no capitalization of differential tax rates or expenditure levels. Many studies have found that individuals will vote with their feet if expenditure levels and/or tax rates in a community do not meet with their satisfaction (see the study by Wallace Oates),[8] at least for certain crucial public goods such as education. If, however, the information conveyed by this activity is

---

[7]U.S. Bureau of the Census, *U.S. Census of Population* (1970), Vol. 1.

[8]Wallace E. Oates, "The Effects of Property Taxes and Local Spending on Property Rates: An Empirical Study of Property Tax Capitalization and the Tiebout Hypothesis," *Journal of Political Economy*, Vol. 77 (1969), pp. 957-71.

ignored by local politicians, differential tax and expenditure patterns will be capitalized. If local politicians do not adjust taxation and expenditure levels to satisfy individual preferences as revealed by population movements, then the allocation of local public goods will not move towards efficiency. Capitalization will occur and Tiebout's results will break down.

Matthew Edel and Elliot Sclar attempt to test this aspect of the Tiebout model.[9] Edel and Sclar try to determine whether the long-run supply of local public goods adjusts to the demand for the goods as revealed through a voting-with-the-feet process. Using communities in the Boston area for their study, they attempt to determine the degree to which taxes and the level of expenditure on public schooling and highway maintenance reflect individual preferences in the long run. They do this by looking at the effects of these and other variables on housing prices in the various communities for each decade from 1930 to 1970.

Edel and Sclar find that capitalization of school expenditures tends to disappear over time. This is in accordance with the Tiebout model, which implies that the expenditure on education may be approaching an efficient level in these communities. However, their results do not show that provision of other services (specifically, highway maintenance) approaches a Tiebout (efficient) equilibrium.

Questions and Exercises

1. Instead of playing bridge, a man works around the house painting and refinishing the walls. Why is this a form of investment?

2. Goods differ in their yield of consumption services or in their durability. Pine lumber deteriorates more rapidly than redwood. If demand for future consumption rights should rise relative to present consumption rights, would pine or redwood experience the greater increase in present price? Show why this can be expressed as a fall in the rate of interest.

3. A rise in the profitability of constructing houses and buildings will tend to push up the rate of interest. Why?

4. Your wealth today is $1,000. If the interest rate is 10 percent, what is your annual income?

---

[9]Matthew Edel and Elliott Sclar, "Taxes, Spending and Property Values: Supply Adjustment in a Tiebout-Oates Model," *Journal of Political Economy*, Vol. 82 (1974), pp. 941–54.

5. Suppose you own a house that yields an annual net rental income of $2,000. The interest rate is 8 percent. If the house is expected to last indefinitely, what is your wealth in the house? Show that you would be indifferent between paying an annual tax of $100 each year levied on the rental receipts and a one-time tax of $1,250 levied on your wealth in the house.

6. The nominal property tax rate in City A is 10 percent of the assessed value subject to tax. This tax rate is levied on 40 percent of the assessed value of the property. What is the effective property tax in this city?

7. "Since present prices depend upon the capitalized value of past income flows, assessors can obtain accurate estimates of the market price of property by capitalizing these flows." What are the two errors in this statement?

8. Why is there a difference between the incidence of the property tax on land and on structures on land?

9. What adjustments take place to equalize the rates of return to development of property in high tax rate areas and low tax rate areas?

10. In the voting-with-your-feet model, capitalization of differing tax rates does not always occur. Under what conditions would we observe no capitalization taking place?

11. What factors lead to a more efficient allocation of resources in the provision of public goods at the local level than at the federal level?

12. Explain the relationship between Tiebout's sixth and seventh assumptions and the supply curve of a competitive industry.

Additional Readings

Maxwell, James A. *Financing State and Local Governments.* Washington, D.C.: The Brookings Institution, 1969.

Peckman, Joseph A. *Federal Tax Policy.* New York: W. W. Norton and Company, 1971. Chapter 9.

Tiebout, Charles M. "A Pure Theory of Local Expenditure." *Journal of Political Economy,* Vol. 65 (October 1956), pp. 416–24.

Index